Domestic Violence Law Reform and Women's Experience in Court

Domestic Violence Law Reform and Women's Experience in Court

The Implementation of Feminist Reforms in Civil Proceedings

Rosemary Hunter

CAMBRIA PRESS

AMHERST, NEW YORK

Printed in the United States of America

Requests for permission should be directed to:
permissions@cambriapress.com, or mailed to:
Cambria Press
20 Northpointe Parkway, Suite 188
Amherst, NY 14228

Library of Congress Cataloging-in-Publication Data

Hunter, Rosemary C.

Domestic violence law reform and women's experience in court : the implementation of feminist reforms in civil proceedings / Rosemary Hunter.

p. cm.

Includes bibliographical references and index.

ISBN 978-1-60497-575-8 (alk. paper)

1. Domestic relations courts—Australia. 2. Family violence—Law and legislation—Australia. 3. Feminist jurisprudence—Australia. 4. Women—Legal status, laws, etc.—Australia. I. Title.

KU541.H86 2008
346.9401'35—dc22

2008045748

Table of Contents

List of Tables

Acknowledgments

I would like to express my particular gratitude to the survivors of violence, support workers, and lawyers who generously gave me their time to be interviewed for this study. I would also like to record my thanks to those who facilitated my research, including Susan Blashki M. (Supervising Magistrate, Family Law Division, Magistrates' Court of Victoria), Ann McDonald M. (Supervising Magistrate, Crimes Compensation Tribunal, Magistrates' Court of Victoria), Robert Kumar M., Brian Wynn-McKenzie M., Justice Frederico (Judge Administrator [Southern Region], Family Court of Australia), Bruce Norris (Melbourne Registry Manager, Family Court of Australia), David Dillon (Operations Manager, Melbourne Registry, Family Court of Australia), Paul Rennison (List Clerk, Melbourne Registry, Family Court of Australia), the various administrative staff of the Family Court who retrieved files for me, the judges' associates who provided me with copies of judgments in the cases I observed, Leanne Abela, Carol Adams, Renata Alexander, Hana Assafiri, Maria Dimopoulos, Cath McCarthy, Thérèse McCarthy, Zoe Rathus, Helen Rhoades, Donna Stuart, and Maggie Troup.

This book is developed from my doctoral dissertation, submitted to Stanford University in December 2005. I would like to offer special thanks to my principal adviser, Professor Deborah Rhode, and also to the other members of my reading committee, Professors Lawrence Friedman and Deborah Hensler. Professor Donna Coker taught a comprehensive and thought-provoking seminar on domestic violence at Stanford in the fall 1994 semester, which provided an invaluable grounding for the dissertation. And several people supported, encouraged, inspired, and cajoled me to get it written, including Rashmi Goel, Kathy Mack, Ann Genovese, Lesley Laing, Julie Stubbs, Shaunnagh Dorsett, Heather Douglas, Bronwyn Statham, and my parents, Jean and Neil Hunter. My heartfelt thanks to them and, most of all, to my patient and long-suffering partner, Dr. Laurie Duggan.

* * *

Part of chapter 3 was previously published as "Styles of Judging: How Magistrates Deal With Applications for Intervention Orders," *Alternative Law Journal, 30*, 231–236 (2005). Parts of chapters 2, 4, and 6 concerning varying understandings of domestic violence were previously published as "Narratives of Domestic Violence," *Sydney Law Review, 28*, 733–776 (2006), and are reproduced with permission of the editors of the *Sydney Law Review*. The sections on consent orders in chapters 3 and 5 were previously published as part of a chapter titled "Consent in Violent Relationships," in R. Hunter and S. Cowan (Eds.), *Choice and Consent: Feminist Engagements With Law and Subjectivity* (Oxford: Routledge-Cavendish, 2007), pp. 158–173, and are reproduced with the permission of Taylor and Francis Books (U.K.). The power and control wheel in appendix E is reproduced with the permission of Springer Publishing Company, LLC, New York, NY 10036.

Domestic Violence Law Reform and Women's Experience in Court

Chapter 1

Introduction

Feminist legal scholarship on the treatment of women as victim-witnesses and as defendants in criminal cases has highlighted the many failures of criminal law to respond adequately to women's voices and experiences, and to comprehend the ways in which women are socially harmed. Civil remedies for violence and abuse seem to offer better possibilities: there is a lower standard of proof and the woman is the subject of her own action, rather than merely being the object of proceedings. The availability of civil remedies has, in many cases, resulted from feminist campaigns to fill the gaps in protection left by the criminal law. It has also been argued that civil actions provide scope to change public discourses and legal understandings of violence against women. Listening to women's stories might force a revision of traditional conceptions and myths about what constitutes violence, what causes violence, and the effects of and "appropriate" reactions to violence.

This study investigates the ways in which women's experiences of one particular form of violence—variously known as "domestic violence," "intimate partner violence," or "family violence"—are heard and understood in civil court settings, and examines women's experiences of telling their stories (or at least attempting to do so) in those settings. The two areas on which the study focuses are domestic violence restraining order (known as "intervention order") proceedings in State Magistrates' Courts, and custody, visitation (known as "residence" and "contact"), and property matters in the Family Court of Australia (a federal court). It also looks at the intersection between these two types of proceedings—that is, how State Magistrates' Courts deal with family law issues arising in intervention order applications, and how the Family Court regards intervention orders obtained by parties to family law proceedings. The two jurisdictions both have a statutory rather than common-law basis, and the relevant legislation is either partly or wholly a product of feminist legal activism. The study therefore seeks to determine whether the feminist claim that the criminal law silences women[1] also pertains in the context of new civil claims specifically designed to respond to women's experiences. And if this is the case, why is it so? What factors and mechanisms contribute to the ongoing silencing of women's voices, and what, if any, lessons can be drawn for the benefit of future feminist law reform efforts?

THE INCIDENCE OF DOMESTIC VIOLENCE

The fact that domestic violence is a serious and ongoing social problem has been well recognized since the women's movement made the hitherto private experience of violence against women in the home into a political issue in the 1960s and 1970s. In Australia, a major, national prevalence study of violence against women conducted by the Australian Bureau of Statistics (ABS) in 1996 found that 23% of women who had ever been married or in a de facto relationship—1.1 million women—had experienced violence from their partner at some stage during the relationship (pp. 42, 50).[2] Of women who were currently married or in a de facto relationship, 2.6%—or 111,000—had experienced violence from their partner during the previous 12 months (p. 50).[3] Half of the women reporting violence in a current relationship and three quarters of those reporting violence in a previous relationship said they had experienced more than one incident of violence (p. 51). Twelve percent of women who had experienced violence from a current or previous male partner—41,700 women—currently lived in fear as a result of the violence (p. 42). Young women (aged 18–24) were found to be most vulnerable to violence from a current or former partner (p. 50). A more recent prevalence survey based on a smaller, randomly selected sample of women aged 18–69 across Australia found that 34% of those who had a current or former intimate partner (spouse, de facto, or boyfriend) had experienced at least one form of physical or sexual violence from that partner at some stage—4% in the last 12 months (Mouzos & Makkai, 2004, p. 44).

Campaigns against domestic violence have sought to measure the economic cost as well as the incidence of violence.[4] For example, in 2004 Australia's leading economic consulting agency, Access Economics, produced a report commissioned under the Australian government's Partnerships Against Domestic Violence program, which estimated that in 2002–2003 there were 408,100 victims of domestic violence in Australia, 87% of them women, with 98% of perpetrators being male; that 263,800 children lived with victims of domestic violence and 181,200 children witnessed domestic violence; and that the total cost of the violence was $8.1 billion (pp. vi–vii). This figure included an estimated $3.5 billion in pain, suffering, and premature mortality and $4.6 billion in costs to health care, production, consumption, administration, second generational costs, and costs of transfers (p. vii). The bulk of the cost of domestic violence ($4.1 billion) was borne by its victims, but $1.3 billion of the cost fell upon federal and state governments, and a further $1.2 billion fell upon the general community (p. vii).

Other statistical studies of domestic violence have been conducted among various subpopulations, such as adults attending hospital emergency departments (e.g., Roberts, 1995) and women visiting general practitioners (e.g., Mazza, Dennerstein, & Ryan, 1996). These are often groups amongst whom a higher prevalence of violence might be expected than in the general population (see, e.g., Mazza et al., 1996, p. 15). The same might be expected for parties engaged in family law proceedings, while, clearly, 100% of applicants for intervention orders will report a history of violence—although, as discussed subsequently, this will not necessarily always be physical and/or sexual violence.

Nevertheless, my focus on court proceedings necessarily excludes some women from view. The first category excluded are those women who experience a one-time act of violence and/or low-level, occasional violence such that they either tolerate the behavior or simply leave the relationship, but do not take legal action. Women who apply for intervention orders are generally in fear for their safety; abusive behavior that does not produce this result is less likely to result in a court application. A wider range of abusive behaviors might be expected to appear in Family Court cases, but if the behavior is not considered material to the particular dispute (or not even identified as "violence"), it may not be raised in evidence. Thus, the women who appear in court (leaving aside the specter of false allegations, which is discussed in later chapters) might tend to be those who have experienced violence at the more serious end of the spectrum.

The second category of women excluded from a study focusing on court proceedings is those women who, for one reason or many, have difficulties accessing the legal system. The potential barriers are discussed more fully in chapter 2, but broadly may include lack of knowledge of the system or lack of assistance to make use of it, fear and intimidation, shame, inability to afford legal proceedings, cultural or physical barriers, racism, homophobia, or, at worst, death at the hands of the violent partner. Women excluded for these reasons may experience very severe and prolonged violence but may be practically unable to do anything about it—or at least anything involving a court of law. This is simply to acknowledge that courts are not effectively open to all and that some groups of women are systematically less likely to appear there. In Australia, Aboriginal women, lesbians, and women with a physical or intellectual disability who have been victims of domestic violence, despite their representation (and in some instances overrepresentation) in the prevalence statistics, tend to be conspicuously absent from either intervention order or family law proceedings, and hence from this study.

Feminist Law Reform

Second-wave feminism's initial activism around domestic violence in Australia focused on the establishment of women's refuges and the achievement of justice for battered women who had killed violent partners (see, e.g., Genovese, 1997, 2000; Laing, 2000a). Attention also turned to the inadequate policing of domestic violence, although, unlike in the U.S., aggressive criminalization has never formed part of Australian feminist strategies around domestic violence, and mandatory arrest and no-drop policies have never been a feature of the Australian scene. Rather, civil protection orders came to be seen as something of a panacea for the problems of policing, whether by encouraging or bypassing police action.

Protection order regimes were enacted throughout the Australian States and Territories during the 1980s[5] following a series of taskforces and reports on domestic violence, which noted its high incidence in the community, as evidenced by the high proportion of police time spent on domestic violence calls, the money spent on women's refuges, the proportion of hospital casualty admissions attributable to domestic violence, and so on (Graycar & Morgan, 1990, p. 277). In Victoria, the relevant legislation was the Crimes (Family Violence) Act (1987).

Concerns about the way in which domestic violence was dealt with (or rather was ignored) in family law cases began to be expressed by academic commentators and women's advocacy groups in the early 1990s, and by the mid-1990s the Family Court's appellate case law was beginning to reflect these concerns. The Family Law Reform Act (1995), which came into force in mid-1996, for the first time specified that any history or future risk of family violence affecting a child was to be taken into account in determining the best interests of the child in residence and contact proceedings.

Feminist engagements with the state to achieve particular legal rules and policies that respond to women's harms and seek to overcome injustices towards women have, however, repeatedly been dogged by what might be termed the "implementation problem." Deborah Rhode (1997) has observed that "[o]nce we pass a law or institute a policy, we often believe we've done our bit for women and move on to other issues" (p. 16). Yet before announcing the successful attainment of feminist goals, it is necessary to determine how the reforms are actually operating in practice. In the words of Betsy Stanko (1985), "The most important part of any legislation is how decision makers put the provisions of the statutes into practice. Unfortunately, once legislation is passed, it is mistakenly credited with solving the problem" (p. 165). Unfortunately, too, studies of the outcomes of feminist law reform efforts have persistently demonstrated that decision makers are often highly resistant to putting the provisions of the statutes into practice and that much-heralded legal interventions may have little or no impact in practice (see, e.g., Horney & Spohn, 1991; Römkens, 2001). Numerous commentators, for example, have documented the failure of feminist rape law reforms, the ways in which battered woman syndrome evidence has been twisted out of its intended shape, and judicial hostility to the civil rights remedy for gender-based violence in the Violence Against Women Act (1994).[6]

Various diagnoses of the implementation problem have been offered. Lawrence Friedman's influential theory of legal culture argues that if reforms are out of step with prevailing "legal culture," that is, "people's ideas, attitudes, values, and expectations with regard to law" (2002, p. 589), they are "doomed to failure" (1994, p. 130). Legal culture imposes limits on the scope of changes that can be made in practice; it is impossible to "cut against the grain" (1994, p. 130). While recognizing that legal culture will not be uniform across the whole of a society, the important culture from the perspective of implementation is the "internal" legal culture of the judges, lawyers, and other legal actors who are called upon to put new legislation into effect (Friedman, 1985). If there is a disjunction between the legal culture of (feminist) reformers and that of (nonfeminist) enforcers, then dismal results are inevitable.

The ability for internal legal cultures to persist and thrive in opposition to legislative mandates may be attributed to the relative autonomy of legal decision makers and the wide areas of discretion they possess. Thus, according to Horney and Spohn (1991),

> The chronic failure of reforms aimed at the court system suggests that reformers have misperceptions about the nature of the judicial process. Most reform proposals assume that we have a hierarchic, centralized, obedient system of courts that will automatically and faithfully adhere to new rules. These misperceptions cause reformers to overestimate the role of legal rules in controlling the behavior of decisionmakers and to underestimate the role of discretion in modifying the legal rules…Numerous studies have demonstrated limited impact of reforms when officials' attitudes were at odds with reformers' goals…Officials may modify or ignore reforms that threaten the status quo by impeding the smooth and efficient flow of cases or that require changes in deeply entrenched and familiar routines. (p. 120, references omitted)[7]

In line with this view, some commentators have suggested that incremental reforms are likely to be more successful than radical reforms, as they do not ask decision makers to shift very far from their existing positions, which means they are more likely to be prepared do so (e.g., Hekman, 1999, pp. 144–146; Kahan, 2000). But this argument begs the questions of whether incremental reforms are of any substantive value and whether it is possible to tell in advance what will be considered "moderate" or "radical." Since feminist legal reforms aim to achieve legal citizenship for a previously excluded group and to provide remedies for previously unrecognized harms, perhaps they must always be, or will always be perceived to be, radical.

More fundamentally, some feminist critical theorists have argued that law is very much a two-edged sword for women, which can end up doing more harm than good. According to these theorists, law is unlikely to deliver the outcomes that feminist law reformers seek because feminist objectives must be translated into existing legal forms and concepts, which do not adequately respond to women's concerns (e.g., Finley, 1989, pp. 891, 909; Jhappan, 1998, pp. 62–64; Smart,

1989, p. 82; Thornton, 1991, p. 461). Moreover, once translated, they take on a different life, and their meaning is controlled not by feminists but by legal actors with their own agendas (Römkens, 2001; Schneider, 2000, p. 6; Smart, 1989, p. 164). Law transforms elements of experience (such as being subjected to domestic violence) into fixed, objectified, and disempowering categories (such as those of "victim," or "battered woman"), and decisions as to whether individual women fit into these categories and therefore qualify for protection are made by unsympathetic law enforcers (Brown, 1995; Hekman, 2000, pp. 296–297; Römkens, 2001, pp. 267, 283; Siegel, 1996, pp. 2119–2120). Feminist interests may even be co-opted to serve other interests (such as conservative "law and order" campaigns) that are antithetical to the original feminist intentions (Ferraro, 1996, pp. 77, 79; Scutt, 1997, pp. 137–143; Thornton, 1991, p. 464). According to this view, the real problem for women may turn out to be not lack of legal recognition, but hostile social discourses of which law is only a part. Thus, rather than accepting law's claims to be a powerful instrument for justice, feminists should focus their attack on those wider discourses as they are manifested in law and elsewhere (Frug, 1992, pp. 148–153; Smart, 1989; 1990, p. 20; 1995, p. 219).

These different accounts of the implementation problem in law reform are perhaps not so far apart in that they each identify ideas or discourses circulating both outside and inside the legal system, which may operate in opposition to particular reforms. The critical account also identifies structural features of law—its tendencies to individualize, decontextualize, and categorize, and the established processes and remedies it offers—which may limit or actually prevent the achievement of desired outcomes. Where they differ most markedly is in their degree of optimism or pessimism about the possibilities for beneficial legal change in the short, medium, or longer term—a question beyond the scope of this study.

What experience of and theorizing around (feminist) law reform activities tells us, however, is that we should expect implementation problems. But the exact nature of those problems is not necessarily predictable. If they were, we might have worked out some appropriate counter moves before now! Lack of predictability is inevitable because law does not operate monolithically. In the context of this study, social discourses (or what I generally call "narratives") about domestic violence and about victims of violence may be constant, but each institutional setting has a different set of rules and structures that may provide more or less space for hearing women and responding to their need for safety, and that presumably interact with broader social narratives about violence in different kinds of ways. There is thus a need for detailed examination and analysis of how these various elements work in different court settings—the task attempted in this study. In doing so, I have two objectives. Firstly, I am looking to see what conclusions can be drawn about the nature of implementation problems in the jurisdictions examined, which may inform future feminist activism around violence against women. Secondly, I want to make a more general point about the importance of procedure in feminist legal theory and praxis. In Australia in particular, feminist legal scholars and advocates have placed a heavy emphasis on doctrinal revision and have largely ignored issues of implementation (apart from noting them, exclaiming loudly in protest, and trying to craft further doctrinal solutions). My argument is that procedure (conceived broadly to encompass the what, where, how, and who of legal proceedings) crucially shapes women's experience of the legal process and is neglected by feminists at their peril.

Methodology

In order to examine the operation of intervention order legislation and the domestic violence provisions of the Family Law Act (1975), the study looks not just at the legal doctrine expounded in appellate decisions but also at the day-to-day processes of giving and evaluating evidence within the courtroom. As just noted, this is a relatively rare focus in the Australian context. Few previous feminist studies have sought to scrutinize court proceedings, especially civil proceedings, in any detail, and even fewer have made this their exclusive subject. Previous studies have tended to concentrate on what happens before and after court, with relatively brief reference to what occurs during the court process.

My research incorporated theoretical, doctrinal, and empirical components. The theoretical component involved a wide-ranging study of feminist and "difference" scholarship on violence against women and related areas of feminist (legal) and critical race theory, reports on violence against women, feminist and nonfeminist work on law reform and women's engagements with the state, voice scholarship, narrative scholarship, and law and society scholarship. This material is mostly found in this and the following chapter, and provides a framework for the subsequent discussion of the empirical material. The doctrinal component consisted of a study of case law under the legislation governing the two courts examined: the Crimes (Family Violence) Act (1987) and the Family Law Act (1975), both up to and subsequent to the period of the fieldwork. There have been far more appellate decisions under the Family Law Act (1975) than under the Crimes (Family Violence) Act (1987), reflecting the relative doctrinal complexity of the two pieces of legislation and the different extent to which doctrine impinges on day-to-day practice under the legislation. Doctrinal discussions are found at the beginning of chapters 3 and 6, prior to the discussion of the empirical material.

The core of the study is its empirical component, discussed in detail in chapters 3–7. My empirical research consisted of court observations in the two courts, a review of files in the Family Court, and interviews with lawyers, support workers, and women litigants. I obtained ethics approval for the conduct of the empirical research from the Stanford University Panel on Non-Medical Human Subjects. I conducted court observations in various city and suburban Magistrates' Courts in Melbourne, and in the Melbourne Registry of the Family Court in 1996–1997. When attending court, I sat at the back of the courtroom and took notes on a form developed for the purpose (see appendix A). The form consisted of three parts: a series of standardized questions about the case, the proceedings, and the outcome; a running sheet, on which I recorded all speaking roles in the proceedings, including the status of the speaker, the start and finish time of the speech, and the content of the speech; and demographic questions about the woman involved in the case. The process of observations in each court and statistics from the court observations are described in chapters 3 and 5. The cases observed are referred to by means of code numbers: "M.C.n" for cases in the Magistrates' Court, and "F.C.n" for cases in the Family Court.

In the Magistrates' Courts, I also observed domestic violence court support programs in action and spoke informally to magistrates and support workers, taking notes of these interactions. These are referred to as "Field notes." In the Family Court, I identified cases to be observed by means of an initial review of files. This process and its results are also described in chapter 5.

I conducted interviews with lawyers and support workers to supplement the data gained from court observations and from women litigants. The interviews were semistructured and were conducted face-to-face at a location of the interviewee's choosing, in accordance with a preprepared interview schedule (see appendix B). I took handwritten notes rather than tape recording during the interviews, as my aim was to gain specific information based on the interviewee's professional experience rather than to generate a rich source of narrative data that could be used for quotation. I recruited interview subjects on the basis of my knowledge of feminist practitioners working in family law/domestic violence, as well as the practitioners I observed in court, and then by the "snowball" method, as my initial interview subjects recommended others with experience and/or a high profile in the field. My aim was not to recruit a representative sample of domestic violence and family law practitioners in Melbourne, but rather to gain the views of those who had the most experience acting for women with a background of domestic violence in the kinds of proceedings in which I was interested.

In total, I interviewed 18 practitioners: 11 solicitors, 4 barristers, and 3 support workers. Nine of the 11 solicitors were in private practice, while 2 worked in community legal centers. Eight of the 11 had experience in both intervention order applications and family law proceedings. Two had experience only in family law, and 1 had experience only in intervention orders. Of the 4 barristers, 3 practiced only in family law while 1 practiced only in intervention orders. The 3 support workers had experience in assisting women to obtain intervention orders. One worked for a domestic violence outreach service, 1 worked in a community legal center, and the third worked in a specialist service for immigrant women who had entered a battered women's shelter (in Australia known as a "women's refuge"). Interviewees were asked as part of the informed consent process whether their identity could be revealed in reports of the study. Most interviewees agreed to be identified, but some wished to remain anonymous. In these cases, I have assigned those interviewees a code name, such as "S.1" (solicitor), "B.2" (barrister), or "S.W.3" (support worker).

I gained direct accounts of women's experiences in intervention order and family law proceedings from a small group of women litigants who had been subjected to domestic violence and who had been through these proceedings, sometimes repeatedly. These litigants were recruited via legal services and domestic violence support services. This was not an easy process, as services were often very protective of their clients and were wary about passing on material inviting participation in research projects, and also because survivors of violence understandably had other priorities and were often reluctant to revisit painful experiences. In total, I interviewed 13 women litigants, 5 individually and 8 in two separate focus groups. Of the 5 women interviewed individually, 2 were interviewed face-to-face and 3 by telephone, according to their preference. One focus group, involving 3 women, was organized and attended by one of the support workers interviewed. The other focus group involved 5 women from non-English speaking backgrounds, organized by the Immigrant Women's Domestic Violence Service. This focus group also included several support workers, who acted as interpreters for the women and interpolated their own experience on occasions.

As with the interviews with lawyers and support workers, I conducted the interviews with women litigants according to a preprepared, semistructured interview schedule (see appendix C). Again, I did not tape the individual interviews, but recorded them by means of handwritten notes.

The focus group interviews were taped, and I then made handwritten notes from the tapes, which I used for the purposes of analysis. In this case, although narrative accounts and extended quotations from interview subjects would have been illuminating, it was more important for these women that their identity and personal affairs remain completely confidential, so reporting in the form of individual stories or case studies was out of the question. In accordance with the requirement for confidentiality, I have ascribed a code name and number to each woman litigant in referencing their interview material, in the form "W.L.n."

The women litigants interviewed were also asked to complete a short, demographic questionnaire (see appendix D). The majority of those interviewed ($n = 8$) were aged between 31 and 40.[8] Only one was in the 18–24 age group identified in the ABS survey as most vulnerable to violence. This may reflect the fact that younger women are the least likely to be involved in family law proceedings and may also have relatively limited contact with support workers, and so may have been excluded by both my focus and my recruitment method. None of the women interviewed were currently in the workforce, and all were reliant on some form of welfare payments. Five undertook home duties and received what were then known as sole parent pensions. Four were students and received student allowances. Three were unemployed and in receipt of unemployment benefits, and 1 was retired on an age pension. This profile probably reflects the fact that domestic violence survivors who are not in employment are more likely to be in contact with support workers and available to participate in an interview during the daytime. There is no reason to believe, however, that their experiences in court would have been any different from those of the broader spectrum of survivors of violent relationships.

Five of the interviewees had no children; the other 8 had anywhere from 1 child (3 interviewees) to 7 children (1 interviewee). In 3 cases, these were adult children. Of the dependent children, 4 were preschool aged, while the rest ranged from ages 6 to 15. Six of the interviewees were from Anglo/Celtic/Australian backgrounds, 6 were from non-English speaking backgrounds,[9] and 1 was from a mixed background.

Eight spoke English as their first language while 5 spoke a language other than English at home.

Nine of the interviewees lived in either the inner city or suburban Melbourne, and hence had experience in some of the same courts that I observed. One now lived in a rural area in the State, but had attended suburban Magistrates' Courts for intervention order proceedings. Three lived in a regional center just outside Melbourne. For intervention orders, they had attended a local Magistrates' Court that I did not observe, but this gave me the opportunity to find out about similarities and differences between different Magistrates' Court practices. People from this regional center did, however, attend the Melbourne Registry of the Family Court for family law matters. Eleven of the women had been to court to apply for an interim intervention order (3 had done so twice) and 8 had also applied for a full intervention order (again, 3 had done so twice, while 1 had done so 3 times and 1 had done so 4 times). Seven had been to the Family Court. Family Court proceedings tended to involve a number of interim hearings, directions hearings, counseling appointments, conferences, and so forth, before cases reached a defended trial. After a matter had been determined, there might also be further appearances for the enforcement of court orders where a party allegedly failed to comply with them, applications for variation of the original orders, or fresh applications for final orders. It was therefore difficult for respondents to say how many times they had attended the Family Court. Two had been through two defended trials, and 1 of these had also experienced an appeal to the Full Court. One respondent answered the question, how many times have you been in the Family Court? simply by saying "a lot," while another said "too many to count."

Finally, the demographic questionnaire asked about the nature of the violence these women had experienced and who had been the perpetrator. Ten of the women had been abused by their husband (5 women) or ex-husband (5 women), while 2 had been abused by an ex-partner, and 1 by her ex-boyfriend. Questions about the nature of the violence were based on the Duluth "power and control wheel" (Pence & Paymar, 1993; see appendix E). This framework understands domestic violence as a pattern of abusive behaviors by the perpetrator designed to exercise power and control over the victim, which causes the victim to fear for her safety. This conception of violence is discussed in greater detail in chapter 2. The forms of violence reported by the 13 interviewees are set out in table 1.

Clearly, all of the women had experienced multiple forms of abuse, with the various behaviors identified tending to be experienced cumulatively, rather than separately. Some of the women had endured abuse over a very long period before they took legal action, including violent marriages that lasted for over 10 years, 15 years, and, in one case, 44 years. At the opposite extreme, one woman had come to Australia as a "mail order bride" but had stayed with her abusive husband for only 5 weeks before escaping to a refuge. The average period of time that the violence lasted before the woman took legal action, excluding the two outliers just mentioned, was over 5 years.

Obviously, such a small group of interviewees cannot possibly claim to be representative; nor was this the intention. Rather, these women's accounts of their experiences in court serve to flesh out the statistical data from the court observations and to confirm (or disconfirm) and add depth to observed phenomena. As Deborah Hensler (1993) noted in relation to the report of the Ninth Circuit Gender Bias Task Force, stories and statistics can be mutually reinforcing and can combine to present a

TABLE 1. Forms of violence reported by women interviewed.

Type of Violence	Number
Emotional abuse	13
Intimidation	12
Isolation	11
Physical abuse	10
Economic abuse	10
Coercion and threats	9
Sexual abuse	8
Sexual harassment	4
Use of children to exercise control	3

fuller picture: "[T]he stories give life to the statistics, and the statistics tell us that the stories are not idiosyncratic or aberrational" (p. 2193).

As will be clear from the preceding description, my study focused solely on *women* as litigants in domestic violence proceedings. The reasons for this were twofold. Firstly, it would be difficult to make any kind of meaningful comparison between men's and women's experiences of speaking about domestic violence in court, because men so rarely appear in court as the targets (as opposed to the perpetrators) of domestic violence. Although, as is discussed in chapter 3, men frequently do make cross-applications for intervention orders, the context of those applications and the evidence raised in them are quite different from the context of and evidence in women's applications. This is largely because, as discussed in the next chapter, women's experiences of domestic abuse per se tend to be qualitatively different from men's. Secondly, the aim of the research was not to examine gender differences or similarities in courtroom experiences, but to test feminist claims about the effect of legal proceedings and to determine how feminist law reforms were being implemented. Since those claims concerned the specific position of women, and since the reforms were designed for the benefit of women, it followed that, in order to answer the research questions, the study would necessarily focus upon women's experiences in attempting to invoke the relevant legal provisions in court.

Finally, the study also draws upon data from other empirical analyses of—or of relevance to—intervention order and family law proceedings, both from overseas and from Australia, undertaken either before or after my own fieldwork. This data is incorporated into the discussion in chapters 3–7.

Endnotes

1. For the argument that criminal law silences women, see, for example, Scutt (1997): "To be a woman, whether as victim of crime or accused, is to be incredible in the context of the law" (p. 5). Jocelynne Scutt is Australia's most high-profile legal feminist.
2. "Violence" was defined as "any incident involving the occurrence, attempt or threat of either physical or sexual assault" (Australian Bureau of Statistics, 1996, p. 2). For a discussion of definitional and methodological issues in prevalence surveys of violence against women, see Johnson (1998). In the U.S., the National Violence Against Women Survey (NVAWS), conducted by the Center for Policy Research, similarly found that almost 25% of surveyed women said they had been raped and/or physically assaulted at some time by a current or former partner (Tjaden & Thoennes, 2000, p. iii).
3. In the U.S., the equivalent figure from the NVAWS survey was 1.5% (Tjaden & Thoennes, 2000, p. iii).
4. See, for example, the campaign to enact the Violence Against Women Act (1994) in the U.S. (e.g., Goldfarb, 1996).
5. Domestic Violence Act (1986, A.C.T.); Crimes Act (1900, N.S.W.), Part 15A; Domestic Violence Act (1992, N.T.); Domestic Violence (Family Protection) Act (1989, Queensl.); Domestic Violence Act (1994, S. Austl.); Justices Act (1959, Tas.), Part XA (at the time of writing, a new Family Violence Act (2004) had been passed by the Tasmanian State parliament but not yet proclaimed); Restraining Orders Act (1997, W. Austl.). In November 1997, the Domestic Violence Legislation Working Group, a subgroup of the Model Criminal Code Officers Committee established by the Australian federal government, released a *Model Domestic Violence Laws: Discussion Paper*, which proposed uniform national legislation for domestic violence protection orders; however, the idea of national laws was not pursued. For criticism of the proposed model laws, see Hunter and Stubbs (1999). Note that the 1980s also saw the passage of similar legislation in most U.S. States (Kinports & Fischer, 1992; Klein & Orloff, 1993).
6. On rape law reform in Australia, see, for example, Easteal (1998); Heath & Naffine (1994); Heenan & McKelvie (1997); N.S.W. Department for Women (1996); in the U.S., see, for example, Nourse (2000); Spohn & Horney (1992); in the U.K., see, for example, Lees (1996); Temkin (2000); in Canada see, for example, Gunn & Linden (1997); Sheehy (1996); Tan

(1998); in New Zealand, see, for example, McDonald (1994). On battered woman syndrome in Australia, see, for example, McCarthy (1995); Sheehy, Stubbs, & Tolmie (1992); Stubbs & Tolmie (1994); Stubbs & Tolmie (1999); Threadgold (1997); Tolmie (1997); in the U.S., see, for example, Ammons (1995); Burke (2002); Schneider (2000); in the U.K., see, for example, O'Donovan (1993); in Canada see, for example, Sheehy (1994); in New Zealand, see, for example, Seuffert (1997). On the civil rights remedy of the Violence Against Women Act (1994), see, for example, Goldfarb (2000); MacKinnon (2000); Nourse (1996); Resnik (1991); Siegel (1996).

7. See also Friedman (1990), noting that "[m]any experts…have come to grief, because they assume that the law is a top-down command system" (p. 522); and Lees (1994), observing that "the law often constitutes gender relations in its discretionary spaces rather than in its explicit rules," which "renders these practices virtually immune to political action" (p. 126).
8. One was aged 21–30, 2 were aged 41–50, 1 was aged 51–60, and 1 was aged over 60.
9. "Non-English speaking backgound" is a term developed in Australia to refer collectively to non-Anglo immigrant communities. It is usually abbreviated NESB, and was used pervasively in both government policy and community activism throughout the 1980s and 1990s.

Chapter 2

Feminism, Violence, and Law

This chapter begins with an examination of feminist understandings of domestic violence, which lay behind legal reforms such as the Crimes (Family Violence) Act (1987) and the Family Law Reform Act (1995). It then turns to the identification of nonfeminist narratives about domestic violence that circulate in society and within the legal system. As noted in the previous chapter, the extent to which these narratives prevail in the understanding of legal personnel will necessarily affect the way in which feminist-inspired legal reforms are implemented in practice. Finally, the chapter considers general legal structures and processes that may impede the realization of feminist objectives to have women's stories heard, understood, and given effect to in law. The following chapters then examine whether and how these narratives, structures, and processes create implementation problems in intervention order and family law proceedings.

FEMINIST UNDERSTANDINGS OF DOMESTIC VIOLENCE

The Mainstream Feminist Account of Domestic Violence

Based on interviews and discussions with battered women, feminist domestic violence advocates and activists have developed a range of stories about women's experiences of violence and abuse. These stories seek to bring to light women's collective accounts and experiences of violence and abuse—which have been excluded from mainstream discourses about violence such as social work, psychology, and criminal justice—as a basis for social and legal efforts to ensure women's safety and survival and to end violence against women. They have also been tested and confirmed in a limited number of prevalence surveys that have looked beyond the incidence of physical violence. These feminist understandings of domestic violence may be represented schematically as follows.

1. Domestic violence is a highly gendered phenomenon. There is a substantial gender disparity in who initiates violence and who is more physically harmed by it. A woman striking back in anger or in self-defense is not engaged in mutual battering. There is also a clear gender disparity in who seeks safety from violence (Pence & Paymar, 1993, p. 5).[1]
2. Violence is not just about physical abuse but about power and control—the exercise of power and control by one partner in a relationship (usually the male in heterosexual relationships) over the other (Fischer, Vidmar, & Ellis, 1993, p. 2141; Mahoney, 1991, pp. 53–60).
3. Power and control is exercised in a great variety of ways. Domestic violence workers in consultation with over 200 battered women in Duluth, Minnesota, developed the "power and control wheel" (appendix E), which depicts violence as a pattern of coercive behaviors. Physical assaults and sexual abuse reinforce other tactics such as emotional abuse, isolation, minimizing, denying and blaming the target of violence, using the children to get at

the target, using male privilege, economic abuse, coercion and threats, and intimidation (Pence & Paymar, 1993, pp. 2–3; see also Dobash & Dobash, 1977–78, p. 438; Fischer et al., 1993, pp. 2121–2122, 2141).[2]

4. Threats and coercion (particularly threats concerning the children) have a serious impact. Many women describe emotional abuse, "mental cruelty," and fear as the worst aspects of domestic violence. The pain from physical injuries fades, but fear does not go away (Bailey, 1995, p. 8; Kelly, 1988; Pence & Paymar, 1993, pp. 155–156). The kind of constant fear that soldiers may feel in a war zone (West, 2000, p. 169), or that may be felt by some men in prison, is experienced by many women in their own homes.
5. Women with violent partners frequently experience abuse during pregnancy and when they are caring for young children, as their partner seeks to reassert his position at the center of her attention. Some women are hit for the first time when they are pregnant.[3]
6. Children living with domestic violence are aware of the violence, even if they do not personally observe it, and are "actively involved in seeking to make meaning of their experiences and in dealing with the difficult and terrifying situations which confront them" (Laing, 2000b, p. 1; see also Pagelow, 1993, p. 77). Children affected by violence experience trauma, behavioral and emotional problems, and effects on their social and cognitive development (Bala, 1996, pp. 335–337; Davidson, 1995, p. 359; Doyne et al., 1999; Jaffe, Lemon, & Poisson, 2003, pp. 22–24; Levin, 2000, p. 833; McIntosh, 2002, p. 230). They may also blame themselves for the violence or develop inappropriate attitudes towards violence (Jaffe et al., 2003, pp. 22–24). And they further suffer from the effects of the violence on the parenting capacity of the abused partner (e.g., Bala, 1996, pp. 235–237). In addition, there is a high degree of correlation between spousal abuse and child abuse (Bala, 1996, pp. 235–237; Bowker, Arbitell, & McFerron, 1988,

p. 158; Davidson, 1995, pp. 357–358; Eastwood & Phillips, 1996, p. 12; Hewitt, Brown, Frederico, & Martyn, 1996, pp. 19, 20–22; Jaffe et al., 2003, p. 30; Krug, Dahlberg, Mercy, Zwi, & Lozano, 2002, p. 68; Rendell, Rathus, & Lynch, 2000, p. 42; Tomison, 2000).

7. Violent men routinely deny, minimize, and excuse their violence (e.g., by reference to anger, stress, insecurity, or alcohol), or blame their partner for provoking the violence. However, violence is a deliberate strategy designed to undermine their partner's ability to act autonomously. This includes supposedly "out of control" behavior, which is rarely unintentional (Cavanagh, Dobash, Dobash, & Lewis, 2001; Fischer et al., 1993, p. 2138; Pence & Paymar, 1993, pp. 2–3, 9–14; Ptacek, 1999, p. 71; Schneider, 1991, p. 984).
8. Women may not initially identify their partner's behavior as "violence," or may initially deny it is happening to them (Fischer et al., 1993, p. 2141; Kelly, 1988, p. 119). They may then seek to rationalize or excuse the violence, blame themselves, and/or attempt to modify their behavior so as not to provoke their partner (Bailey, 1995, p. 9; Fischer et al., 1993, pp. 2129–2130; Gondolf & Fisher, 1988; Walker, 1987; West, 2000, p. 167). However, a woman cannot change a violent man's behavior by changing her own (Pence & Paymar, 1993, p. 13; Walker, 1987). Rather, the frequency and severity of violence tends to escalate over time (Gondolf & Fisher, 1988).
9. In addition to modifying their behavior, women's strategies for coping with violence include dissociating themselves from the violence, "forgetting" about abuse, retaining vague and sketchy memories of violent incidents, minimizing the seriousness of the violence, vigilance, helpseeking, and attempting to leave (Bailey, 1995, p. 9; Kelly, 1988, p. 124; Lawless, 2000, pp. 73–77; Mahoney, 1991, pp. 18, 22; Schneider, 1991, p. 984).
10. The effects of violence are cumulative. Women understand all of their partner's actions in the context of their prior violence

and controlling behaviors. They become experts in "reading the signals"—cues that signify danger that may not be evident to anyone else. Their perceptions of danger are accurate. "Many women describe a certain 'look in the eye' that signals extreme danger," and that may precipitate an extreme response, such as killing the batterer (Dutton, 1992).

11. Women who are targets of violence are "active survivors" (Gondolf & Fisher, 1988). They make frequent efforts to seek help, but these attempts may not be effective in increasing their safety (Dutton, 1992; Fischer et al., 1993, p. 2136; Gondolf & Fisher, 1988; Mahoney, 1991, p. 61). Police responses are often inadequate (see chapter 3). Social institutions (e.g., families, schools, churches, the welfare system, and the legal system) cannot necessarily be relied upon for support. Instead, they often support violent men's beliefs that their partners should be subordinate to them and should comply with their demands (Dobash & Dobash, 1977–78, p. 438; Mahoney, 1991, p. 55; Pence & Paymar, 1993, p. 15), and also tend to engage in denial, minimization, excuses, and victim blaming, rather than holding men accountable for their behavior (Busch, Robertson, & Lapsley, 1995, p. 194). Women's efforts to seek help may also be met with violent retaliation from their partners (Fischer et al., 1993, p. 2141; Ptacek, 1999, p. 79).

12. Women often do not wish to leave their violent partners. Some still love their partners (Seuffert, 1999; Threadgold, 1997, pp. 222–225). They wish to rescue the relationship; maintain the connection between themselves, their partner, and their children; and live together in safety (Coker, 2000, p. 1019; Espinoza, 1997, pp. 901, 906, 919; Langer, 1995, pp. 86, 88; Mahoney, 1991, p. 20). Other women see no realistic alternative to reliance on their partner's financial support for their own and their children's well being (Coker, 2000, pp. 1017–1018). In response to queries as to why women remain in abusive relationships, Martha Mahoney (1991) asks, "Do we 'stay' or are we simply married?" and

notes women's understandable resistance to defining their entire experience of marriage by the episodes of violence (pp. 15–16; see also Bailey, 1995, pp. 7–8). Several writers have observed that society and the legal system expect women to separate from violent partners, while paying insufficient attention to the possibilities for achieving safety within relationships (e.g., Littleton, 1989, p. 52; Merry, 1997, p. 304; Rhode, 1997, p. 114).

13. Women also frequently do attempt to leave, but this can be difficult and dangerous. Practical obstacles include leaving safely without attracting a violent response, finding alternative housing, and surviving economically, and these are compounded if (as is often the case) there are children to provide for as well (Ptacek, 1999, p. 73). The violent partner may be contrite and loving, and may beg forgiveness and promise never to do it again (Walker, 1987). Or he may threaten to kill her and/or the children if she leaves. And he will often come after her when she does.
14. Abuse frequently escalates at the point of separation. This is when women are possibly in the greatest danger of being killed, as the violent partner seeks to reinstate his power and control over her (Mahoney, 1991, pp. 5–6; Walker, 1987). "Separation assault" names "the particular assault on a woman's body and volition that seeks to block her from leaving, retaliate for her departure, or forcibly end the separation" (Mahoney, 1991, p. 6).[4] Marital rape can be one particular form of separation assault (Lees, 1997, p. 129). Another can be harassment through the court system (e.g., in applications for child custody), and harassment and abuse surrounding counseling, mediation, and court hearings (Hart, 1990; Seuffert, 1996, p. 536).

Women's Accounts From Positions of "Difference"

Although the feminist account of domestic violence as power and control is widely accepted, it has been variously extended, modified, and in some respects rejected by nonwhite women, women with disabilities, and lesbians. The particular and different experiences of domestic violence that have been asserted by these groups may be summarized as follows.

1. Intralesbian domestic violence cannot adequately be understood in the context of patriarchal gender relations (Cecere, 1986, p. 29). Female-female violence involves different dynamics to male-female violence, has a different social meaning, and receives different responses to male-female violence (e.g., Dziggel, 1986, pp. 62, 67; Vickers, 1996, ¶ 23, 30–31, 72). Homophobia at both institutional and personal levels plays a major role in the experience of lesbian violence (e.g., Bennet, 1997, pp. 17–20; Eaton, 1994, pp. 197–198, 216; Vickers, 1996).
2. Women with disabilities experience forms of abuse not experienced by able-bodied women, such as the withholding of food or medicine, the removal or sabotage of accessibility devices (wheelchairs, ramps, TTYs, etc.), unnecessary institutionalization, and chemical restraint (Frohmander, 2001; Nosek, Howland, & Hughes, 2001, p. 484; Womendez & Schneiderman, 1991, p. 276). They also experience abuse from carers and other residents in group homes, as well as from intimate partners (Frohmander, 2001; National Committee on Violence Against Women [NCVAW], 1993, pp. 14, 29; Nosek et al., 2001, p. 482; Womendez & Schneiderman, 1991, p. 277).
3. Black women are less likely to be economically dependent on their husbands (Collins, 1991, p. 59) and are at least as likely to experience state coercion in relation to their children as coercion from a violent partner (Kline, 1989, p. 130). Women whose immigration status is uncertain (e.g., those who are applying for refugee status or for permanent residence as a spouse of a citizen) are threatened with deportation (Easteal, 1996, pp. 117, 119; Loke, 1997; Martin & Mosher, 1995, p. 20). Their limited or nonexistent English-language ability and lack of information sources give their abusive husbands total power to define their world and the potential consequences of taking steps to seek help

(Kelly, 1998; Keys Young, 1994, p. 51; Marginson, 1996, p. 19; Martin & Mosher, 1995, p. 27). Filipino women sponsored as spouses or fiancées by Australian men are particularly vulnerable to domestic violence if they fail to conform to stereotyped images of Asian women as passive, subservient, domesticated, and pliable, and as a result of the racial, economic, gender, and social power differences in mixed marriages (Cuneen & Stubbs, 1997; Easteal, 1996, pp. 152, 155; Marginson, 1996, pp. 18–19). Emotional abuse of immigrant women includes racist abuse of them and their children (Easteal, 1996, pp. 24, 108, 116).[5]

4. The practical difficulties of leaving a violent relationship for an immigrant woman or a woman with a disability can be enormous. Women with intellectual disabilities or psychiatric illnesses have greater difficulty in getting people to believe they have been abused (NCVAW, 1993, p. 14). At worst, it is impossible for a woman with no English, no knowledge of services available, and no family in the country to leave her husband and live on her own (Easteal, 1996, p. 97). Women in this situation may also be trapped by the need to provide continuing financial support to families in their homeland (Easteal, 1996, p. 10). Similarly, women with disabilities may have no practical means of escape from a carer who is also an abuser (NCVAW, 1993, p. 14).
5. Internalized cultural beliefs also affect immigrant women's efforts to seek help to end the violence and their ability to leave an abusive relationship. These include beliefs about women's responsibility to the family and the importance of family solidarity (Easteal, 1996, p. 9; Marginson, 1996, p. 19; Rimonte, 1991, p. 1313), concerns about bringing shame on their family and community (Martin & Mosher, 1995, p. 28; Rimonte, 1991, p. 1319), and the extreme stigma attached to marriage breakdown (Easteal, 1996, pp. 34, 36). Thus, the possibility of leaving will be attended by a strong fear of family and community rejection. A woman may escape her partner's violence at the cost of family and community membership ("A Strategy on Domestic

Violence and Sexual Assault for non-English Speaking Background Women," 1996, p. 85). Women also experience direct community pressures to stay and put up with the violence (Bricker, 1993, pp. 1398–1399; Cecere, 1986, p. 29; Easteal, 1996, p. 124; Vickers, 1996, ¶ 23, 30–31, 72; Yue, 1996, pp. 24–25).

6. Calling the police to a domestic violence incident is far more difficult when a woman fears a homophobic or racist response towards herself and/or towards her partner (Bennet, 1997, pp. 23–24; Bricker, 1993, p. 1396; Easteal, 1996, p. 10; Fenton, 2003; Hampton, Oliver, & Magarian, 2003, p. 534; Martin & Mosher, 1995, pp. 26–28; "'Out' of sight," 2000, pp. 14–15; Vickers, 1996, ¶ 36, 39, 41), when her history of persecution in her home country has engendered a deep fear of the police (Easteal, 1996, pp. 93–94; Keys Young, 1994, pp. 52–54; Martin & Mosher, 1995, p. 20), when she worries that drawing police attention to her situation may have immigration or child protection implications ("A strategy," 1996, p. 85; Coker, 2000, pp. 1042, 1048; Easteal, 1996, pp. 93–94; Martin & Mosher, 1995, pp. 26–28), and when she is unable to communicate with the police due to limited English-language ability and to their failure to provide interpreters (Easteal, 1996, p. 129; Keys Young, 1994, pp. 52–54; Martin & Mosher, 1995, p. 23).[6] Australian studies have found that the police are far more likely to be called by Australian-born than by overseas-born victims of domestic violence, that very few victims calling the police could speak no English, that police are reluctant to use interpreters when attending domestic violence calls, and that some police employ racist and cultural stereotypes about non-English speaking background women and so fail to take appropriate action (Easteal, 1996, pp. 49–50; Hitter, 1996, pp. 46–47; see also Martin & Mosher, 1995, pp. 20, 23, 25). Some women with disabilities may need to rely on a third person to contact the police on their behalf, which is difficult if that person does not believe that the woman has been abused or thinks that police involvement is unnecessary or inappropriate. Women with psychiatric illnesses

also report negative experiences with the police, which tend to discourage further reporting (NCVAW, 1993, p. 29).

7. In general, women from non-English speaking backgrounds (Antonios, 1996, pp. 5–6; Easteal, 1996, pp. 35, 70, 75, 99, 131; Katsabanis, 1993, pp. 41–42, 50–51, 55, 78–79) and women with disabilities (Frohmander, 2001, p. 28; Ireland, 2002, p. 9; NCVAW, 1993, pp. 17, 23–25, 27) face a lack of specialist support services, together with difficulties of communication with and/or access to most mainstream services.[7] Even where interpreters are available, it is very difficult to speak about domestic violence through an interpreter, and more so when the woman and the interpreter are known to each other as members of a small community (Easteal, 1996, p. 100). Interpreters generally receive no training in domestic violence, and Australian support workers have encountered many interpreters who have tried to convince the woman to reconcile with her husband, and some who have criticized the woman for going to court (Sous, 1996, pp. 14–15).
8. Australian Aboriginal women are 45 times more likely than non-Aboriginal women to experience domestic violence (Ferrante, Morgan, Indemaur, & Harding, 1996, pp. 34–35; Memmott, Stacy, Chambers, & Keys, 1999; see also Bolger, 1991, p. 4; Greer, 1994, pp. 64–66) and are more likely to be seriously injured than non-Indigenous victims (Aboriginal and Torres Strait Islander Women's Task Force on Violence [ATSIWTFV], 2000, p. 97; Ferrante et al., 1996, pp. 34–35). Abuse of Indigenous women by their partners often takes place within a broader context of violence in Indigenous communities, including fighting between men and between women, suicide and self-harm, rape of women and girls of all ages by men and boys of all ages, child abuse, verbal harassment, and economic deprivation.[8]

   Indigenous women also experience particular problems with calling the police, leaving a violent relationship, and community pressures to stay. Women may be reluctant to invoke police assistance due to fear of a racist and/or abusive response, fear of retribution from their partner, pressure from the man's relatives, or unwillingness to expose their partner to possible incarceration in the context of the massive overrepresentation of Indigenous people in police and prison custody in Australia, as well as the high incidence of Indigenous deaths in custody (Atkinson, 1990, pp. 6–9; Bolger, 1991, pp. 58–59, 68; Greer, 1997, pp. 13, 16; Moore, 2002, pp. 7–8).9 Leaving one's community is also extremely traumatic and difficult to sustain, involving dislocation from the physical and emotional support of families, from country, and from identity (ATSIWTFV, 2000, p. 59; Bolger, 1991, pp. 54, 62). Members of the woman's and the man's family, along with other community members, may blame the woman for the violence or exert pressure on her to stay (Bolger, 1991, pp. 54–57). As is the case with immigrant women, Indigenous women encounter excuses for violence based on (mis)representations of traditional culture, such as the notion that men are entitled under traditional law to beat (or even kill) their wives for supposed infractions, or to claim sexual services from them (Payne, 1990, p. 10; Upton, 1992, p. 872). These excuses have been accepted by white authority figures such as social workers, police, lawyers, magistrates, and judges in purported "sensitivity" to Indigenous culture (ATSIWTFV, 2000, p. 59; Atkinson, 1990, pp. 6, 8; Bolger, 1991, pp. 50–51, 53, 71, 80–81; Payne, 1990, p. 10; Randall, 1995; Upton, 1992, p. 873).10 In addition, Indigenous women experience strong cultural feelings of shame in talking about personal problems in front of a white and/or male audience (Moore, 2002, p. 8).

Aboriginal women insist upon three points that are absent from white feminist theorizing about domestic violence. Firstly, they argue that Indigenous family violence is not a result of patriarchal domination, since Aboriginal women were not and are not economically, politically, or socially subordinate to men within their families and communities (Behrendt, 1993, p. 33; Huggins, 1994, p. 71; O'Shane, 1976, p. 32; Pettman, 1992, p. 65). Rather, they contend that violence against Indigenous women must be seen within the broader context of colonization, dispossession, and racial discrimination experienced by Aboriginal and Torres Strait Islander people. This experience includes massacres of Aboriginal people, forced relocations, disruption of traditional gender relations, removal of children, state control on missions, labor exploitation, and denial of human rights. Much of this treatment has occurred within living memory and is, indeed, ongoing and unresolved, resulting in transgenerational cycles of trauma and violence (ATSIWTFV, 2000, pp. xxxi, 22–23, 25–26, 58, 60; Atkinson, 1997, p. 6; Bolger, 1991, p. 44; Goodall & Huggins, 1992, p. 418; Payne, 1990, p. 10; Wanganeen, 1990, pp. 69–70; see also Coker, 1999, pp. 26–27; Razak, 1998, pp. 64–66). Current legacies of the white invasion include high rates of mortality and morbidity,[11] unemployment, isolation, poverty, the effects of child removal, cultural disorientation, the decline of traditional law, hopelessness, and despair (ATSIWTFV, 2000, pp. xxxiv–xxxv; Bolger, 1991, p. 44).

Secondly, while mainstream feminist analysis sees men's abuse of alcohol as an excuse for violence, Aboriginal women see alcohol abuse as a symptom of and response to the rage, pain, and despair engendered by the effects of colonization, which has become a major cause of violence in Indigenous communities (ATSIWTFV, 2000, pp. xxxi, xxxiii, 28, 31, 59; Bolger, 1991, pp. 29, 34–35, 45). Some accounts of family violence in Indigenous communities refer to "alcohol violence" as a separate category of violence.

Thirdly, due to their shared history of racial oppression, Indigenous women are concerned to stand alongside rather than in opposition to Indigenous men in the struggle for basic rights, including efforts to end family violence (ATSIWTFV, 2000, p. xxx; Behrendt, 1993, pp. 27, 42; Flick, 1990, p. 66; Goodall & Huggins, 1992, pp. 401–402; Huggins, 1991, p. 6; Moreton-Robinson, 2000, pp. 160, 161–165, 177; O'Shane, 1976, pp. 32–34). Indigenous men suffer high levels of unemployment, have access to few services, and have seen their position in the family and the community erode (ATSIWTFV, 2000, p. 193; Bolger, 1991, p. 44).[12] Combating violence involves helping men to heal, and reviving and reuniting extended families and communities (ATSIWTFV, 2000, p. 50).

The civil justice response to domestic violence certainly reflects more of a mainstream feminist position than one inflected by understandings of difference. The expectation that women should go to court in order to secure safety for themselves and their children is clearly one with which some groups of women find it far more difficult to comply—hence the general absence, as noted in the previous chapter, of Indigenous women, women with disabilities, and lesbians from intervention order and family law proceedings. In Australia, immigrant women have made use of the court system, and specialist services have developed to assist them to do so. As already suggested, however, they still face communication barriers in court in having their experiences of violence and their cultural contexts heard and understood.

Nonfeminist Understandings of Domestic Violence

In her history of family violence, Linda Gordon (1988) outlined the shifting understandings and constructions of wife beating before the 1970s, in line with shifts in institutional power to define the phenomenon between the church, the police, social workers, and the discipline of psychology (see also Mahoney, 1991, pp. 27, 60). While feminism entered the struggle for definition in the 1970s, positing arguments about structural male dominance against earlier institutional views about family or individual pathology, the development of the discourse of "domestic violence" by no means represented a complete "feminist victory" (Ferraro, 1996, pp. 77, 83). Other discourses about violence continue to circulate. For example, Nan Seuffert (1999) has explored in detail the ways in which violence is entwined with romantic love in literary and popular texts, so that "women who are subject to physical, sexual and emotional abuse may position themselves within the sedimented layers of constructions of romantic love in order to 'make sense' of their situations" (pp. 216, 224–225). And in Australian federal public policy, discussions of domestic violence have been framed by conservative discourses concerning the nuclear family. Thus, while domestic violence is seen as a threat to family stability, feminist activists against domestic violence have themselves been accused of trying to undermine families.

In the context of court proceedings, the discourses most likely to shape the implementation of legislation relating to domestic violence are those that are entrenched within "internal" legal culture—that is, the understandings about domestic violence commonly held by judicial officers and lawyers. This section explores social and legal stories about domestic violence, as identified by previous commentators, that diverge from those put forward by feminists. The analysis of intervention order and family law proceedings in chapters 3–7 will draw upon and extend this discussion.

Social Narratives

"Fright" narratives are a common trope found in social discourse. One of the most enduring "fright" narratives in criminal law is that of the state abusing its power to arbitrarily deprive individuals of their rights and liberty. In order to stave off this story, the law has devised an extensive array of protections for accused persons, including *Miranda* rights, rights of confrontation, the presumption of innocence, burdens and standards of proof, rules of evidence, and the privilege against self-incrimination. Other "fright" narratives feature feminine characters rather than the state. These include stories about bad, mad, and vengeful mothers and wives, the "monstrous feminine," and the woman who makes a false complaint.[13] The notion that women may make false allegations of domestic violence, rape, and sexual harassment for purposes of revenge or tactical gain is widely held and actively promoted by some antifeminist groups (see, e.g., Kaye & Tolmie, 1998b, p. 54; Scheppele, 1992, pp. 149–150). A prominent masculine "fright" narrative involves the stranger-rapist "lurking in the bushes." By contrast, there is no strong cultural story expressing fear of men's violence against their partners, or their abuse of power in the private sphere of the home.[14]

Stories about domestic violence tend rather to deny, minimize, and trivialize violence than to regard it as a serious social issue. Many of these stories center on the sanctity of the family and the importance of family privacy, including the notion that the state should not interfere in the private business of the family (see Graycar & Morgan, 2000, pp. 10–27; Minow, 1990, p. 1672)—or, at least, in the private business of the white, heterosexual, nuclear family.[15] The social understanding that violence is a product of conflict between spouses may, however, justify intervention in the form of conflict resolution, in order to restore the family to its desirable, intact state (Fischer et al., 1993, p. 2137; McGregor & Hopkins, 1991, p. 118). The view that violence is a matter of relationship conflict also suggests that both parties are responsible for domestic violence, a view that underpins the proposition asserted by some antifeminists that women are as violent as men (see, e.g., Kaye & Tolmie, 1998b, pp. 57, 61; Pence & Paymar, 1993, p. 14; cf. Graycar & Morgan, 2002, pp. 309–310).

In addition, social stories about violence define "violence" to mean (serious) physical assaults. As a consequence, violence is seen as an exceptional or rare event rather than as a pervasive phenomenon (Langer, 1995, p. 87). Renée Römkens (2001), for example, has noted the ambivalence in social attitudes towards domestic violence: it is abhorred in the abstract, but individual claims to victimhood are treated with suspicion, otherwise domestic violence would appear too prevalent for comfort (pp. 287–288). Similarly, Adrian Howe (1998) has commented on the apparent unease in media reporting at acknowledging the scale of men's violence against women.

> It is as if the stark "reality" of men's violence against women is simply too awful to contemplate. It must be hedged in with discursive strategies which have the effect of deflecting attention away from the harshness of the verdict that men are responsible for their own violence. (p. 38)

The discursive strategies to which Howe refers include labelling feminist claims about the extent of men's violence as "extreme" and telling stories about the behavior of women and men that obscure and provide excuses for the extent of men's violence (1998, p. 38). These include, for example, the notions that alcohol abuse is the major cause of violence against women and that women provoke men into violence by nagging, failing to discharge their domestic duties, otherwise failing to conform to a "normal" or conventional feminine/wifely role, sleeping with another man, or trying to leave the relationship. An Australian national survey of attitudes towards violence against women in 1995 found that only 6% of respondents attributed the causes of violence to "male socialization, dominance or power" (cited in Bailey, 1995, p. 17). Respondents were more likely to attribute domestic violence to factors such as financial pressures, relationship problems, and alcohol abuse. More recently, men's violence has been excused in the media as a product of frustrations engendered by the family law system (Kaye & Tolmie, 1998b, p. 59).

At the same time, since the autonomous liberal subject does not put up with prolonged abuse, stories about violence seek to explain women's failure to leave abusive relationships. These include the notions that women who endure abuse are willing victims—masochists—or somehow attract abusive men (Pence & Paymar, 1993, p. 11). Alternative explanations center on the woman's lack of credibility—that is, she must be lying about or exaggerating the severity of the violence, because if it were true she would not have stayed (Espinoza, 1997, p. 915; Lees, 1997, p. 137; Mahoney, 1994, p. 78; Schneider, 2000, p. 104; Threadgold, 1997, p. 217; Westlund, 1999). In the same Australian national survey just noted, fully 77% of respondents found it difficult to understand why women often stay with violent partners (Bailey, 1995, p. 17).

Finally, social stories may represent domestic violence as a feature of certain ethnic communities. According to Howe, "[W]hen it reports family violence, the press…appears to be more comfortable if it is located in conveniently racialized ethnic minority families, far removed from the sanctity of the Australian (read: non-racialized Anglo-Celtic) family" (1998, p. 53). Domestic violence in non-Western cultures is often understood in the West as being a product of religion or tradition and as a sign of the inferiority of the culture in question compared to Western culture (Lazreg, 1990, pp. 327, 329; Narayan, 1989, p. 259). The association between culture and violence means that immigrant women seeking to escape violence are expected to reject their ethnicity and tradition and to adopt modern, Western values—or may be accused of doing so by their own communities (see, e.g., Antonios, 1996, p. 6; Min-ha, 1989, pp. 104, 106).

Legal Narratives

Nonfeminist stories about domestic violence are widely reflected and reproduced in law. These stories are evident in both criminal and civil law and in the attitudes of individual judges. U.S. Task Force reports on gender bias in the courts during the 1980s and 1990s were replete with examples of judges trivializing male violence and displaying gross insensitivity towards is victims (Rhode, 1997, pp. 110–111; Schafran, 1995, p. 1065).[16] Legal doctrine focuses on violence as physical assaults and provides a partial defense for men who claim they were provoked into killing their wives, but makes it very difficult for women who kill abusive partners to fit their experience into the legal definition of self-defense (e.g., Australian Law Reform Commission [ALRC], 1994, pp. 274, 278; Victorian Law Reform Commission [VLRC], 2004b, pp. 17, 27–30, 62–64). The irrelevance of domestic violence to most legal actions means that it is rarely acknowledged or described in legal judgments, thereby reinforcing its perceived exceptionality (Fenton, 1999, pp. 996, 1027–1028; Mahoney, 1991, p. 3). Graycar's (1996a) close reading of tort, contract, and other civil cases involving husband and wife, de facto partners, or other family litigants disclosed many semisuppressed histories of violence lurking in the pages of the law reports, though violence was never the central issue in the cases studied (see also Sarmas, 1994).

Even when violence is in issue, by reason of feminist law reform efforts or litigation strategies, legal descriptions still tend to deny or minimize domestic abuse. For example, judgments in child custody cases where the father has been violent towards the mother, and in homicide cases where battered women have killed their partners, tend to provide distanced, detached, and dispassionate descriptions of the violence; to employ passive constructions; and otherwise to obscure male agency in perpetrating violence (Busch, 1994, p. 107; Graycar, 1996b; Minow, 1990, p. 1673; Stubbs & Tolmie, 1994, p. 193). "In the course of the legal reproduction of the abused woman's story…the abuse becomes decentered, minimalized or even eliminated from the official version of the relevant facts" (Beaman-Hall, 1996, p. 132; see also Langer, 1995, p. 66). Consequently, courts may find that there was "not enough violence" to support the woman's claim or defense (e.g., Scutt, 1995, pp. 131–132, 137–141; Meier, 2003, pp. 673–674).

The phenomenon of minimization is exemplified in the Australian High Court decision of *Osland v. R* (1998). Heather Osland and her son killed their husband/father after enduring years of severe abuse. One of the judges in the case gave a detailed description of Frank Osland's violence, including physical, sexual, and psychological abuse; domination; abuse of and threats towards the children; cruelty to family pets; and multiple strategies to defeat Mrs Osland's attempts to leave the relationship. He described life with Frank Osland as "a pattern of threats, physical violence, short-lived reconciliations, illness, repression and fear," and also noted evidence of escalating violence and greater physical abuse prior to his death, to the point where Mrs Osland feared for her life (Callinan J, pp. 388–390). By contrast, the other four judges referred only to Mr Osland's "deplorable" conduct (Kirby J, p. 379), "the violent incident" on the night of his death and "other evidence of the past conduct of Frank Osland" (McHugh J, p. 363), and "an evidentiary background of tyrannical and violent behaviour by Mr. Osland over many years" (Gaudron & Gummow JJ, p. 321). Heather Osland's appeal against her conviction for murder was unsuccessful.[17]

In family law cases, too, violence is minimized in support of more powerful stories about the value of the nuclear family: that maintenance of the family, resolution of marital "difficulties," and reconciliation following temporary separation are generally desirable (Busch, 1994, pp. 106–107; Langer, 1995, p. 82); that joint custody and shared parenting are the best arrangements following separation (Beaman-Hall, 1996, p. 132; Fineman, 1988; Meier, 2003, p. 710; Zorza, 1996); and that wife abuse and parenting are entirely separate matters (Bancroft & Silverman, 2002, pp. 115–128; Beaman-Hall, 1996, p. 129; Busch, 1994, p. 130; Meier, 2003, pp. 675–681). The latter view is based on the understanding that violence is caused by the stresses of the marriage and hence, once the parties are separated, the violence will stop (Busch, 1994, pp. 131–132). This, in turn, reinforces the notion that violence is exceptional, enabling courts to characterize perpetrators as not *essentially* violent. Rather than being held responsible for their violence or considered dangerous, violent men are often presented as objects of pity, essentially gentle or quiet but driven to extremes—to act out of character—by marital tension or by their partner's provocative act of leaving or taking up with another man (Busch, 1994, pp. 108–109).

Notions of the exceptionalism of "real" domestic violence and the liability of women to make false claims (see, e.g., Meier, 2003, pp. 683–684) also result in requirements for some form of corroboration of women's accounts of violence. This might include physical injuries or, failing that, evidence of psychological injury provided by a qualified expert. Expert evidence of "battered woman syndrome" is the most obvious example of this form of corroboration. But while expert testimony may render women's claims of violence more believable, it also tends to present being a victim of domestic violence as a disabling, individual psychological condition, further deflecting attention from the responsibility of the perpetrator for the consequences of his violence (see, e.g., Coughlin, 1994; Hunter, 1996a, pp. 153–154; Rhode, 1997, p. 116).

Legal Structures and Processes

As the previous chapter noted, feminist-inspired legal reforms may strike implementation problems not only because they clash with contrary social and legal discourses, but also because they cannot effectively be pursued within established legal forms, structures, and processes. These two factors may interact in particular legal locations. This final section of the chapter examines legal forms, structures, and processes that may impede the implementation of legislation relating to domestic violence. The extent to which they in fact do so, and the extent to which other structures and processes may play a part in the legislative regimes examined, are discussed in chapters 3–7.

Legal Categories

Legal categorization is the first level of filtration imposed by law on social experience. The law recognizes only certain kinds of harm, defined in specific ways. If a particular experience does not fit within one of the existing categories, it is not legally cognizable. And if a person's experience is held to fall outside the boundaries of an existing category, that person is "found" to have suffered no remediable harm. Gilkerson (1992) has argued that established legal categories reflect the experiences, perspectives, and images of those in power, while excluding the voices and perspectives of the powerless (p. 871), and feminist legal theorists have highlighted the disjunction between legal categories and women's lives (Graycar, 1996b, p. 309; Graycar & Morgan, 2002, pp. 1–3). Because the categories of criminal law, tort law, contract law, property law, equity, and so forth, were developed without women in mind, harms experienced particularly by women—such as sexual harassment, restrictions on reproductive freedom, loss of children, and so forth—cannot readily be articulated as legal claims (Troup, 1993, p. 71).

This is especially true in relation to domestic violence. The paradigm "wrong" in civil cases occurs in an encounter between autonomous individuals in the public, social world; in criminal cases, it is a single act or course of conduct with determinate material consequences (Hunter, 1996a, p. 130). Moreover, legal harms are considered to be abnormal, not frequent or pervasive (Levitt, 1995, p. 532). These paradigms do not fit the feminist profile of domestic violence outlined earlier in this chapter. Legal responses to violence against women are also divided amongst a range of doctrinal categories, requiring women to resort to a variety of legal fora in order to achieve adequate protection from and redress for the violence they have suffered (Graycar, 1996b, p. 300). As discussed in chapter 7, these fora are not necessarily coordinated with each other, nor do they provide complete coverage of the issue.

Legal Doctrine: The Cause of Action

As well as having to contend with general legal categories, litigants must also establish their case by reference to the applicable legal doctrine and the structure of the particular claim or defense being put forward. Legal doctrine performs a dual function in this regard. Firstly, it provides a further, localized set of categories into which claimants must fit. Thus, while feminist law reform interventions have succeeded in making domestic violence visible within the legal system as a kind of harm that was not previously recognized as such, an individual woman's ability to obtain a restraining order, for example, is constrained by the legal frameworks used to define eligibility for an order, which may cover only a limited range of relationships, restrict the forms of violence against which protection may be sought, or require applications to be based on specific kinds of triggering incidents (see, e.g., Finley, 1989, p. 909; Hunter & Stubbs, 1999, pp. 13–14; Römkens, 2001, p. 267; and chapter 3, next). In the very process of defining a new harm in law, some experiences will be excluded from the category.

Secondly, legal doctrine acts as the touchstone by which the "relevance" of evidence is judged. Many commentators have observed that "what is relevant to many plaintiffs and defendants cannot be heard, cannot be made sense of, cannot be allowed to be spoken in legal discourse" (Cain, 1994, p. 40; see also Bezdek, 1992; Conley & O'Barr, 1990; O'Barr & Conley, 1985). In Carol Smart's (1989) words, "[T]he legal process translates everyday experience into legal relevance, it excludes a great deal that might be relevant to the parties, and it makes its judgement on the scripted or tailored account" (p. 11). In the domestic violence context, women may be prevented from giving an account of the history of their relationship with their abusive partner, which explains their partner's ongoing efforts to exercise power and control over them and their current fear of their partner, on the basis that much of that history is "too old" or involves actions not covered by the legislation (see chapters 3–6).

These two points come together in the observation that, contrary to some of the arguments of "voice" scholarship, courts do not invite people to "tell their stories" "in their own voices." Rather, they wish to hear from characters—the "aggrieved family member," "defendant," "wife," "husband," and so forth—who are to a considerable extent already scripted. The experience for litigants of being written into the relevant doctrinal script is one of abstraction, the submersion of their subjectivity in order to become the necessary kind of legal subject. This abstraction of ordinary people into legal characters is arguably a necessary element of the rule of law. The delivery of equal and impartial justice requires the working out of "neutral principles whose application is believed to transcend human variation" (Conley & O'Barr, 1990, p. 9). But it is also a disciplinary process in the Foucauldian sense, "a process of objectification and subjection" (Bumiller, 1988, p. 69), in which complexities and contradictions are ultimately erased in favor of a clear, black-or-white story (Davies & Seuffert, 2000, p. 289; see also Berns, 1999, pp. 104–105; Frohmann, 1998).

The Rules of Procedure and Evidence

The rules of procedure and evidence are the means by which doctrinal categories are applied to social experience. They determine who will be heard, how they will be heard, and what information is considered relevant and reliable, as opposed to misleading or prejudicial (Scheppele, 1992, pp. 164–165). The rules of evidence function both as a means of bringing the outside world into the courtroom, and as an aporia—that which will not allow passage (Berns, 1999, p. 39). "Law's knowledge is limited by the rules of evidence"; they determine what is permitted to be legally known (O'Donovan, 1993, p. 428).

As many commentators have noted, the rules of procedure and evidence embody radically different epistemological premises from those of everyday life. As a consequence, the requirement for the adversarial presentation of evidence—through direct examination and cross-examination, where the witness is straightjacketed by the questions asked and certain types of expressions, such as opinions and hearsay, are excluded—is experienced by virtually all lay litigants as both intensely frustrating and a means by which the story they wish to tell is actively suppressed rather than freely elicited (e.g., Conley & O'Barr, 1990, pp. 14, 39; O'Barr & Conley, 1985, pp. 666–667, 672). When adversarial procedure is relaxed and litigants are freed of the restraints of the rules of evidence, they tell very different kinds of narratives, although these still run the risk of being deemed legally irrelevant (O'Barr & Conley, 1985, pp. 661–662, 676).

As with the inclusions and exclusions of legal categories, the rules of procedure and evidence, while appearing neutral, operate in a partial and specifically gendered fashion. For example, forms of social disadvantage experienced by women and minority groups, such as discrimination and domestic violence, must be proved in each individual case rather than by means of group experience or statistical patterns.[18] At the same time, evidence that might help to prove the individual case, such as similar fact, propensity, or broad contextual evidence, may be inadmissible or otherwise structurally excluded (Ewick & Silbey, 1995, pp. 215–216; see also Delgado, 1989, p. 2428).

I have written previously of the ways in which the rules of evidence are gendered through their basis in Enlightenment epistemology, their focus on discrete incidents or transactions, and their reliance on "universal cognitive competence" (Hunter, 1996a). Firstly, Enlightenment epistemology operates according to a set of hierarchized dualisms in which, for instance, reason is privileged over emotion, presence is privileged over absence, and physical is privileged over psychological (e.g., Scheppele, 1994, pp. 1000, 1012–1014). This makes it particularly difficult, for example, for a woman not bearing evidence of violence on her body to come into court and convince a judicial officer that she is fearful of her former partner, or for protection orders made ex parte to be given credence in other contexts.

Secondly, the rules of evidence complement substantive legal doctrine by eliciting information about discrete incidents or transactions, while obstructing fact finding in nonparadigm cases involving patterns of abusive behavior, or a person's interpretation of and reaction to incidents within a cumulative series of events (Mahoney, 1991, pp. 28, 34; Scheppele, 1994, pp. 1014–1015). Regarded in isolation, much abusive or threatening behavior can be explained away, given a benign interpretation, or made to appear innocuous. The decontextualized examination of disaggregated incidents can leave a case in shreds (Hunter, 1996a, p. 131).

Thirdly, evidentiary rules and adversarial proceedings assume "universal cognitive competence," that is, the notion that normal, unbiased people are able to assess the information presented to them and to reach the same conclusion. This in turn rests on a view that common experience gives rise to universally accepted generalizations about human behavior that are available to all triers of fact (MacCrimmon, 1991, pp. 37–38). In reality, however, as demonstrated earlier in this chapter, gender-, race-, and sexuality-based experience may give rise to very different generalizations and intuitions about human behavior. When judges make discretionary decisions about whether to admit or exclude certain evidence, or what weight to give to that evidence, they tend to rely on generalizations from a masculine, socially dominant point of view, and one that is influenced by the prevailing legal culture (Hunter, 1996a, p. 131). This is not usually good news for women litigants (Hunter, 1996a, pp. 133–150). Examples from the domestic violence field noted earlier include the notion that if the violence was as bad as the woman claims, she would have left—or left sooner—or not "reconciled" with her abuser. Or that if a man behaved in that way, he must have been provoked, drunk, under pressure, or acting out of character.

Speaking in Court

Finally, the actual court process can have a silencing effect upon victims of violence. First, speaking in court usually means telling one's story through a lawyer (see, e.g., Coombs, 1993, p. 291). The lawyer therefore acts as yet another filter, determining what will be said and how it will be said. The power relations between lawyer and client may involve more or less control on the client's part, and more or less understanding, empathy, and empowerment on the part of the lawyer (Espinoza, 1997, p. 914; Seuffert, 1996, pp. 525, 531–532, 544, 547).

Power relations in the courtroom are another matter. When women do have the opportunity to speak for themselves in court, either in proceedings without a lawyer or in giving evidence, their ability to do so is hampered by the unfamiliarity of the court setting and their reactions to it. Interviews with women who have applied for restraining orders indicate that they are generally frightened and nervous about going to court and intimidated by the institution. Some mention feeling overwhelmed, numb, or faint (Ptacek, 1999, p. 149). Others feel embarrassed, humiliated, or degraded at having to speak in open court about the violence they have endured (Chaudhury & Daly, 1992, p. 244; Ptacek, 1999, p. 148). They may find it very difficult to relate their histories of domestic violence and to articulate their ongoing fear and need for protection (Busch et al., 1995, p. 204). Telling a detailed story about trauma is the last thing some survivors are willing or able to do.[19]

More generally, as Lucie White (1990) has pointed out,

> [T]he web of subterranean speech norms and coerced speech practices that accompany race, gender, and class domination—undermine the capacity of many persons in our society to use the procedural rituals that are formally available to them. (p. 4)

"Powerless" speech forms, developed by women and other subordinated speakers to manage verbal encounters with those more powerful, fail to project authority or credibility (Bezdek, 1992, pp. 583–585; Cahn, 1993, pp. 2517–2518; Conley & O'Barr, 1998, p. 65; Mack, 1993, pp. 330–331; White, 1990, pp. 15–17). This problem is exacerbated for nonnative speakers of English, whose speech patterns and communication styles may be seriously misread by the court, or whose story may be substantially affected by the need to tell it through an interpreter (see, e.g., Bezdek, 1992, pp. 594–595; Cooke, 1995; Goldflam, 1995; Oh, 1992, p. 127; Tolmie, 1997, pp. 488–501).

Conclusion

Legal method claims to ensure detached, objective, and impartial adjudication (Mossman, 1986, p. 39; Sarmas, 1998), free of emotionality (Henderson, 1987, 1575–1576) and of any political, cultural, social, or gender bias (Troup, 1993, p. 63). The "forensic constraints" of witnesses being required to tell their stories within a formal court setting, on oath, in a witness box, in response to lawyers' questions, and in accordance with the rules of evidence, apply equally to all litigants, whether the case is gender or race sensitive or not (Heerey, 1996, p. 16; Heerey, 2000, p. 686). The experiences of previously excluded groups in the legal system, however, highlight the fact that courts are not equally accessible to all,[20] that legal categories are not inevitable and are not always fair, that the rules of evidence "provide…a particular frame that produces a particular truth" (Seidman, 1996, p. 164), that assessments of relevance may exclude the particular concerns and motivations bringing litigants to court in the first place, and that human behavior cannot necessarily be fully understood by reference to the particular social and legal narratives that the judge believes to be true.

Feminist law reformers may have hoped that the acceptance of domestic violence as a legal category would help to "end the silence" about male violence in the home, as women would speak about it publicly in court, thereby educating judges and the general community about the prevalence, dynamics, and effects of domestic abuse. But the process of going to court and making a legal claim is itself one that disciplines, regulates, abstracts, and possibly silences the subject so that the chances of "her" story being heard are limited. James Ptacek (1999), in his study of two courts hearing domestic violence protection order applications, noted that some of the judges' understandings of violence had changed, but this was through participating in workshops and reading feminist literature, not through listening to women's stories in court (p. 119).[21] The following chapters consider whether the theoretical arguments and empirical observations set out in the foregoing discussion hold true in the courts hearing claims about domestic violence that were the subject of my study.

Endnotes

1. For U.S. statistics on the gender disparity in the perpetration of domestic violence, see United States Department of Justice (2000), estimating that in 1998, women were 5 times more likely to experience violence at the hands of an intimate partner than were men, and were also much more likely to report physical injury as a result of the violence; Straus & Gelles (1990), noting that men are likely to inflict greater pain or injury by acts of violence than are women, and that "a great deal of violence by women against their husbands is retaliation or self-defense" (p. 120); and Tjaden & Thoennes (2000, p. 31), concluding that intimate partner violence is perpetrated primarily by men.
2. The ABS *Women's Safety Australia* study (1996) found that 8.8% of women in a current relationship had experienced some form of emotional abuse by their partner, defined as "manipulation, isolation or intimidation." In 59% of these cases, emotional abuse was experienced in conjunction with physical violence. In addition, 25% of those who experienced physical or sexual violence had also had their partner damage or destroy property, and 13% reported difficulties with their partner over family finances (p. 51). In the more recent Australian International Violence Against Women Survey (IVAWS), 37–40% of women reported controlling behaviors from a current intimate partner, and controlling behaviors were found to be the strongest risk factor for physical violence. "If the woman's intimate partner engaged in controlling behaviors, the odds of experiencing physical violence over the lifetime are increased by a factor of six" (Mouzos & Makkai, 2004, pp. 48, 61). Similarly, the U.S. NVAWS survey found a strong association between women reporting rape and/or physical assault and women reporting controlling behavior, jealousy, and verbal abuse by their partners (Tjaden & Thoennes, 2000, p. iv).
3. The *Women's Safety Australia* study estimated that 701,200 women had been pregnant at some stage during a previous relationship with a violent partner, and that 42% of these had experienced violence during the pregnancy; 20% experienced violence for the first time when pregnant (ABS, 1996, p. 52).
4. In the *Women's Safety Australia* study, around half of the women who had experienced violence in a previous relationship had separated from the previous partner and then returned before the final separation, 35% of these had

experienced violence during the time of separation, and 7% of the women who had experienced violence from a previous partner reported that the violence occurred only after the relationship ended (ABS, 1996, pp. 51–52). One U.S. study found that up to three quarters of reported domestic assaults occur after the victim has left the abuser (see Hart, 1990, p. 324).

5. This was a feature of one of the family law cases I observed (F.C.9, January 20–24, February 10–11, & February 14, 1997).
6. U.S. proarrest and mandatory arrest regimes compound women's fears about exposing their partners to racist treatment (see, e.g., Coker, 2000, p. 1042; Fedders, 1997; Ruttenberg, 1994, p. 182).
7. For similar observations in the U.S., see Crenshaw (1994, pp. 94, 107–110) on access to battered women's shelters for Black women; Klein & Orloff (1993, p. 1021–1022) and Rivera (1994, p. 252) on lack of bilingual services in shelters. Lesbians may also experience homophobia and discrimination when attempting to access refuges/shelters and other mainstream services (see Bennet, 1997, pp. 21–22; Eaton, 1994, p. 198; Geraci, 1986, p. 77; "'Out' of sight," 2000, p. 14; Vickers, 1996, ¶ 53–56, 90).
8. Indigenous people use the term "family violence" to capture the range of violence and abuse experienced in and affecting all members of Indigenous communities (ATSIWTFV, 2000, p. 2, citing Mow, 1992, p. 10; Atkinson, 1997, p. 6; Laing, 2000a, p. 2; Memmott et al., 1999; Victorian Government, 2004, p. 4).
9. For a comprehensive account of police treatment of Indigenous women, including false imprisonment and rape of women in custody, see Human Rights and Equal Opportunity Commission (HREOC) (1991). On Indigenous deaths in custody, see Royal Commission into Aboriginal Deaths in Custody (1991); Aboriginal and Torres Strait Islander Social Justice Commissioner (1997).
10. On similar problems in Canada and the U.S., see Razak (1998, pp. 69–72), citing instances of sexual violence by Aboriginal men against Aboriginal women in Canada being excused on the basis of "culture"; Rimonte (1991) and Volpp (1994), on the invocation of the so-called "cultural defense" to excuse domestic violence in the U.S.
11. See, for example, Moreton-Robinson (2000, pp. 158–159), who lists the following social indicators illustrating the difference between Indigenous and white women in Australia: Indigenous women have a life expectancy 20 years lower than non-Indigenous women, and have a 5 times greater risk of dying in the 25–44 age group; 30% of the Indigenous population has diabetes; Indigenous infant mortality is 3 to 5 times higher than

non-Indigenous infant mortality; Indigenous families are 20 times more likely than non-Indigenous families to be homeless; 33% of Indigenous children complete high school compared to 77% of non-Indigenous children; the Indigenous unemployment rate is 30–40%, with a further 20–30% receiving unemployment benefits for work on community development projects; and in 1994 Indigenous people earned 65 cents in the white dollar. Indigenous women in the Northern Territory are 28 times more likely to be victims of homicide than are non-Indigenous people. Bolger (1991, p. 69) notes that these homicide figures do not include Indigenous women who die from the cumulative effects of violence on their health over a number of years, often exacerbated by alcohol abuse and malnutrition.

12. Bolger notes, however, that some Indigenous men who abuse their partners are not powerless and poor: they are well educated and have good jobs as teachers, bureaucrats, and so forth. However, the stories of these men and their partners more closely resemble those of violent relationships in the Anglo-Australian community (1991, pp. 35–37, 44).
13. See, for example, Creed (1993), citing instances including Clytemnestra of Greek mythology, witches, vampires, and castrating mothers; Heberle (2001), discussing capital murder cases involving female defendants, and concluding that these cases "show how cultural anxieties about gender difference and gender identity persistently overdetermine legal outcomes and that there is no predictably safe way to enact femininity before the law"; Schneider (2000, p. 121), noting that women who kill their abusers are viewed as mad or bad; Stubbs and Tolmie (1994, pp. 193–194), discussing the case of *R v. Whalen* (1991) and contrasting the judge's description of the long history of terrible physical and emotional abuse suffered by the defendant as "matrimonial discord," with his description of the defendant's "savagery" in killing her husband while he lay "helpless" in bed; and Threadgold (1997, p. 228) on the "monstrous feminine" in connection with battered women who kill their abusers.
14. See also Brown (1995), who argues that liberalism assumes that masculine dominance within the family is nonviolent, because "[l]iberal state-of-nature theory presumes that violence inheres among equals, not between dominant and subordinate persons. Liberalism, presuming rational men, has no theory of violence practiced for reasons—psychic, erotic, etc.—independent of material gain" (p. 150).
15. On the limited or nonexistence of the zone of family privacy for racial minority families, see Collins (1991, p. 150), HREOC (1997), Hunter (1996, p. 150), and Kline (1989, p. 130). On the denial of family privacy

to gay men and lesbians, see Backer (1998, pp. 620, 659) and Mason (1995, pp. 67, 80).

16. Schafran (1995, pp. 1066–1067) also suggests that male judges often project themselves into domestic violence cases in sympathy with the man. For example, their own experience of divorce, and the anger and resentment it engendered, enable them more readily to believe that the man appearing before them was provoked by his wife's leaving, or by her relationship with another man.
17. The primary issue in the appeal concerned the fact that at trial, the son (who actually struck the fatal blow) had been acquitted on the basis of self-defense, while Mrs Osland had been found guilty of murder. Two of the "minimizing" judges would have allowed the appeal on the basis that the verdicts were inconsistent; however, the majority did not find any inconsistency and allowed Mrs Osland's conviction to stand.
18. See, for example, Ewick and Silbey (1995), who note, "The law's insistent demand for personal narratives achieves the kind of radical individuation that disempowers the teller by effacing the connections among persons and the social organization of their experiences" (p. 217).
19. See Scarry (1985), noting that pain cannot be shared because it is resistant to language—the scope for linguistic expression of pain is very limited; and Tolmie (1997, p. 483), explaining, in the context of a survivor of the Cambodian genocide, that it is problematic to ask trauma survivors to explain their circumstances in court, that symptoms of posttraumatic stress disorder include avoiding talking about and "forgetting" the experience, and that, as previously noted, women who have survived a violent relationship may share these symptoms. Compare Lawless (2000), discussing "narrative failures" in battered women's stories, and initially considering that "language and words cannot do justice to the pain and the violations," and that "[t]he unspeakable is, in fact, unspeakable" (pp. 71–72), but eventually concluding that such gaps signify the woman's survival and transformation: she "refuses to recount the disaster and privilege the subjectivity of her abuser" (p. 78).
20. The normal forensic constraints have been modified in some Australian contexts, for example, in native title claims by Indigenous groups, in which evidence of a cultural or customary matter may be given by way of singing, dancing, or storytelling, and in trade practices cases, in which the reception of expert economic evidence allows for presentations by and dialogue between the experts, in a round-table setting (Heerey, 2000, p. 689). It is not clear why these modifications are possible but modifications that would,

for example, allow raped or abused women to tell their stories more easily would apparently represent a breach in the edifice of forensic impartiality.

21. See also Braithwaite and Daly (1995), suggesting community conferencing as a forum in which the voices of rape and domestic violence victims are more likely to be heard and respected than in court; Coombs (1993, pp. 304–305), suggesting that nonlitigation forums for telling women's stories, such as "quiet conversations with those we know," classroom discussions, and published stories of a fictional, autobiographical, or scholarly nature, hold out greater prospects for challenging dominant narratives.

CHAPTER 3

THE INTERVENTION ORDER PROCESS

INTRODUCTION

This chapter and the following chapter look at women's experience in applying for intervention orders against domestic violence. This chapter deals with the process of applying for and obtaining an intervention order, while chapter 4 deals with the understandings of domestic violence revealed in intervention order proceedings.

As noted in chapter 1, in Victoria intervention orders are made pursuant to the Crimes (Family Violence) Act (1987). Prior to the enactment of this legislation, the only avenues available to protect victims of domestic violence against further violence were common law peace orders, which bound the perpetrator to "keep the peace"—a fairly limited remedy—or criminal prosecution of the perpetrator, which depended upon proof of an assault to the criminal standard of beyond reasonable doubt. Even if a criminal conviction was secured, the victim would not necessarily be protected from further violence, since convictions tended to result in relatively minor penalties, with incarceration reserved only for very serious cases. Domestic violence intervention orders, on the other hand, are (at least in theory) tailored specifically to protect victims of violence from future acts of domestic violence, and the grant of an order requires only the civil standard of proof. Breach of an order is a criminal offense, which can (but in practice most often does not) result in prosecution and conviction.[1]

Intervention order applications are heard in Victoria—and in most other Australian States and Territories—by Magistrates' Courts, the lowest level court in the generalist State court hierarchy.[2] Magistrates' Courts also deal with summary offenses (criminal matters not involving a prison sentence), indictable offenses when the defendant elects to plead guilty or to be tried summarily, committal hearings (to decide whether sufficient evidence exists to send a matter to trial in a higher court), and civil matters up to a specified monetary limit. Since the advent of intervention order legislation, applications for intervention orders have become a substantial component of Magistrates' Court work, without, as a general proposition, the courts having been provided with additional resources to deal with these matters.[3] As a consequence, intervention order applications have been assimilated into the courts' general workload and tend to be dealt with in similar, routinized ways as other matters. In some courts, however, magistrates have experimented with different ways of dealing with intervention order applications—setting aside a separate hearing room, setting aside a particular time and/or day to hear intervention order applications, or having applications heard by a particular magistrate who has developed expertise in the jurisdiction or is thought to be particularly sympathetic towards the issue of domestic violence.

The heavy usage of intervention order provisions and similar provisions in other States and Territories, in contrast to extremely limited criminal prosecution of either domestic assaults or breaches of protection orders, has led some commentators to describe protection order regimes as having produced a "decriminalization of domestic violence"

(Douglas & Godden, 2003; McGregor & Hopkins, 1991, p. 114; Scutt, 1990, p. 293).[4] In actuality, however, domestic violence has never been criminalized in Australia, and feminists are divided as to whether the criminal law could ever be an effective tool for the elimination of violence and the protection of its victims (Holder, 2001; see also Cahn, 2000, pp. 820–821).

The Legislation

At the time the fieldwork was undertaken for this study, the Crimes (Family Violence) Act (1987) provided for complaints for an intervention order to be made by or on behalf of an "aggrieved family member."[5] "Family member" was defined very broadly to include the spouse (including former or de facto spouse) of the alleged perpetrator, a person who has or has had an intimate personal relationship with the alleged perpetrator, a relative (as further defined) of the alleged perpetrator, a child who normally or regularly resides with the alleged perpetrator or of whom the alleged perpetrator is a guardian, or any person who is or has been ordinarily a member of the alleged perpetrator's household (s. 3).[6]

The court was empowered to make an intervention order in respect of a person if satisfied on the balance of probabilities that that person had

(a) assaulted a family member or caused damage to the property of the family member, and was likely to again assault the family member or cause damage to their property; or
(b) threatened to assault or cause damage to the property of a family member, and was likely to assault the family member or cause damage to their property; or
(c) harassed, molested or behaved in an offensive manner towards a family member, and was likely to do so again. (s. 4)

The Act thus set up a two-part test for an order. The court had to be satisfied that there had been either an assault or property damage; a threat to assault or cause property damage; or harassment, molestation, or offensive behavior; *and* that there was a likelihood of (further) assault or property damage, or further harassment, molestation, or offensive behavior. Past assault, threats, or offensive behavior without the likelihood of repetition would not be sufficient for an order.

The doctrinal weaknesses of the legislation included the absence of a preamble or set of guiding principles explaining the objectives of the Act, the exclusion of some commonly experienced abusive and controlling behaviors from the definition of domestic violence, and the requirements to prove both harm and likely repetition before an order could be granted.[7] The legislation did not provide a clear statement of its rationale—the prevalence of domestic violence in the community and the aim of the legislature to reduce the incidence of violence—nor did it state any background facts (such as the fact that the majority of domestic violence is perpetrated by men against women and children), guiding principles (such as the need for perpetrators to take responsibility for their actions and for stopping their violence), or overriding goals (such as to ensure the safety of family members subjected to violence and abuse) (see Hunter & Stubbs, 1999, p. 12; Victorian Community Council Against Violence [VCCAV], 1991, p. 10). The only preliminary information provided was that "[t]he main purposes of this Act are to provide for intervention orders in cases of family violence and to amend the Crimes Act 1958" (s. 1). The absence of an interpretive framework for magistrates in applying the Act left them unconstrained in invoking their own beliefs and assumptions about domestic violence. Further, as discussed subsequently, the definition of violence in the Act and the requirements for the granting of an order tended to produce a focus on incidents and deflected magistrates' attention from indicators important to feminist understandings of violence, such as intimidation, a pattern of coercive behavior, or behavior inducing fear or emotional distress (see also Hunter & Stubbs, 1999, pp. 13–14). Moreover, given research indicating that the majority of women applying for intervention orders had already experienced repeated violence (Stubbs & Powell, 1989, p. 43; Trimboli & Bonney, 1997, p. 30; Wearing, 1992, p. 363; Wearing, 1996, p. 133; see also Fischer & Rose, 1995, p. 416 and chapter 1 of this book), the requirement to prove likelihood of repetition was arguably an unnecessary evidentiary barrier to securing applicants' safety and protection (Hunter & Stubbs, 1999, p. 14).

Complaints for an intervention order could be made by either a member of the police force or an aggrieved family member (or a parent of a child if the aggrieved family member was a child) (s. 7). In practice, in Melbourne during the period of the fieldwork, virtually all applications were made by aggrieved family members themselves. I observed only two cases in which the police applied for an intervention order on behalf of a victim of violence (M.C.10, April 22, 1996; M.C.30, July 4, 1996).[8] This was not necessarily the practice everywhere. For example, interviewees and the literature suggested that police were more active in other parts of Victoria and in other States (e.g., Alexander, 2002, p. 90; Easteal, 1996; p. 192; Seddon, 1993, p. 132; Trimboli & Bonney, 1997; Vucko, 2001; Wearing, 1996, pp. 14, 15).[9] But certainly in Melbourne aggrieved family members made their own applications, which obviously affected their experience of the court process.

Intervention orders could be made on an interim or a final basis. Interim orders could be made in the absence of the defendant

> if the court is satisfied that it is necessary to ensure the safety of the aggrieved family member or to preserve any property of the aggrieved family member pending the hearing and determination of the complaint. (s. 8(1))

Interim orders could be applied for by the police out of hours by telephone or fax (s. 8(4)–(10)), but, as previously noted, this occurred very rarely. Otherwise, interim orders could not be made unless the complaint was supported by oral evidence (s. 8(2); see also Hunter & Stubbs, 1999, p. 15). Interim orders could only be made for a limited period (s. 8(3)). Final orders could also be made in the absence of the defendant if he had been served with a summons and had failed to appear in court on the specified date (s. 12).[10] If the defendant did appear, he could either contest the matter (in which case the magistrate would hear evidence and make a decision) or consent to an order. Although the legislation provided that "[t]he court may make any order under this Act with the consent of all the parties to the proceedings" (s. 14), in practice, as explained later in this chapter, the consent of the aggrieved family member to a "consent" order was almost never sought.

Magistrates' Courts in fact granted many more interim than final orders. According to the leading study on this issue, in the period 1991–1995 in Victoria, 35–40% of applications were not proceeded with after an interim order had been obtained (Wearing, 1996, p. 1; see also Egger & Stubbs, 1993, p. 31). In 1994–1995, 26% of applications for final orders were struck out and 9% were withdrawn, while only 4% were dismissed (Wearing, 1996, p. 10).[11] The main reason for applications being struck out was that the applicant failed to appear on the return date (Wearing, 1996, p. 24). An investigation of struck-out and withdrawn cases revealed that the applications often involved allegations of serious and prolonged violence, and had been made by both the police and aggrieved family members themselves (Wearing, 1996, pp. 29–52).[12] However, two thirds of the women interviewed who had not proceeded after obtaining an interim order said that the impact of the order was either negative or at best unhelpful. The violence had continued in 37% of these cases and had become worse in 30% (Wearing, 1996, p. 140). The study concluded that withdrawals after interim orders were mainly attributable to events outside the courtroom (including defendants' threats or pleas for reconciliation), but that there was a lack of support in helping women to get (back) to court and to negotiate the court process (Wearing, 1996, pp. 233–237).

Terms of orders could include restricting or prohibiting the defendant from approaching within a specified distance of the aggrieved family member; entering premises where the aggrieved family member lived, worked, or attended regularly; being in a specified locality; contacting, threatening, or intimidating the aggrieved family member; or damaging the aggrieved family member's property (s. 5(1)(a)–(e)). Orders could also include the revocation of the defendant's license or permit to possess or carry firearms (s. 5(1)(h)). In relation to the making of "sole occupancy" orders evicting the defendant from the family home, the Act provided that

> [b]efore making an order which restricts the defendant's access to any premises, the court must take into account—
>
> (a) the need to ensure that the aggrieved family member is protected from violence; and
> (b) the welfare of any children who may be affected by the order; and
> (c) the accommodation needs of all persons who may be affected by the order—
>
> and give paramount consideration to the matters in paragraph (a). (s. 5(2))

Although the last paragraph of this subsection attempted to make the safety of the aggrieved family member paramount, the effect of the subsection was clearly to suggest to the court that it should exercise particular caution before making such orders, since no similar, additional considerations were specified in relation to the making of any other kinds of orders.

Final orders remained in force "for the period specified by the court" (s. 6).[13] At the time the fieldwork commenced, many final orders were made "until further order"—in other words, indefinitely. However, during the course of the fieldwork, debate among magistrates as to whether this was permitted under the legislation resulted in an increase in orders being made for a specified period—usually 12 months, although some were made for longer periods of between 2 and 5 years (Field notes, Broadmeadows Magistrates' Court, February 21, 1997; Sunshine Magistrates' Court, June 17, 1997).[14] Orders could be revoked, varied, or extended on application by the aggrieved family member or by a party to the original proceedings (s. 16(1)–(2)). This required the applicant to serve a copy of the application on the other party (s. 16(4)–(5))—an obvious difficulty for a target of violence who wished to extend a time-limited order without having contact with the defendant. At the very end of the fieldwork period, the Crimes (Family Violence) Act (1987) was amended specifically to allow for orders of indefinite duration—if no period was specified in the order it remained in force until further order—and to retrospectively validate indefinite orders made prior to the amendment

(s. 6, inserted by Law and Justice Legislation Amendment Act (1997), s. 7). This potentially alleviated the problem for applicants of having to return repeatedly to court to keep orders in place. As discussed later in this chapter, however, this provision has not been fully exploited.

In general, very little evidence about the operation of the Crimes (Family Violence) Act (1987) is available from the reports of superior court cases. At the time of the fieldwork, 9–10 years after the Act came into force, there had only been three appellate court decisions interpreting its terms. Even at the time of writing, in 2005, a search of cases on the Crimes (Family Violence) Act (1987) revealed only 16 decisions of the Victorian Supreme Court involving the Act. The life of this legislation, therefore, is to be found not in the appellate record of doctrinal interpretation, but in the day-to-day functioning of the Victorian Magistrates' Courts.

OBSERVATIONS

In the typical case, on the basis of my observations and interviews, the aggrieved family member would first come before the Magistrates' Court to apply for an interim intervention order, in the absence of the defendant. The applicant would be interviewed initially by a member of court staff (then variously called the court clerk, registrar, or family law coordinator, now uniformly known as the registrar), who would assist them to complete the application form. The applicant would then go into court and give sworn evidence in support of the application and answer any questions that the magistrate might have in satisfying him- or herself that there were sufficient grounds for an order. Interim orders were usually (though not invariably) granted (see also Wearing, 1992, p. 18) for a period of 2–4 weeks. Each court tended to schedule intervention order return dates on a particular day or days of the week, so a court date would be set for one of these days in 2–4 weeks' time. The interim order had then to be served on the defendant (which was done by the police) before it had any effect.

On the return date, in almost half of the matters I observed (47.1%), the defendant did not appear in court.[15] In these cases, the applicant would appear briefly before the magistrate to confirm her continuing desire for an order, and the order would be made final. In the cases in which the defendant did appear, the court clerk would present his options: he could contest the matter, which would require witnesses and could involve a lengthy delay; or, if he wanted to get the matter over with, he could consent to having an order made against him. In order to sweeten the consent option, clerks routinely informed the defendant that he could consent to the order without admitting the allegations. Not surprisingly, this option was frequently adopted by defendants. Both parties would then appear before the magistrate, who would make the order final and explain to the defendant the consequences of breaching the order. The aggrieved family member was almost never asked whether she agreed to allow the defendant to consent without admitting the allegations.

In a small proportion of cases (5.6%), the defendant had not been located or had otherwise evaded service of the interim order (see also Wearing, 1992, p. 335). In these cases, the only option open to the court was to extend the interim order for a further period to allow further attempts at service. A final order could not be made without the defendant being notified. Thus, if the defendant could not ultimately be located, the interim order would lapse and the applicant would be left without a remedy.

If the defendant insisted on contesting the matter, it would proceed to a formal hearing. Hearings were usually postponed until all consent matters had been disposed of and, in some cases, were adjourned to another date if the court could not hear the matter on the particular day. Hearings were adversarial, with each side in turn presenting their case, supported by sworn evidence from the parties and any witnesses they wished to call. At the conclusion of the evidence, the magistrate would announce his or her decision. As discussed further in this chapter, the applicant was successful in only around half of the contested matters observed.

I observed 100 domestic violence protection order applications in nine Magistrates' Courts in the Melbourne metropolitan area, during the 18-month period of February 1996–July 1997. The cases were heard by 17 different magistrates: 13 male and 4 female. The average number of cases heard per magistrate per observation session (a day or half day) was six. The great majority of applicants (91%) were women (see also Putt & Higgins, 1997, p. 29; VCCAV, 2002, p. 8; Wearing, 1992, p. 315). The breakdown of types of applications is shown in table 2.

Applications for final orders constituted approximately three quarters of the observation sample. This is not surprising given that interim orders may be applied for at any time, but returns tend to be scheduled on specified hearing days, which in turn were the days when it made most sense to attend a particular court to undertake observations. As noted above, however, many more interim than final orders are made in practice, so the more "typical" experience overall was that of the applicants for interim orders.

The defendant's relationship to the applicant in each of the cases is set out in table 3.

Men who had been in an intimate relationship with a female applicant made up over half of all defendants, with other family relationships receiving fairly limited representation. Notably, though, in over one quarter of the cases, the relationship between the defendant and the aggrieved family member was never stated during the court proceedings. Without access to the written complaints, it was difficult to infer the nature of these relationships.[16] This occurred mostly in applications for final orders when the defendant either was not present or consented to an order, so that there was virtually no discussion of the matter in court.

TABLE 2. Types of intervention order applications.

Application Type	Female No.	Male No.	Total
Interim orders	17	0	17
Final orders	66	8	73[a]
Revocation	5	1	6
Variation	3	1	4
Total	91	10	100

[a]One of these applications was for mutual orders, involving both female and male applicants.

The largest group of applicants in the observation sample (34%) were aged 21–30, with 21% aged 41–50, and 19% aged 31–40.[17] Ten percent of applicants were aged under 20. It was impossible to determine the applicant's occupation and source of financial support in the great majority of cases. Approximately one third of applicants were from non-English speaking backgrounds (including Eastern and Southern European, South East Asian, Middle Eastern, African, and South American). In turn, approximately one third of these applicants ($n = 11$) had an interpreter with them in court, while a further 6 applicants had poor or limited English and would have benefited from the use of an interpreter. A significant number of applicants brought children with them to court—either very young children or older/adult children. However, if children were not present and there was no discussion of children in the courtroom, it was impossible to determine the applicant's parental status in most cases. A small number of applicants ($n = 8$)—generally older women—presented with obvious mobility disabilities, while 3 applicants appeared to have an intellectual disability, and 1 presented with visible injuries from a recent assault by the defendant.

TABLE 3. Defendant's relationship to applicant for intervention orders.

Relationship	No. Cases
Husband or ex-husband	33
De facto or ex–de facto husband	11
Boyfriend or ex-boyfriend	12
Ex-wife or ex–de facto wife	4
Father	2
Son or daughter[a]	6
Sibling[b]	3
Other	3
Unknown	27
Total	101

[a]Including adoptive son and son-in-law.
[b]Including brother, sister, and ex-sister-in-law.

The great majority of applicants were successful in their applications, as shown in table 4.

Final order applications were adjourned either because, as previously noted, the defendant had not yet been served with the interim order, or because the defendant indicated that they wished to contest the making of the order, and the contested matter could not be heard immediately.

The way in which decisions and orders were made is shown in table 5.

It can be seen from this table that over half of all dispositions in the intervention order cases observed were made ex parte. This included all but one of the interim orders (as would be expected) and, as previously noted, almost half of the final orders. The next largest group of final orders—over one third—were made by consent, and the majority of these were by consent without admitting the allegations. Only a small proportion of matters overall were contested.

TABLE 4. Outcomes of intervention order applications.

Type of Application	Granted	Refused	Adjourned
Interim order	15	1	1
Final order	54	5	12
Revocation	4	1	1
Variation	3	1	0
Total	76	8	14

TABLE 5. Basis on which intervention orders were made.

Type of Application	Consent	Consent Without Admitting Allegations	Contested Determination	Ex Parte
Interim order	0	1	0	16
Final order	8	18	12	35
Revocation	2	0	1	3
Variation	1	0	1	2
Total	11	19	14	56

Representation and Support

The Need for Representation

An information paper issued by the Women's Legal Resource Group (WLRG) in Melbourne noted that

> although the Crimes (Family Violence) legislation was enacted with a purpose of enabling self representation in court, this is not always possible because:—
>
> a. Violence usually has a disabling effect on its victims often rendering them unable to properly identify and articulate the complaint;
> b. The Act has a very wide definition of violence and representation may be required to direct a Magistrate to grant an Order with respect to…the "grey" areas;
> c. Lack of education and experience in the court process;
> d. Fear of the perpetrator being in court; and
> e. A general lack of confidence by the victim in their own abilities to initiate and carry through legal action and in the system which so often lets them down. (Abela, Opat, Wilkes & van Moorst, 1994, pp. 3–4)

To this might be added the observation that many abused women are unable to remain calm and rational in court, but if they express anger or become emotional or confused, their credibility in the eyes of the magistrate is diminished (Kinports & Fischer, 1992, p. 204; McGregor & Hopkins, 1991, pp. 100–101; Wearing, 1992, p. 155; S.W.1, interview, December 23, 1997).

The particular situation of domestic violence survivors thus suggests a need for support and representation in court. Support workers and legal service workers interviewed said they would particularly advise women to have representation on the return day for an intervention order if they thought their partner was likely to contest the application (e.g., F. Culpen, interview, March 17, 1997). Legal aid was available (subject to means and merit tests) if it was known that an application would be contested. One flaw in the system, though, was that there was no requirement for the defendant to serve notice of his intentions prior to the return date. He could decide to appear or not appear on the day as he chose, with or without his own representation.[18] Thus, it was very difficult for applicants to know what to do, and in the absence of certainty, most could not afford to pay a lawyer for the return date "just in case" (see also Nunn & D'Arcy, 2001, p. 21). My observations included several instances when the defendant had appeared unexpectedly, and the applicant then sought an adjournment to obtain legal assistance (e.g., Field notes, Moonee Ponds Magistrates' Court, November 1, 1996; also H. Assafiri, interview, June 24, 1997).[19]

In the previous chapter, three potential problems were raised in relation to the legal representation of survivors of domestic violence. Firstly, there is the possibility that lawyers will share nonfeminist understandings of domestic violence as part of their "internal" legal culture, and hence will have only a limited understanding of their client's position. Secondly, there is the possibility that women's voices will be silenced by the fact that court proceedings are dominated by the voices of lawyers. Thirdly, there is the possibility that lawyers will disempower their clients by transforming their stories into standardized legal narratives that misrepresent the client's actual experience and/or fail to respond to their actual needs. The following sections explore these possibilities in relation to intervention order proceedings.

The Availability of Representation and Support

Women applying for intervention orders had a range of support options available to them. First, it was open to women to obtain their own legal representation. Free legal representation from a community legal service or Legal Aid office was rarely available, however, due to limited resources and, consequently, restrictive guidelines as to the circumstances in which assistance would be provided. Legal representation most often had to be paid for. Around half of the women interviewed had had legal representation, but the women from non-English speaking backgrounds in particular stressed that they and most of the women they knew could not afford to pay for a solicitor to represent them for an intervention order (NESB Focus Group, interview, December 23, 1997; see also Kinports & Fischer, 1992, pp. 174–175; Wearing, 1992, p. 22).

In order to attempt to alleviate the difficulties of affording representation and not knowing whether the defendant would appear to contest the order, a series of domestic violence court support services had been established since 1992, which operated at various Magistrates' Courts on designated return dates. These generally involved both a solicitor and a domestic violence support worker. Solicitors were drawn from local community legal services or were volunteers from private practice, while support workers generally came from one of the regional domestic violence outreach services. The solicitor would advise applicants for intervention orders on their legal position and options, and sometimes (though not always) would represent them in court. The support worker would provide applicants with emotional support, information, and referrals to other services if needed, including women's refuges. Similar court support services existed (on a more or less coordinated basis) in other States (Abela et al., 1994, p. 1; ALRC, 1994, pp. 130–131; Domestic Violence Advocacy Service, 1998). However, like my observations, court support programs focused on return dates. None was in a position to staff the relevant court every day to assist women applying for interim orders.

Court support services operated on intervention order return days in four of the nine Magistrates' Courts in which my observations took place: Broadmeadows, Sunshine, Preston, and Dandenong. Applicants arriving at court to apply for an interim or final order would be referred by court staff to the support program, which would then interview the applicant and assess her or his support needs. Three of the programs assisted all applicants, but the program at Sunshine was exclusively available to women applicants, with non-English speaking background women having the highest priority on the basis that they were the ones with the greatest need for support and assistance (C. McNamara, interview, June 14, 1996).

The solicitors at Broadmeadows explained that they did not necessarily accompany the applicant into court if the defendant was not present, unless the woman had a real need for support and assistance. In interim matters, there was little for the solicitor to do in any case. And in final matters, they thought it was more compelling for the woman to tell her own story to the magistrate. Even if the matter was contested (which generally meant it would proceed in the afternoon), the solicitor would not usually stay to represent the applicant, unless the defendant had legal representation or the applicant had no English and was accompanied by an interpreter (Field notes, Broadmeadows Magistrates' Court, October 25, 1996; February 21, 1997).

Similarly, lawyers in the court support programs at the Sunshine and Dandenong Magistrates' Courts would not usually accompany applicants into court (Field notes, Dandenong Magistrates' Court, November 4, 1996; Sunshine Magistrates' Court, July 2, 1996). One of the Sunshine lawyers argued that they were too busy interviewing and advising applicants and did not have time to go into court, although they would do so if they knew the woman would have problems otherwise (C. McNamara, interview, June 14, 1996). Sunshine was a somewhat unusual court, however, because the magistrate was known to be very sympathetic to applicants, and the court also only operated in the mornings and did not hear contested matters (all contested cases were adjourned to another court at a later date). Only the Preston court support solicitor routinely appeared in court on behalf of applicants. It was clear that the solicitor had a good relationship with the magistrate and would discuss the pending matters with him prior to their coming on. Armed with this foreknowledge, the magistrate would then work through the cases without requiring much input from the solicitor (Field notes, Preston Magistrates' Court, February 22, 1996; July 4, 1996).

The value to the court of the intervention order support program was recognized, for example, by the fact that the Preston Magistrates' Court provided financial support for the program out of the court poor box (Field notes, Preston Magistrates' Court, July 4, 1996). One of the ways in which support program lawyers performed a valuable service for the court was in conducting discussions and negotiations with the defendant and/or his lawyer, thereby relieving the court of the need to mediate between unrepresented litigants. The magistrate at Sunshine noted, for example, that the court support solicitor was very helpful to the court by talking to both sides and getting agreement (Field notes, Broadmeadows Magistrates' Court, February 21, 1997; see also Hickey & Cumines, 1999, p. 39).

Apart from limited representation, assistance to applicants included more practical matters such as arranging a safe place for a woman to wait before her hearing, arranging a professional interpreter for a woman who would otherwise have been relying on the defendant to interpret the proceedings for her, and driving a woman to the local school because she needed to collect her child while waiting for her order to be issued (Field notes, Broadmeadows Magistrates' Court, October 25, 1996; February 21, 1997). One worker in the field also argued that the important role of the court support solicitor was to give women time and the chance to be heard and believed *before* going into court. Thus, even if little was said in court, there was at least someone with a good understanding of the woman's situation, and she had been accorded some dignity and privacy in telling her story. As a result, this worker argued, women who used a court support program had a more positive experience of going to court than those who did not (Field notes, Women's Legal Resources Group [WLRG], 1996). Another interviewee contended, however, that this difference was made not by solicitors but by support workers. The woman knew that the support worker believed her and was there for her, which was also different from having the support of family or friends who, like the woman herself, were emotionally involved in the matter (S.W.1, interview, December 23, 1997). Evaluations of court support schemes in New South Wales had shown a decrease in the proportion of withdrawn complaints, an increase in the proportion of successful applications, good relationships with the court, and clients feeling supported and empowered (ALRC, 1994, pp. 132–133).

At the same time, it was clear that the court support programs in the four courts observed operated somewhat differently, with no coordination between them. Neither did court support program participants receive any particular training for their role. At the time of the observations, the

WLRG in Melbourne had commenced a project to identify best practices and to provide training and minimum standards for court support schemes, but this had not yet been completed.[20] Among the matters identified by the WLRG in its background paper for the project was the lack of any specific court support available for non-English speaking background women in the community who were seeking intervention orders (Abela et al., 1994, pp. 8, 10; also H. Assafiri, interview, June 24, 1997; Keys Young, 1994, p. 59; and see further VLRC, 2004a, p. 139).

Finally, applicants in most Magistrates' Courts had access to assistance from members of an organisation called Court Network. Court Network consisted of volunteers (typically nonworking or retired, middle-class, Anglo-Australian women) who provided support to unrepresented litigants (applicants or respondents, male or female) throughout the court system in Victoria.[21] Court Network occupied a room at most of the Magistrates' Courts attended, and the networker would approach litigants who appeared to be alone, offering anything from cups of tea to a sympathetic ear to a quiet place to sit. They did not give legal advice, but could provide information about procedures and what to expect in court. Sometimes a networker would accompany an applicant into court for moral support. At the Sunshine Magistrates' Court, the intervention order court support program was actually coordinated by Court Network, and involved the court support solicitor and a networker working with women applicants, while another networker and the Legal Aid duty lawyer worked with defendants (Field notes, Sunshine Magistrates' Court, July 2, 1996). More usually, however, Court Network and the court support program operated separately. And unlike the court support programs, networkers were present every day and therefore were likely to have greater contact with applicants for interim intervention orders (see also Babbel, 2002, p. 17).

In the cases observed, the largest group of applicants appeared in court for themselves with no form of representation or support, while the second largest group appeared for themselves with support from a family member or friend. Only 28 applicants had legal representation in court, and only 12 of these were privately represented. The overall pattern of representation and support in court is shown in table 6. Note that this table refers to appearances *in court*. As previously noted, a number of applicants may have been assisted by a court support program outside the courtroom, but appeared for themselves in the court.

Not surprisingly, applicants were significantly more likely to have legal representation (either court support or private) when the defendant was present in court and when the defendant was legally represented.[22] There was no significant difference between legal representation for interim and final orders, although this observation is probably a result of the fact that the majority of applications were observed on return days when a court support lawyer, if present, would represent applicants applying for both interim and final orders (no private lawyers appeared to represent applicants for interim orders). Orders were granted equally to applicants who had legal representation and to those who appeared for themselves.

Some of the lawyers interviewed noted that when women did have legal representation, they often did not want to say anything in court and just wanted the matter over with (J. Peirce, interview, August 21, 1997). Part of the lawyer's role, therefore, was to say things on behalf of clients that the women were too frightened to say themselves (S. Borg, interview, October 17, 1997). The women interviewed who had had legal representation generally felt happy about having a lawyer speak

Table 6. Applicants' representation in court.

Representation/Support	No. Cases
Self alone	39
Self + family member/friend	21
Court support program	16
Private lawyer alone	9
Private lawyer + family member/friend	3
Support worker alone or + family member/friend	6
Police alone or + family member/friend	4
Total	98

on their behalf, although their reasons for this varied. In some cases, the point was not the lawyer speaking for them, but the lawyer running the case. For example one woman, whose ex-husband always contested her applications for renewal and continuously applied for variations and revocation of orders against him, said one of the reasons she was frightened of going to court was that she never knew what he was going to come out with. Thus, it was tremendously helpful to have a lawyer acting for her. It took the weight off her shoulders, and, although she still felt sick, she knew she could at least sit back and let the solicitor handle the case (W.L.3, interview, August 18, 1997). Another had been in a fragile mental state when she obtained her intervention order and thought it was probably good to have a lawyer advocating for her and taking care of everything (W.L.1, interview September 8, 1997). In other cases, women perceived that a lawyer was more effective at presenting their case. One said she did not know what to say to the magistrate, so it was great to have a solicitor to guide her through the process (W.L.9, interview, December 19, 1997). Two others had the distinct impression that lawyers were necessary as magistrates would not listen to women speaking on their own (W.L.5, interview, December 19, 1997; W.L.10, interview, December 23, 1997).

The evidence from the court observations and interviews thus suggests that the potential problem of women being silenced by lawyers speaking on their behalf tended not to arise in intervention order proceedings. The majority of applicants were not represented by a lawyer in court, while those who were represented were generally happy to be relieved of a speaking role. At the same time, while representation and support might have made little difference to whether or not an order was granted, it did have the potential to significantly improve the woman's experience of the application process, suggesting that applicants would be much better off if representation and support were more widely available. In this context, it is notable that the voices of support workers remained silenced within the courtroom.[23] They were not authorized to speak on behalf of the women they were supporting, but allowing them to do so would be an obvious way of addressing the shortage of legal representation (see, e.g., Chief Justice's Taskforce on Gender Bias, 1994, p. 172; Klein & Orloff, 1993, p. 1060; Stewart, 2005, p. 14). Support workers also work within feminist and empowerment models, while lawyers may not do so.

Lawyers' Understandings of Domestic Violence

In Nan Seuffert's interviews with women survivors of domestic violence, the women consistently said that their lawyers did not understand the dynamics of domestic violence, did not understand their levels of fear and perceptions of danger, and considered their fears to be exaggerated (1994, pp. 90–92; 1996, pp. 525, 532). Lawyers shared a tendency to minimize and trivialize domestic violence, to disbelieve women's stories, and to blame the victim (1995, pp. 326–328, 333–334; 1996, p. 525). Women interviewed by Molly Chaudhuri and Kathy Daly had their best experiences with students from a specialist law school restraining order clinic and with legal aid lawyers, who "listen[ed] to battered women, giving them time and attention," but were critical of (male) private attorneys, who evinced little empathy for their situations (1992, p. 242). Domestic violence workers have also found some private lawyers to be unsympathetic to the aims of the legislation in general, and to represent victims and perpetrators indifferently (McGregor & Hopkins, 1991, pp. 102–106). In other words, the legal culture shared by many (if not all) of the lawyers in these various studies incorporated nonfeminist rather than feminist understandings of domestic violence.

In my own interviews, some of the lawyers displayed a high level of feminist understanding about the dynamics of violence and empathy towards their clients, while others took a more technical, decontextualized or even judgemental approach. For example, one acknowledged safety issues for women in coming to court on the return date, and their fear and distress at being in close proximity with the defendant (J. Pierce, interview, August 21, 1997), while another said she assumed women felt threatened when attending court, but she had never spoken to her clients about this (A. Palumbo, interview, April 1, 1996). Several lawyers in casual conversations around court or in informal discussions about my research expressed the view that intervention orders were being abused as a tactic in family law proceedings (see, further, chapter 7) and recounted cases in which they had represented women who had experienced little in the way of physical violence and who they thought really did not need an intervention order.

None of the lawyers interviewed had received any formal, specialist training in domestic violence, although some had gained an understanding through a community development course, seminars, reading, and working with social workers or psychologists and psychiatrists. Nor was any specialist training available in Victoria at the time, either in law schools or in continuing legal education programs (although training programs were available in the community sector for domestic violence workers). Rather, lawyers (like magistrates) gained most of their knowledge of domestic violence from experience in the courts, and they inevitably interpreted that experience through the lenses of the prevailing legal culture. One barrister said that it had been a real learning curve for her hearing clients' stories of violence in the first 25–50 intervention order cases she had handled (S. Borg, interview, October 17, 1997). Others, clearly, either felt they had nothing to learn or heard their preconceived ideas reinforced over and over.

Lawyering for Survivors of Domestic Violence

In his classic article, "Why the 'Haves' Come Out Ahead" (1974), Marc Galanter predicted that lawyers for "one-shotter" litigants would tend to provide stereotyped and uncreative legal services, due to their episodic and isolated relationship with the client. For these lawyers, Galanter argued, the permanent client is the forum, or the intermediary supplying clients (p. 117). Applicants for intervention orders may not technically constitute "one shotters," since the same lawyer will often represent them for both intervention order and family law proceedings; however, it is certainly true that their encounters with the legal system, and hence the business they bring to the lawyer, are likely to be limited.

On the other hand, there is a body of academic literature associated with "voice" scholarship that argues that lawyers representing battered women ought to provide feminist or "affective" representation infused with empathy, equality, empowerment of the client and relinquishment of power on the part of the lawyer, avoidance of judgement, self-reflection, and understanding of the dynamics of domestic violence, which includes a duty to educate the court about violence (e.g., Mills, 1996, pp. 1228–1229, 1245, 1259; Seuffert, 1994, p. 79; Seuffert, 1996, pp. 523, 541–544, 549). Such an approach inevitably requires specific training, preferably of an interdisciplinary nature involving techniques and insights from psychology, psychoanalysis, and/or social work, as well as in lawyering methods (Mills, 1996, pp. 1243, 1257).

In Seuffert's study, lawyers tended to provide mystificatory explanations of the legal process and to exercise their power to reinterpret women's stories (1996, pp. 531, 534; see also Kinports & Fischer, 1992, p. 177). Although she acknowledges the need for lawyers to translate clients' experiences into legal categories, Seuffert argues that this process should begin only after the client is given the space to tell her own story, the lawyer explains the law to her, and they jointly formulate a strategy for the case (1996, p. 547). Mills goes further in arguing that lawyers for battered women should build their relationship with the client first, then think about what legal or nonlegal recourse the client may need, providing the client with "the space, the time, and the fluidity necessary for self-guided resolution" (1996, pp. 1230, 1241).

These prescriptions, however, assume at least one consultation in the lawyer's office prior to a court hearing—a luxury clearly not available to court support program lawyers. Some of the support program lawyers interviewed for the research made this point explicitly: they had very limited time to obtain and impart information and could not always ensure that the client understood their explanations (F. Culpen, interview, March 17, 1997; J. Peirce, interview, August 21, 1997). On the other hand, a support worker interviewed considered that court support programs did help to demystify court procedures for clients and provided them with good opportunities to make informed decisions (H. Assafiri, interview, June 24, 1997).

Three of the eight private lawyers interviewed who regularly represented women applying for intervention orders explained the way they worked in terms that conformed in at least some degree to Seuffert's and Mills' injunctions. One said she always asked a new client about violence, and explained what that meant (including physical and non-physical abuse and intimidation), provided the woman with options, told her about the availability of intervention orders, and left the decision to the woman as to whether or not she pursued that option. She had learned from experience and from listening to clients that she should not tell them what to do but should let them make the decisions, in accordance with their own understanding of their situation and circumstances (S.1, interview, January 16, 1997). Another said it was important to let women talk as much as they wanted, to make them feel that their participation was genuine, to explain the legal issues, and to give them the opportunity to ask questions and express preferences (S. Borg, interview, October 17, 1997). The third noted that if a woman came to see her in crisis, she would respond to the crisis first and discuss legal options later. She also said it was important to empower clients and liked them to be involved in their own cases, for example, by getting an interim order on their own—although if they did not want to or could not do this, she would represent them. Pragmatically, too, she recognized that getting clients to do as much as possible saved them money (S. Macgregor, interview, March 1, 1996). By contrast, another private lawyer encouraged women to go to court by themselves and to get their own interim orders simply because this was much quicker than waiting until she was available to accompany them—apparently regardless of the woman's actual capacity to cope on her own (D. Dawson, interview, June 5, 1996). The private lawyers also noted, however, that most women had already obtained interim orders, either with the assistance of refuge workers or at the suggestion of the police, before they reached the lawyer's office.

While intervention order cases provided some limited evidence of feminist or affective lawyering for women who had been targets of violence, they also provided evidence supporting Galanter's point about the identity of the permanent client in such cases. Magistrates' appreciation of court support program lawyers, already noted, constituted part of that evidence. Moreover, it appeared that court support program lawyers were more likely to attempt to respond to the magistrate's wishes than to take on the role of educating magistrates about domestic violence. One court support lawyer said that how she prepared applications for final orders depended on who was sitting on the court that day. If it was the regular magistrate, she would speak to the defendant or his lawyer and try to reach an agreement for a consent order. If some other magistrate was sitting, she would speak to the court registrar and try to find out how that particular magistrate liked to approach applications (J. Peirce, interview, August 21, 1997). Another court support lawyer said that she tried to provide the court with the information it wanted to know. If there was a history of violence, she would focus on two or three incidents within the last year, because magistrates were looking for recent, physical violence. If there had been no physical abuse, she would try to draw out the client's feelings at the time she was verbally or mentally abused, knowing that "he yells at me" would not be enough to get an order. The magistrate would simply say, "I yell too" (F. Culpen, interview, March 17, 1997).

Only one private lawyer mentioned a court strategy of focusing on a particular incident on the basis that magistrates responded better to evidence of a particular incident than to a general history (M. Mann, interview, March 8, 1996). By contrast, two of the private lawyers took a more robust approach to developing magistrates' understandings. One said she would always try to elicit evidence about several incidents, in order to demonstrate that the violence was not isolated or accidental, and so that the magistrate would understand there was a strong likelihood of recurrence (S. Macgregor, interview, March 1, 1996). The other considered it important to put as much detail in front of the magistrate as possible so that he or she could empathize with the woman (S. Borg, interview, October 17, 1997).

The arguments of Galanter and feminist lawyering advocates converged in those instances in which the "repeat player" was a women's refuge or domestic violence service. These services tended to refer clients to lawyers known to take a feminist approach, and these feminist lawyers in turn were concerned to provide representation in a way that would ensure continuing referrals. Thus, if a woman had had the good fortune to be referred into the legal system via one of these agencies, she was likely to receive empathetic, empowering, and informed legal services (see also Chaudhuri & Daly, 1992). My observations suggest, however, that this occurred in only a very small minority of cases.

PHYSICAL FACILITIES

Survivors of domestic violence may be deterred from going to court or impeded in their ability to speak effectively in court by reason of physical fear of being in close proximity to the defendant, and/or intimidation by the court setting itself. Courts dealing with significant numbers of domestic violence survivors may or may not recognize these potential difficulties and take steps to alleviate them. This section explores the experience of women applying for intervention orders waiting for their case to be heard, and then in the hearing venue itself.

The Waiting Area

When an applicant for an interim order first attended court, she would be interviewed by the registrar and would then wait until a magistrate was available to determine the application. On the return date, after reporting her appearance at the front counter, the applicant would again sit and wait for her case to be called. If a court support program was operating at the court on that day, some of the waiting time might be spent being interviewed and given advice by the program's lawyer and support worker. But otherwise, there was a significant amount of time to kill.

For most applicants, the time spent waiting in court for their matter to be heard far exceeded the amount of time they spent in court. Waiting times and hearing times for different categories of cases are shown in table 7.

The table shows that in all cases, the median waiting time was 1 hr 15 min, while the median hearing time was only 3 min. Only in contested matters did the maximum hearing time (just over 5 hr) exceed the maximum waiting time (almost 4 hr 30 min). As previously noted, contested matters had the longest waiting times (*Mdn* 2 hr 15 min) and the

TABLE 7. Waiting and hearing times in intervention order cases.

	Waiting Time (Minutes)[a]			Hearing Time (Minutes)		
Hearing Type	*Min.*	*Mdn*[b]	*Max.*	*Min.*	*Mdn*	*Max.*
Interim order[c]	15	98	149	2	3	19
Final order ex parte	7	61	306	1	3	23
Final order by consent	11	85	180	1	3	22
Final order contested	15	137	266	2	63	310
All	7	76	306	1	3	310

[a]Waiting time was calculated from the time the court began sitting (usually 10:00 a.m.), until the time the case came on for hearing. This gives an underestimate of total waiting time, since most applicants would have arrived at court between 9:00 and 9:30 a.m.
[b]Median is used rather than mean since this gives a better measure of central tendency and is less skewed by outliers, thus is more appropriate for use with time data.
[c]It was difficult to judge waiting times for interim orders, since applicants could arrive at any time and the time they actually did so could not always be determined. The waiting time given here relates to only 10 of the 17 interim order matters.

longest hearing times (*Mdn* 1 hr). All other matters had broadly similar hearing and waiting times.

The amount of time applicants spent waiting for their matters to be heard was in most courts a function of scheduling practices, which listed all matters on a particular day for 10:00 a.m., but then gave a higher priority to police matters (summary crime) and other civil matters than to Crimes (Family Violence) matters (Field notes, Broadmeadows Magistrates' Court, October 25, 1996; February 21, 1997; Prahran Magistrates' Court, June 27, 1996; Sunshine Magistrates' Court, July 2, 1996; June 17, 1997; see also Bezdek, 1992, pp. 551–552; Kinports & Fischer, 1992, p.199).[24] Only two of the courts (Melbourne and Dandenong) had both a courtroom and a magistrate exclusively dedicated to hearing intervention order applications. In the other courts, intervention order applications were slotted in among the rest of one or more magistrates' workloads, usually towards the end. At Preston Magistrates' Court, one of the clerks explained that they wanted to get the police matters finished before beginning "the others" so the police prosecutor would not have to wait around (Field notes, July 4, 1996), while a magistrate at Broadmeadows referred to the difficulty of interrupting criminal cases to fit in intervention orders because it broke his concentration and required him to turn his mind to completely different issues (Field notes, February 21, 1997).

The amount of waiting time compared to court time meant, however, that much of women's "experience in court" consisted of experience of the court's waiting facilities (see also Wearing, 1992, pp. 22–23). In most cases, applicants for intervention orders waited in general, open, crowded waiting areas, where it was almost impossible to avoid contact with the defendant if he was present (Field notes, Broadmeadows Magistrates' Court, October 25, 1996; February 21, 1997; Frankston Magistrates' Court, June 27, 1997; Prahran Magistrates' Court, June 27, 1996; Preston Magistrates' Court, February 22, 1996; July 4, 1996; March 2, 1997; Sunshine Magistrates' Court, July 2, 1996; June 17, 1997; see also Kinports & Fischer, 1992, p. 199; Naffine, 1995, p. 29). I observed defendants harassing applicants in waiting areas on more than one occasion, and interviewees also noted the lack of privacy and safety for women and the subtle forms of violence and intimidation defendants were able to exert in these circumstances (Field notes, Prahran Magistrates' Court, June 27, 1996; Preston Magistrates' Court, March 2, 1997; Sunshine Magistrates' Court, June 17, 1997; C. McNamara, interview, June 14, 1996; M. Mann, interview, March 8, 1996; J. Peirce, interview, August 21, 1997; see also Babbel, 2002, p. 15; Chief Justice's Taskforce on Gender Bias, 1994, p. 172; Klein & Orloff, 1993, p. 1048; Taylor, 2001, p. 22; VLRC, 2004a, p. 211). In the words of one observer, "People who are terrified of an assailant or a voice on the phone have to sit and look at their persecutor. There is no place to run or hide" (Greenwood, 1996, p. 574).

Court support program support workers and Court networkers could alleviate this situation to some extent if they were present, but could not always spend all their time with just one woman. Lawyers, court support workers, and registrars knew that they could call court security to provide protection for an applicant, but this tended only to occur in particularly serious cases.[25] One court had downstairs and upstairs waiting areas, and defendants were supposed to be kept downstairs, but this became problematic when defendants made cross-applications. During one visit, a defendant/cross-applicant had gotten to the upstairs waiting area first, which meant that his female partner, the original applicant, had to be kept in an interview room downstairs for her own protection (Field notes, Broadmeadows Magistrates' Court, October 25, 1996). This same court had also established a special waiting room for intervention order applicants, which had comfortable armchairs, toys for children, coffee and tea facilities, magazines to read, and was supervised by a Salvation Army couple. However, the room looked immaculate and barely used. On one of my visits, it was certainly not used by women who consulted the court support program that day, and it was not clear that the support program workers were aware of its existence (Field notes, Broadmeadows Magistrates' Court, February 21, 1997). Women who brought family members, friends, or their own support workers (such as refuge workers) with them appeared to be best supported during the waiting process (NESB Focus Group, interview, December 23, 1997; W.L.2, interview, December 18, 1997; W.L.3, interview, August 18, 1997; W.L.8, interview, November 7, 1997; W.L.12, interview, December 19, 1997; Field notes generally); however, as already indicated, this was a minority (around one third) of those observed.

The Hearing Venue

Once cases came on for hearing, the great majority were heard in regular courtrooms, in open court. As previously noted, only two of the courts I observed had dedicated courtrooms for intervention orders. These were configured in the same way as ordinary courtrooms, with a bar table, witness box, and raised benches for the clerk and magistrate. However, they were much smaller and more intimate spaces than ordinary courtrooms, with little room for witnesses or spectators, and were generally not open to the public, thus providing a rare degree of privacy. A third court, Broadmeadows, had a special Hearing Room for intervention orders, which was small and configured informally with flat tables in an H shape and chairs around the walls. But views differed as to when and in what circumstances the Hearing Room would be used. During one visit, the supervising magistrate told me that it was normally used on Fridays for all interim orders; however, on that particular day, it was not being used because of a shortage of magistrates (Field notes, February 21, 1997). Other magistrates said they were happy to use the Hearing Room for ex parte hearings, but preferred to use a regular courtroom if the defendant was present, particularly for contested matters. In those situations, they wanted clear separation between themselves and the defendant, and the authority of the court to keep the defendant under control (Field notes, July 11, 1997; also F. Culpen, interview, March 17, 1997). On the other hand, court support program workers said that most magistrates other than one committed supporter always preferred to be in court and had barely used the Hearing Room after the first few months of its establishment (Field notes, October 25, 1996; February 21, 1997; July 14, 1997).

One of my interviewees said that the first time she went to court to get an interim order had been "terrifying," particularly since she had thought that she only needed to speak to the clerk and did not know she would be expected to go into court and into the witness box. In general, she felt very nervous and frightened about being in court, which made her mind go blank (W.L.3, interview, August 18, 1997; see also Chief Justice's Taskforce on Gender Bias, 1994, p. 171; Klein & Orloff, 1993, p. 1048; Wearing, 1992, p. 22). Other women also expressed concerns about speaking in open court about the violence to which they had been subjected, when anyone present could hear, and they never knew when they might meet one of those people again (W.L.5, interview, December 19, 1997; see also Chaudhuri & Daly, 1992, p. 244; Stubbs & Powell, 1989, pp. 91, 106). The immigrant women's focus group also thought it was worst when a magistrate wanted the applicant to give details and dates of abuse and to repeat what had happened over and over. They said this felt very uncomfortable, and that it was particularly uncomfortable for women from different cultures to have to speak about sexual abuse (NESB focus group, interview, December 23, 1997). From my observations, it appeared that women applying for interim orders were likely to be nervous, hesitant, fearful, and/or upset and crying ($n = 9/17$). However, on the return day, in uncontested cases, relatively few applicants ($n = 15$) remained hesitant, distressed, or softly spoken, with a larger number appearing reasonably confident and assertive ($n = 20$)[26]—although, admittedly, these were the applicants who had come back to court on the return day, and there would have been others who were too intimidated to return.

Apart from dedicated, closed courts, informal Hearing Rooms, and other privacy strategies (e.g., Kinports & Fischer, 1992, pp. 212–213; VLRC, 2004a, p. 97), it was also possible for magistrates to help women to overcome their fear and shame in the courtroom. For example, one (unusual) magistrate observed that the first time women came into court for an interim order it was a big thing for them. They were often tearful, their life was disintegrating, something bad had happened in their marriage, and they might be very shy talking about some aspects of what had happened to them. But he described how he tried to be gentle (not patronizing) in eliciting their story and how he could see the tension starting to ease as they talked (Field notes, Broadmeadows Magistrates' Court, July 11, 1997).

Efforts to mitigate the intimidation and humiliation that victims of violence might experience in court appear to have been sporadic, however, and efforts to mitigate the fear and harassment they might experience in sharing a waiting area with the defendant, even more so. In the majority of cases, no account was taken of these factors, and applicants for intervention orders were expected to access the court in the same way as any other litigant. Some applicants for final orders clearly did so without undue difficulty; but other applicants—particularly for interim orders—obviously found the experience distressing and traumatic, and this must have contributed to the level of attrition between interim and final orders.

The Brevity of Proceedings

The most salient feature of the hearings I observed, whether in an open court, a closed court, or a hearing room, was their extreme brevity. As shown in table 7, the median hearing time for all proceedings other than contested final orders was 3 minutes.

The general explanation given for the brevity of intervention order proceedings was that the court did not have sufficient resources to hear every case in full. A supervising magistrate at one of the courts explained that the court was operating under the pressure of a huge caseload, which meant it could not possibly hear every case or all of the evidence that people wanted to give (Field notes, Broadmeadows Magistrates' Court, February 21, 1997). Other magistrates lamented the lack of resources to do a good job with Crimes (Family Violence) matters (Field notes, Preston Magistrates' Court, July 4, 1996). Similar problems with courts having excessive workloads, and domestic violence matters being "processed" or "handled" rather than given individual attention, have been found in other jurisdictions (e.g., Gondolf, McWilliams, Hart, & Stuehling, 1994, p. 513; Kinports & Fischer, 1992, p. 209; Stanko, 1985, pp. 129–131).

This section discusses what occurred during the typical 3 minutes of an intervention order hearing and considers some of the implications of the standardization and abbreviation of intervention order proceedings.

The Substance of the Hearing

For interim orders, when the applicant entered the courtroom, she was usually directed to go into the witness box and was sworn in.[27] In most cases (n = 12/17) the magistrate then questioned the applicant briefly about why she wanted an order, although in some cases the magistrate simply asked the applicant to affirm the statement made in the complaint (n = 2/17) or did not ask the applicant to speak at all (n = 3/17). A typical interim order script ran as follows:

> APPLICANT: Stands in witness box, sworn.
> MAGISTRATE: Asks what defendant has been doing to her.
> APPLICANT: Explains recent incident.
> MAGISTRATE: Agrees to make order; reads out the terms of the order; advises A that if the defendant breaches those terms, she should phone the police and show them the order; advises A to come back to court on the return date; and if the magistrate is then satisfied there is a likelihood of further violence, he will make the order permanent.
> APPLICANT: Leaves.

For final orders, revocations, and variations, applicants were only asked to give sworn evidence in one quarter of cases (23.2%), consisting of around half of the contested matters ($n = 7/13$) and one quarter of the matters in which the defendant did not appear ($n = 11/40$). In the majority of final order, revocation, and variation cases (66%), no evidence was given in court, by the applicant or anyone else, including virtually all the cases in which the defendant consented to the order being made. In the remaining 11% of cases, the applicant either was simply asked to affirm her original complaint for the interim order, or made an unsworn statement. A typical final order script in which the defendant did not appear in court ran as follows:

> MAGISTRATE: Invites A to take a seat; reads file; satisfies self that defendant has been served with the interim order; asks A if she still wants the order.
> APPLICANT: Recounts recent episode of violence (subsequent to or immediately preceding the interim order).
> MAGISTRATE: Agrees to make final order; asks how long A wants the order to last.
> APPLICANT: Suggests length of time (or "forever").
> MAGISTRATE: Makes order for nominated time or determines length of order; specifies whether order made in terms sought or imposes different terms; advises A that she can apply to have the order varied, revoked, or extended, to call the police if the defendant breaches the order, that the order will be served on the defendant, and to wait outside until the order is ready.

A typical final order script in which the defendant consented without admitting the allegations ran as follows:

> MAGISTRATE: Checks identities of parties; invites parties to sit down; checks understanding that they have reached agreement.
> [To D] "You're going to consent without admitting the allegations?"
> DEFENDANT: "Yes."
> MAGISTRATE: [To A] "Do you still want the order?"
> APPLICANT: "Yes."
> MAGISTRATE: Requests D to stand up; reads through the order; checks D's understanding, lectures D on the seriousness of breaching

the order; specifies length of order; advises parties to wait outside until the order is ready.

Thus, it can be seen that much of the speaking in court was done by magistrates, that speaking parts for applicants were fairly limited, and that in consent proceedings when the defendant was present, the defendant received more of the magistrate's attention than did the applicant. To quote an observation made of different but analogous proceedings, "So little that is particular rather than *pro forma* is said in each case" (Bezdek, 1992, p. 579).

The Magistrate's Demeanor

Given the dominant role played by the magistrate in these brief intervention order hearings, the way in which they performed their script and their manner towards the applicant and (when he was present) the defendant assumed particular importance. In his observation of 147 civil restraining order applications in two Massachussetts courts in 1992–1993, James Ptacek categorized the 18 judges he observed by reference to a typology of 5 judicial demeanors: good-natured, bureaucratic, firm/formal, harsh, and condescending/patronizing (1999, p. 98; see also Mileski, 1971). Good-natured judges were affable, courteous, and respectful, appearing sometimes like a concerned, helpful social worker (Mileski, 1971, pp. 523, 526). In the domestic violence context, they were concerned to put women applicants at their ease and to ensure that they understood the proceedings, they made clear that the applicant's request for protection was taken seriously, they expressed concern for the applicant's safety, they explained the possibility of criminal proceedings in respect of the violence if the description in the applicant's affidavit warranted it, and they referred applicants to other support services for battered women (Ptacek, 1999, pp. 99–100). Bureaucratic judges, on the other hand, remained passive and detached, were emotionally flat, displayed little empathy for the applicant, and tended to focus more on the documents than on the woman before them. They dealt with matters in a routine, businesslike, and impersonal manner; they asked fewer questions; they did not explain things; and their hearings were often very brief (p. 101). Firm/formal judges were more active, but this tended to be in accentuating their own power and demanding deference (p. 102). In the tone, force, and content of their words and demeanor, they conveyed their moral and legal authority over the parties before them (Mileski, 1971, p. 524). In the domestic violence context, they could be unsupportive of either party. For example, firm/formal judges might give defendants a lecture about their behavior or deliver a stern warning about not breaching the orders made (Ptacek, 1999, p. 107). Condescending/patronizing judges were both unsupportive and somewhat critical of applicants for restraining orders. If the defendant was present, these judges tended to be more supportive of him than of the applicant (pp. 103–104). Harsh judges displayed a nasty, abrasive style. They went beyond firmness to personal vindictiveness (saying, for example, "Don't give me that disgusting look"), often in response to some disrespectful or argumentative behavior on the part of a litigant (Mileski, 1971, pp. 524, 527). In his study, Ptacek encountered only one instance of harshness, in which the judge was very unsympathetic to the applicant for the restraining order, while displaying considerable sympathy for the defendant (Ptacek, 1999, p. 104). Judges could adopt different styles on different occasions, and might also adopt different styles in relation to the different parties, such as good-natured to the applicant but firm/formal to the defendant, or condescending/patronizing to the applicant but good-natured to the defendant (Mileski, 1971, pp. 523–527; Ptacek, 1999, p. 102). Nevertheless, bureaucratic judges tended to be uniformly bureaucratic with all parties alike (Ptacek, 1999, pp. 105–109).

Analyzing the cases in my observation sample in terms of this typology yielded the results set out in table 8.

Clearly, the overwhelming style adopted by Victorian magistrates in intervention order applications was bureaucratic, an obvious product of the time pressures on magistrates, leading them to adopt a routinized approach to applications (see also Wearing, 1992, p. 25). In line with this finding, magistrates often used formal or technical language, leaving some

TABLE 8. Magistrates' demeanor towards intervention order applicants.

Demeanor Towards Applicant	No.	Percentage
Bureaucratic	65	72.2
Good-natured	11	12.2
Firm/formal	6	6.7
Condescending/patronizing	6	6.7
Harsh	2	2.2
Total	90	100.0

doubt as to whether the parties had understood what they were saying (see also VLRC, 2004a, p. 223).

My interviews yielded several observations about the court process that illustrated magistrates' bureaucratic approach. For example, one of the women interviewed, who had been to court on several occasions to extend intervention orders, said that she had only encountered one magistrate who had actually responded to her as a person. Mostly, they had their heads buried in the papers on their desk, did not even look at her during the proceedings, and hence could not get any idea of how she was feeling (W.L.5, interview, December 19, 1997). A group of court support workers described a particular magistrate dealing with intervention orders like a sausage machine. He could be so quick that the applicant hardly had a chance to sit down. This magistrate had taken on board criticism that he was not giving women the opportunity to be heard and had slowed down a bit, but it did seem that he assumed that all the work had been done outside by the court support program, lawyers, and court staff, and that his role was simply to formalize the order (Field notes, Sunshine Magistrates' Court, July 2, 1996).

My observation notes, too, were replete with evidence of magistrates going fast, cutting women off, and failing to engage with them or their stories. Only in a minority of cases were magistrates recorded as being thorough and interested (M.C.19, June 27, 1996), explaining and trying to be helpful (M.C.22, June 27, 1996), going fairly quickly but helping the applicant as far as possible, asking about her situation, clarifying what she wanted and finding out about her particular circumstances (M.C.65, March 20, 1997), and being brisk but not hurried or dismissive (M.C.86, June 27, 1997).

There was no relationship between magistrates' demeanor and their sex (see also Wearing, 1992, p. 25). Neither did the magistrate's demeanor differ depending on whether the application was for an interim or final order, other than the fact that they were never firm/formal or harsh towards interim order applicants. Magistrates were more likely to be good-natured and less likely to be bureaucratic towards applicants who were legally represented.[28] This illustrates another advantage of legal representation, in that magistrates were more likely to show respect and concern for represented parties, while remaining bureaucratic and detached from parties appearing in person. Likewise, magistrates were less likely to be bureaucratic and more likely to be either good-natured or firm/formal in contested cases than in cases decided either ex parte or by consent.[29]

Ptacek argues that judges deciding protection order applications should express their support and empathy for the victims of domestic violence, while impressing upon perpetrators the unacceptability of violence and the seriousness of breaching the orders being made. Thus, ideally, judges in these cases should be good-natured towards the applicant and firm/formal towards the defendant. They should not be condescending/patronizing or harsh towards the applicant, or good-natured towards the defendant. Neither should they be bureaucratic towards either party, because this style fails to send any message either of support or sanction (Ptacek, 1999, pp. 106–109).

Given the large proportion of cases in my observation sample decided ex parte, it was possible to determine the magistrate's demeanor towards the defendant in only 41 cases. In these cases, however, it was evident that magistrates were indeed inclined to be less bureaucratic and slightly more firm/formal towards defendants than towards applicants, in particular, lecturing defendants on the serious consequences of breaching intervention orders. However, magistrates were also inclined to be somewhat more good-natured and less condescending/patronizing towards defendants than towards applicants, as shown in table 9.

TABLE 9. Magistrates' demeanor towards intervention order defendants.

Demeanor Towards Defendant	No.	Percentage
Bureaucratic	17	41.5
Firm/formal	15	36.6
Good-natured	7	17.1
Condescending/patronizing	1	2.4
Harsh	1	2.4
Total	41	100.0

In cases where the magistrate's demeanor towards both parties was discernible ($n = 38$), magistrates were most likely to be bureaucratic to both parties (42%), or to adopt some other style with both parties (24%). Thus, in around two thirds of cases when both parties were present, the magistrate failed to distinguish between perpetrator and victim. The "ideal" combination of good-natured towards the applicant and firm/formal towards the defendant occurred in only 3 cases in my sample.

The Applicant's (Missing) Voice

As previously noted, there was very little scope for applicants to insert their own voice into the intervention order hearing script. This was often a function of the rapid, routinized nature of the proceedings, but other barriers—and some justifications—also came into play.

Insufficient Time

One of the court support program coordinators observed that women were not given time to tell the court what had happened to them (F. Culpen, interview, March 17, 1997). While they might have had the opportunity to tell their story to the clerk or registrar when they went for an interim order, they would not have the same opportunity to tell the magistrate. Yet, according to this interviewee, some women wanted and needed to be heard *in court*. In particular, if the defendant appeared on the return date, they wanted to be able to tell the court what he had done. In these circumstances, the woman would try to blurt out everything that had happened to her and be cut off by the magistrate, who was only interested in the minimum information to determine whether there were grounds for an order. Women in this situation found it difficult to isolate and focus on just one aspect of the violence they had experienced, and the procedure did not allow for their whole story to be heard (F. Culpen, interview, March 17, 1997). This point was borne out by one of the women interviewed, who had expected that the magistrate would at least ask her why she wanted an intervention order. Rather, the defendant had consented to the order while denying the allegations, and she was outraged that the magistrate had not asked her anything about the allegations and had just ignored her presence (W.L.4, interview, December 23, 1997; see also Wearing, 1992, p. 28).

Few of the women interviewed who had obtained intervention orders had had much idea of what was going on in court during their brief appearance (see also Keys Young, 1994, p. 59; VLRC, 2004a, p. 222). One said that she had had no chance to understand what was going on because it was so quick, almost just walk in—walk out (W.L.4, interview, December 23, 1997). Another thought that if the support worker from the women's refuge had not explained to her beforehand what would happen when they went into court, she would have found it very confusing and scary (W.L.6, interview, December 23, 1997). Two who had had legal representation had also not understood what was going on. One of these said, "It's all run by someone else; you don't quite know what's happening" (W.L.7, interview, October 28, 1997; see also Wearing, 1992, p. 27), while the other had been hospitalized prior to her court appearance and was not taking in very much at all (W.L.1, interview, September 8, 1997). Only one woman litigant said she had felt in control at the last renewal of her intervention order, since by then she had been to court so many times that she knew how to do it and what she had to do to be heard (W.L.5, interview, December 19, 1997).

Magistrates admitted that they had no time to listen to everything that people wanted to say (Field notes, Broadmeadows Magistrates' Court, July 11, 1997). One recounted the case of a woman in a matter he had heard recently who would not stop talking and wanted to bring in lots of irrelevant material, and he had had to be forceful and cut her off. He added that it would be alright if he did have time to hear the whole story, though it would still be a waste of time to do so (Field notes, Broadmeadows Magistrates' Court, July 11, 1997). Lawyers also observed that magistrates got impatient and frustrated when women "said too much" (especially if an interpreter was also involved), because of the time pressures under which they were working (S. Borg, interview, October 17, 1997; M. Mann, March 8, 1996).

Language Barriers

The mystification and silencing of women in intervention order proceedings was experienced particularly acutely by women whose first language was not English and who required an interpreter, both to communicate to the court and to understand the proceedings. In the first place, women had difficulties gaining access to suitably qualified interpreters. It was the court's responsibility to identify the need for and to book interpreters, but various obstacles existed, including the making of inappropriate judgements about the applicant's need for an interpreter (her English deemed to be "good enough" by court staff, even though it would desert her under stress in the courtroom); policy decisions to limit the use of interpreters for funding reasons (so that, for example, interpreters would be booked only for contested matters); clerks/registrars not using an interpreter for the initial interview, even if they acknowledged an interpreter was needed in court; not being able to get an interpreter in urgent situations; and insistence that family members, friends, children, or even the perpetrator could do the interpreting (see Babbel, 2002, p. 15; Nunn & D'Arcy, 2001, p. 23; VLRC, 2004a, pp. 138, 243; H. Assafiri, interview, June 24, 1997; F. Culpen, interview, March 17, 1997; C. McNamara, interview, June 14, 1996; NESB Focus Group, interview, 23 December, 1997; Field notes, Broadmeadows Magistrates' Court, October 25, 1996).[30] Assafiri and Dimopoulos (1995, p. 21) give examples of a Greek woman and a Vietnamese woman applying for intervention orders without interpreters. The Greek woman's request for an interpreter was denied on the basis that the magistrate believed her 16-year-old daughter could interpret for her. In order to spare her daughter from having to hear and speak about such intimate details (and possibly endangering her in the process), the woman withdrew her application. The Vietnamese woman attempted to explain herself with limited English, but the magistrate became frustrated that he could not understand her and asked her to “act out” the violence to which she had been subjected. Although the woman was granted an order, she felt totally humiliated and dehumanized by the proceedings.

Even if an interpreter was obtained, women experienced further difficulties in telling their story through the interpreter. Some interpreters behaved unprofessionally, for example, by breaching client confidentiality, giving gratuitous advice to the woman about what she should do, arguing about what information should be presented to the court, or communicating messages to the woman from the defendant (VLRC, 2004a, p. 243; F. Culpen, interview, March 17, 1997; M. Mann, interview, March 8, 1996; NESB Focus Group, interview, December 23, 1997). This became a particular problem when only one interpreter was booked for both parties (Babbel, 2002, p. 15; VLRC, 2004a, p. 243).[31] And above all, even with a professional interpreter, it was very hard for women to talk about intimate and shameful details of abuse—or to express their feelings, emotions, and fears—through a third person, especially if that person was male (F. Culpen, interview, March 17, 1997; see also Pe-Pua & Echevarria, 1998, p. 63). Non-English speaking background support workers were adamant that women applying for intervention orders for domestic violence should be provided with women interpreters (H. Assafiri, interview, June 24, 1997; NESB Focus Group, interview, December 23, 1997; see also Keys Young, 1994, pp. 60, 95). Even so, there were some things that women would not say, or could not adequately get across, which might sometimes impact on the magistrate’s willingness to grant an order. Magistrates also needed to be prepared to give the extra time necessary for a woman to tell her story through an interpreter, but in accordance with the dominant bureaucratic mode of proceeding, this did not always occur (K. Anderson, interview, March 8, 1996; H. Assafiri, interview, June 24, 1997).

Protective Silence?

My observations also revealed some variation in the amount of attention given to applicants by different courts and magistrates. In applications for final orders, applicants were more likely to be asked to give oral evidence in the Melbourne Magistrates' Court, one of the venues with a dedicated, closed intervention order court. By contrast, no applicants were asked to give sworn evidence in the Frankston or Sunshine Magistrates' Courts in any final order applications, and these were also the courts that were most likely to dispose of such applications without hearing any evidence.[32] Interestingly, the two magistrates hearing all or most of the matters in these two courts would have been considered most sensitive and sympathetic to applicants in terms of their readiness to grant orders.

This raises the possibility that giving women a limited speaking role in intervention order proceedings might in fact be considered to be protective of these women. Various versions of this rationale were raised in interviews. A court support program worker thought it might be fine for women not to have to say much or to feel they were being questioned. Perhaps it was not so important for women to speak at the interim order stage in particular, and more important for them to just get in and out with their order (F. Culpen, interview, March 17, 1997). A solicitor was more definite about this, believing that women who had just separated from their partners wanted to feel protected, but did not necessarily want or need to have their say in court and to give evidence against their ex-partners at that time. They were likely to lack the confidence, strength, and preparation to do so, but would build up this strength for their later Family Court proceedings (S.1, interview, January 16, 1997). Others pointed to the fact that women were sometimes too terrified to get into the witness box, and so would much prefer to dispose of the matter without having to speak (M. Mann, interview, March 8, 1996).

Magistrates certainly felt they were doing women a favor. For example, one of the two magistrates just mentioned thought it was inappropriate to make women tell their whole story in front of everyone in the courtroom. Rather, he tried to get it over for them quickly, and was satisfied as long as there was enough material in the written application to provide grounds for an order. It was simply unnecessary to swear everyone and "hold a Royal Commission into every case" (Field notes, Sunshine Magistrates' Court, June 17, 1997). And the second magistrate, in one of the interim order cases I observed (M.C.100, June 27, 1997), quite clearly attempted to shield the applicant by asking her simply to read to herself and affirm her written statement rather than requiring her to speak about what had happened to her in front of me and anyone else in the courtroom.

As noted earlier, some women interviewed had no desire to speak in court. On the other hand, others had wanted to speak personally and were denied the opportunity, or were pleased to have had the chance to speak. One of these women was disgusted that she had not been able to speak during her final order application because the defendant had consented while denying the allegations (W.L.4, interview, December 23, 1997). Another said that speaking about what had happened to her felt good (if also frightening because she knew that what she was saying would make the defendant angry), and that if you fought hard and persevered, the court would hear something (W.L.5, interview, December 19, 1997). A third was grateful for the chance she had been given by the magistrate to respond to her ex-husband's denial of the allegations while consenting to an intervention order. "They couldn't shut me up!" she said. In particular, she had successfully convinced the magistrate that the defendant was sufficiently dangerous to warrant banning him from ever holding a gun license. Having her story heard (and believed) made her feel proud and strong (W.L.12, interview, December 19, 1997).

Consent Without Admissions

As noted earlier, if a defendant appeared at court on the return date, he would be given every encouragement, by counter staff and by the magistrate, to consent to an order rather than to contest the matter. In order to persuade defendants to consent, the practice had developed of allowing them to consent to an order while denying the allegations made in the complaint. This option proved extremely popular. Of the 30 final order applications observed in which the defendant appeared and a decision was made, 17 (57%) were disposed of by consent without admissions, while only 6 (20%) were disposed of by consent with admissions, and 7 (23%) were contested.

Consent without admissions was openly promoted as a time-saving device. Pressures to settle are always present when courts have unmanageable caseloads (Galanter, 1974, pp. 121–122). The emphasis on consent was also consistent with the fact that a mutually agreed settlement is the systemically preferred outcome in civil cases in general. Liberal societies believe that individuals are in the best position to determine their own solutions and should be given maximum freedom to do so. Private agreements are thought both to enhance individual autonomy and freedom of choice, and to maximize social welfare, since parties will (at least theoretically) only agree to arrangements that make them both better off (Neave, 1994, p. 111). Thus, proponents of the practice argued that consent without admissions represented a win-win-win solution for all parties. It saved time for the court, the applicant got her order without having to wait around and without having to go into the witness box and endure a potentially traumatic hearing, and the defendant was able to "save face" to some extent (e.g., Wearing, 1992, pp. 110–111, 184; S.W.1, interview, December 23, 1997; Field notes, Moonee Ponds Magistrates' Court, November 1, 1996).

Support workers and lawyers were more equivocal about the practice of allowing defendants to consent to an order without admitting the allegations. On the one hand, the woman achieved the outcome she sought. She was protected by an order, and the defendant was still subject to criminal penalties for any breach of the order (Wearing, 1992, p. 111; H. Assafiri, interview, June 24, 1997; S. Borg, interview, October 17, 1997; F. Culpen, interview, March 17, 1997; J. Peirce, interview, August 21, 1997; S.2, interview, October 28, 1997; S.W.1, interview, December 23, 1997). She also achieved this outcome without having to go through a contested hearing, which many women were too frightened to contemplate, which would possibly include being cross-examined directly by the defendant if he were unrepresented, and whose outcome would be highly unpredictable (S. Borg, interview, October 17, 1997; F. Culpen, interview, March 17,

1997; J. Peirce, interview, August 21, 1997; S.1, interview, January 16, 1997; S.2, interview, October 28, 1997). One lawyer described contested hearings as having "no goalposts" and as "anything goes" (S.1, interview, January 16, 1997; and see chapter 4, next). A consent order was thus more certain, and was also speedier and less costly for the woman (H. Assafiri, interview, June 24, 1997; S.1, interview, January 16, 1997; S.W.1, interview, December 23, 1997). Giving the perpetrator a "soft option" might also serve to curb his aggression, and thus might be better for the applicant's safety in the long run (F. Culpen, interview, March 17, 1997).

On the other hand, the procedure of allowing the defendant to consent without admissions had a number of drawbacks. First, the practice violated the usual rules of settlement in civil cases in that it was entirely unilateral. The defendant was given the option to consent without admissions. The applicant was, in my observation, never asked whether she agreed to the order being made on that basis, or whether she would prefer to tell her story and prove her case. Some women were frustrated and outraged by this process—how *could* he deny what he had done? How *dare* he be given a choice? (F. Culpen, interview, March 17, 1997; J. Peirce, interview, August 21, 1997; S.W.1, interview, December 23, 1997). A support worker argued that in this respect, women's experience of the court process mirrored that of living with a violent man—they both rendered the woman powerless (S.W.1, interview, December 23, 1997). Thus, some interviewees believed that women ought to be given the option to accept or reject an order based on the defendant's denials (F. Culpen, interview, March 17, 1997; J. Peirce, interview, August 21, 1997; S.1, interview, January 16, 1997), with one noting that where (as in the majority of cases) the applicant was unrepresented, this would place a responsibility on the court system to explain carefully to women the meaning of consent without admissions so that they could exercise an informed choice (J. Peirce, interview, August 21, 1997). Another, however, questioned whether, in the context of the power and control exercised by violent men over their partners, it was at all appropriate to deploy a regime of "consent" in relation to intervention orders. In particular, she considered that it would be a farce to obtain a non-English speaking background woman's "consent" under those conditions (H. Assafiri, interview, June 24, 1997; see also Fenton, 1999, pp. 1024–1025; O'Donovan, 1997, p. 47).

While one lawyer claimed that she had never had a client who was dissatisfied with an order made by consent without admissions (S.1, interview, January 16, 1997), the views of the women interviewed were not so uniform. Six of the women had obtained orders on this basis, but only one was completely sanguine about this result, saying that she was just happy to have the order and to be far away from the defendant (W.L.6, interview, December 23, 1997). Two specifically noted that they had not been asked whether *they* were consenting. One said she was happy to have the order, but was very angry about the defendant's denials, which she considered to be cowardly. She would have liked to have been given a choice, for the magistrate to have asked for her opinion (W.L.4, interview, December 23, 1997). The other said she had expected her ex-boyfriend to deny the allegations, since he was also facing criminal proceedings in respect of his assaults on her, but she did not know that she had any alternative—it was up to the defendant to consent or not. At the time she was dazed and in shock, and did not really think about it, but she did feel betrayed because he had lied to the court (W.L.1, interview, September 8, 1997). A third was not at all happy with the outcome of her application. The magistrate had tried to convince her that it was good to have the order regardless, but she thought that was ridiculous and could not understand how the magistrate could give the order but still accept the defendant's denials (W.L.10, interview, December 23, 1997).[33] The husband of another of the women had sent a letter to the court agreeing to the order but denying the allegations, and she had not been able to say anything. She argued that he should have been compelled to come to court to say why he was denying the allegations, and was angry that his word had been accepted against hers, so that she got the order but was not believed. She acknowledged that the procedure would make it easier for some women who would be very stressed about facing the perpetrator of violence against them in court, but also considered that it made it too easy for perpetrators, who were not made accountable for their actions (W.L.2, interview, December 18, 1997).

This raises the second major drawback of the practice of consent without admissions—its institutional and public consequences. If the great majority of intervention orders are granted either ex parte or by consent without admitting the allegations (and in combination with applicants' limited success in contested proceedings, as discussed in the next chapter), there is an overall lack of institutional affirmation of women's stories of abuse (F. Culpen, interview, March 17, 1997; J. Peirce, interview, August 21, 1997; see also Fenton, 1999, p. 1004). There are few findings by magistrates that these stories are *true*. The lack of such affirmation, in turn, tends to reinforce the nonfeminist notions that women invent or exaggerate stories of abuse and use the legal process for collateral purposes (H. Assafiri, interview, June 24, 1997; S.W.1, interview, December 23, 1997). Further, there is a lack of public, legal condemnation of abusive behavior. What happened is not clearly labeled as unlawful, and abusive men are not required to take responsibility for their actions (H. Assafiri, interview, June 24, 1997; F. Culpen, interview, March 17, 1997). More generally, the existence of violence against women, and the scale of the violence, fail to enter the realm of public knowledge. Men's denial and minimization of violence is echoed by the state, not just in individual cases but also on a grand scale. Consent without admissions contributes significantly to the view that "real" domestic violence is rare and exceptional (S.W.1, interview, December 23, 1997; see also Fenton, 1999, p. 1012). One interviewee argued that if the police were to play a more active role in applying for intervention orders, the existence of police support for the applicant's allegations would render consent without admissions much less of an option (F. Culpen, interview, March 17, 1997).

The third substantial drawback of intervention orders obtained by consent without admitting the allegations was the subsequent effect of these orders in Family Court proceedings. Lawyers considered that intervention orders made on this basis would not disadvantage women in the Family Court, because the issue of violence in the relationship could still be alleged and proved separately in that court (S.1, interview, January 16, 1997; Field notes, Broadmeadows' Court Support Program,

October 25, 1996). They also considered that consent to an intervention order without admissions would not disadvantage men in Family Court proceedings (S. Borg, interview, October 17, 1997; Field notes, Sunshine Court Support Program, July 2, 1996). As discussed further in chapter 7, on the basis of observations in the Family Court, it appeared to be true that consent without admissions did not disadvantage violent men—in fact, it worked to their advantage. Women who had been targets of violence, on the other hand, were more likely to be disadvantaged. Intervention orders made by consent without admissions tended to be discounted in the Family Court. In this situation, according to two of the women interviewed, it was the husband's denials rather than the need for an order to protect the safety of the wife and children that the court believed (W.L.2, interview, December 18, 1997; W.L.10, interview, December 23, 1997).

Standardized Terms of Orders

One final effect of Magistrates Courts' focus on crunching through their intervention order caseload rather than paying attention to the specificity of the cases before them was that the prohibitions in intervention orders were often not tailored to the particular allegations. The defendant could be ordered not to assault, harass, molest, threaten, or intimidate the aggrieved family member; not to approach, telephone, or contact the aggrieved family member; not to go within a specified distance (standardly 200 meters) of any premises at which the aggrieved family member lived, worked, or frequented; and not to damage the aggrieved family member's property (Crimes (Family Violence) Act (1987), s. 5(1)). The defendant's license or permit to use a firearm could also be suspended, and he could be ordered to surrender any firearms to the police. There was also provision for the making of any other order, but this was rarely if ever used. Since clerks/registrars drafted the complaint, they were the ones who chose which terms to specify, and very often they chose either a limited order (not assault, harass, etc.), or everything (see VLRC, 2004a, p. 160; Wearing, 1992, pp. 353, 355). Magistrates would then occasionally tailor the terms sought in the complaint to the specific situation, vary the distance at which the defendant was excluded depending on the perceived seriousness of his actions (Field notes, Broadmeadows Court Support Program, October 25, 1996), and check to see if the defendant actually owned a firearm, and hence whether the clause concerning firearms was relevant. More typically, however, the order resembled what one interviewee referred to as a "hamburger with the lot" (D. Dawson, interview, June 5, 1996), and a magistrate described as "a Chinese menu: numbers 8, 14, 24 and special fried rice" (Field notes, Moonee Ponds Magistrates' Court, November 1, 1996).

One problem with the breadth of standard orders was that they could more easily be breached inadvertently or trivially by the defendant, compelling the applicant to waive certain breaches, which would then be held against her if she sought to take action in relation to nontrivial breaches (see also VLRC, 2004a, p. 161). Another problem was that applicants (and presumably also defendants) did not always understand what the order allowed and did not allow (see also Hickey & Cumines, 1999, p. 79). This was particularly the case when the orders included exceptions to allow defendants to have contact with their children under certain circumstances. For example, one of the women interviewed had an intervention order that prohibited the defendant from contacting or approaching her, except to have contact with the child "as agreed with the aggrieved family member or pursuant to Court Order." It was clear that the woman did not understand the meaning of this clause. She was not sure if it allowed the defendant to demand contact with the child, or if it would be breaching the order to give him contact (W.L.8, interview, November 7, 1997). In fact, neither would be the case.

Conclusion

In summary, as a result of inadequate resourcing and consequent time constraints on the Magistrates' Court, intervention order applicants only rarely received inclusive, particularized attention from the magistrate. In this respect, although applicants may have generally achieved the outcome they wanted (an order), the manner of disposition of these cases was unsatisfactory. Moreover, magistrates' fear that if you "give them an inch, they'll take a mile" may have been exaggerated. It is likely that the majority of applicants did not wish to tell a long story. But there should have been room for those who did. This conclusion echoes that of Conley and O'Barr (1990), who noted that when a litigant is given time to tell their (possibly legally irrelevant) story, "the law has a different face…it is presented as an institution that is attentive to human needs" (p. 120). Thus, they emphasized the importance of procedure as much as outcome and observed that sometimes a litigant's desire to tell their story is not a huge demand on the court system, and may consume minimal time and resources (pp. 130–131).

Failure to hear applicants in intervention order cases also had broader, public consequences, in terms of the implicit endorsement of nonfeminist narratives about domestic violence and the systematic exclusion of evidence and findings that might have resulted in a wider acceptance of the alternative, feminist narratives about domestic violence on which the legislation was based. And even though the great majority of women did receive an order, those outcomes were compromised by inattentive, routinized practices in relation to the terms of orders, making the orders less effective and more difficult to enforce.

Endnotes

1. On police failure to prosecute breaches of protection orders in Australian jurisdictions, see, for example, Chief Justice's Taskforce on Gender Bias (1994, p. 176); Katzen & Kelly (2000); Nunn & D'Arcy (2001, pp. 18–19); *Report of the Taskforce on Women and the Criminal Code* (2000, p. 111); Trimboli & Bonney (1997, pp. 58–59); VLRC (2004a, p. 187). Similar problems of inadequate police responses to breaches of protection orders have been found in the U.S. (e.g., Kinports & Fischer, 1992, pp. 223 ff.)
2. In Victoria, the State court hierarchy consists of the Magistrates Court, County Court and Supreme Court. The same hierarchy is duplicated in other States, although with slightly different terminology. For example in New South Wales, courts at the lowest level are called Local Courts, and in most States, the intermediate level court is known as the District Court.
3. There were 18,662 applications for intervention orders in Victoria in 1996–1997, consisting of 15,951 applications relating to domestic violence and 2,711 applications relating to stalking. This was an increase of 9.4% from 1995–1996, following increases of 20.1% from 1994–1995 and 29.5% from 1993–1994. 11,402 orders were made in 1996–1997, compared to 5,335 in 1991–1992 (*The Age*, October 23, 1997). The number of domestic violence intervention order applications lodged per year has stabilized since 1996–1997 at around 15,000 applications per year (VLRC, 2004a, p. 68). Protection-order applications have similarly become a substantial proportion of lower court workloads in other State jurisdictions (e.g., Hickey & Cumines, 1999).
4. On failures to prosecute domestic assaults and breaches of protection orders in Australia, see Alexander (2002, pp. 31–33); Wearing (1992, pp. 283–289); Nunn and D'Arcy (2001, pp. 18–19), and references in note 1. In 1995–1996 in Victoria, police attended 15,613 family incidents, made 4,508 intervention order applications, and laid criminal charges in only 1,974 cases. The number of intervention orders applied for and criminal charges laid as a proportion of incidents attended increased only marginally over the 3 years to 1995–1996 (*The Age*, November 1, 1996).
5. In addition, the Crimes Act (1958), section 21A, enabled the court to make an intervention order in respect of a victim of "stalking" (as defined), which did not require any relationship between the victim and perpetrator, but is not relevant to the current discussion.

6. In *Kingsland v. McIndoe* (1989), however, the Victorian Supreme Court held that a "family member" as defined did not include an unrelated person with whom the applicant had shared a house.
7. See Hunter & Stubbs (1999), noting in particular that

   > verbal, economic and emotional abuse, intimidation, possessiveness, [and] sexual jealousy...when taken in isolation, may fall short of the notion of "harassing or offensive behaviour", but nevertheless are well recognised and frequently experienced elements on the domestic violence spectrum, which place their targets in fear for their safety. (p. 13)

   See also the forms of abuse experienced by the women litigants interviewed (chapter 1), among which the most common were emotional abuse, intimidation, and isolation, followed by both physical and economic abuse. Again, most of these would not clearly be covered by section 4 of the Crimes (Family Violence) Act (1987).
8. In both cases, unusually, the victims were young women and the defendants were their fathers. The application in M.C.30 (July 4, 1996) was for a final order. M.C.10 (April 22, 1996) involved confirmation of an interim order that had been obtained by the police out of hours. The police officer made it clear that he was appearing only to provide "moral support" to the victim, that he did not wish to be listed as the complainant on the file, and that he did not intend to reappear at the final hearing. The offer of "moral support" may have been intended to circumvent a court ruling that police officers could not appear on behalf of complainants in intervention order matters, and only had a right of audience if they themselves were the complainant (*Fisher v. Fisher*, 1988, p. 1038). In a third case (M.C.54, November 4, 1996), the male defendant had sought a variation of the intervention order made against him, and the application was opposed by a police prosecutor—the victim of violence herself did not appear.
9. Overall in 1996–1997, police made only 14% of intervention order applications in Victoria (*The Age*, October 23, 1997). The proportion of police complaints had not changed 5 years later in 2001–2002 (13.2%), but by 2002–2003, the proportion of applications made by police had risen to 24%. This change was attributed to new police protocols. However it remains the case that despite these protocols, police attending domestic violence incidents are more likely simply to refer victims of violence to court rather than to initiate an intervention order application, and 74.4% of applications are still made by "aggrieved family members" themselves (VLRC, 2004a, pp. 69, 142–143). Moreover, police complainants are hindered by

evidential rules, such as an inability to give hearsay evidence of conversations with the aggrieved family member (*Kirby v. Phelan*, 2003). By contrast, the N.S.W. legislation limits police discretion and *requires* them to apply for an order under certain circumstances.

10. The use of the pronoun "he" in relation to defendants is justified by the fact that in the years preceding the fieldwork (1991–1995), 86% of intervention order defendants were male (Putt & Higgins, 1997, p. 29).
11. By 2002–2003, the proportion of applications struck out (23.3%) and dismissed (5.3%) remained largely unchanged, but the proportion of withdrawals (16.8%) had almost doubled (VLRC, 2004a, p. 70).
12. Compare Egger & Stubbs (1993, p. 53), noting a higher success rate of applications and a lower rate of withdrawals in South Australia, where the police were more active in applying for orders.
13. When originally enacted, the legislation provided a fixed duration of 12 months for intervention orders; however, this was amended and the version of section 6 in place at the time of the observations was inserted in 1994 by the Crimes (Amendment) Act (1994).
14. Some Magistrates had held orders expressed to be made "until further order" to be void, which exposed victims to the risk of further violence, and made it impossible to prosecute breaches of the order. See also *Tsutsulis v. Tsutsulis* (1997), holding that orders made "until further order" only had the status and effect of interim rather than final orders.
15. This observation is not unusual. For example, Victorian court statistics indicated that in 1990–1991, 59% of final orders were granted ex parte and only 40% were granted with the defendant present (Wearing, 1992, p. 328). Similarly, in Chaudhuri and Daly's U.S. research on domestic violence temporary restraining orders in New Haven, in the majority of cases, the defendant did not appear at the show-cause hearing (1992, p. 231).
16. In Wearing's (1992) study, 50% of defendants were spouses or ex-spouses, 32% were de factos or ex-de factos, 3% were parents, 10% were other relations, and 0.4% were ex-boyfriends (p. 316). On this basis, it is likely that many of the "missing" cases in my observation sample would have been (former) spouses or de factos, although it also appears that my sample included a significantly higher proportion of boyfriend/ex-boyfriend defendants than did Wearing's.
17. This is consistent with the data cited in chapter 1 concerning the high incidence of violence experienced by women aged 18–24.
18. By contrast, the Domestic Violence Act (1995, N.Z.), section 76, requires the defendant to give notice of his intention to defend a domestic violence protection order application, and if he does not respond within 3 months,

the order automatically becomes final. A similar provision is found in the Restraining Orders Act (1997, W. Austl.), sections 31–32.

19. The Court's *Family Violence and Stalking Protocols* (Magistrates' Court of Victoria, 2003, ¶ 5.2) now provide that registrars must advise applicants to contact the court at least 2 days before the return date in order to determine if the court has notice of the defendant's intentions, whether the applicant intends to proceed, whether the applicant will be legally represented, and the number of witnesses the applicant intends to call. However, it will not usually be possible for the applicant to say whether she will be legally represented and how many witnesses she will call until after she knows whether the defendant intends to appear and contest the matter.
20. At least one interstate model did exist, however (see Blazejowska, 1996). The principles for court support schemes specified by this publication included that such schemes should only act for women (p. 62), and that solicitors should appear on behalf of women (p. 74).
21. The NESB Focus Group (interview, December 23, 1997) noted that there were no NESB women in Court Network. This apparently remains an issue (see VLRC, 2004a, p. 139; Babbel, 2002, pp. 12, 16–17).
22. Defendant present in court: χ^2 (1, $N = 90$) = 7.695, $p < .01$; defendant represented: χ^2 (2, $N = 88$) = 13.855, $p < .01$.
23. Pursuant to legislation prohibiting anyone other than a qualified lawyer from engaging in legal practice (see now Legal Profession Act (2004), s. 2.2.2(1)). It is possible, however, for specific authorization to be granted, either within the Legal Profession Act or Regulations, or within another piece of legislation such as the Crimes (Family Violence) Act (1987), or for the court to give leave to a person to represent another person (s. 2.2.2(2)(a), (f), (h), (3) and (6)).
24. The *Family Violence and Stalking Protocols* (Magistrates' Court of Victoria, 2003, ¶ 17.1) now provide that the Court Coordinator and Family Violence Registrar should liaise "to ensure family violence/stalking matters receive priority and are managed to provide some time certainty to clients on the day they are listed," but it is not known how this protocol has been implemented.
25. The current *Family Violence and Stalking Protocols* (Magistrates' Court of Victoria, 2003, ¶ 18.1) only oblige the registrar to take steps to secure the applicant's safety when "the Aggrieved Family Member has advised they are in fear of contact with the defendant whilst at Court." This suggests that fear of contact with the defendant on the part of the applicant is seen as

exceptional rather than normal, and also places the onus on the applicant to seek assistance, when she may not know that she is able to do so.

26. Numbers exclude those who had no opportunity to speak or spent so little time in the courtroom it was impossible to assess their demeanor.
27. The applicant was sworn in 14 out of the 17 interim order cases observed. Swearing was exclusively on the Bible. In no cases observed was the applicant given the option to make an affirmation or to swear on the Koran or other holy book. One magistrate explained that the court had a Koran available that could be provided if necessary, but the witness would have to ask for it. If he had a busy list, he did not have time to give all the options and explain them to everyone (Field notes, Broadmeadows Magistrates' Court, July 11, 1997; see also Assafiri & Dimopoulos, 1995, p. 21, describing an observation of a magistrate trying "to coerce a Muslim woman to swear on the Bible, insisting that it was the same as the Koran." When the woman resisted, the magistrate informed her that, "unless she was prepared to swear on the Bible, he would throw the case out of court").
28. Magistrates were good-natured 25% of the time when the applicant was represented, but only 9% of the time when the applicant was unrepresented; they were bureaucratic only 50% of the time when the applicant was represented as opposed to 79% of the time when the applicant was unrepresented. In general, magistrates were significantly less likely to be bureaucratic when the applicant was represented: χ^2 (1, N = 81) = 6.787, $p < .01$.
29. Magistrates were good-natured in 57% of contested cases and firm/formal in 29% of such cases, but were never bureaucratic. By contrast, magistrates were bureaucratic in 80% of cases decided ex parte and 75% of cases determined by consent.
30. It is notable that all of the NESB women interviewed had been supported in court by workers from the Immigrant Women's Domestic Violence Service, who could act as interpreters if necessary. But where NESB women had not been to a refuge or had not made contact with the service, their access to an interpreter was entirely dependent upon the court's good graces. The court's responsibility to arrange for interpreters to be available is now enshrined in the *Family Violence and Stalking Protocols* (Magistrates' Court of Victoria, 2003, ¶ 4.2, 5.2, 16). The protocols provide that qualified interpreters must be used, specify that court interpreters accredited to a certain minimum level must be used "whenever available," and prohibit the use of children or relatives as interpreters. They provide that the registrar must attempt to obtain a qualified interpreter "if necessary," but do not offer any guidance

to registrars in determining whether an interpreter is necessary. Moreover, the form given to the applicant to complete asks, "do you need an interpreter?" in English!

31. The *Family Violence and Stalking Protocols* (Magistrates' Court of Victoria, 2003, ¶ 16.1.1, 16.1.2) now state that "[i]f both parties require an interpreter it is usually preferable, especially in contested matters, that two are provided," but if only one interpreter is available, everyone involved must understand that the interpreter is independent and responsible to the court. Given the relatively limited number of contested matters, it is arguable that the protocols do not place sufficient emphasis on separate interpreters, and the injunction about impartiality is likely to be a fairly fragile defense against abuse.
32. No evidence was heard in 17 of the 18 matters in the observation sample at Sunshine, and 13 of the 15 matters in the sample heard by the most frequently observed magistrate at Frankston.
33. The same logical flaw was identified in *Stephens v. Melis* (2002). The case raised the question of whether intervention orders could be made by consent without any findings of fact. Smith J held that the court needed to be satisfied that jurisdictional facts specified in section 4 of the Crimes (Family Violence) Act (1987) did indeed exist, and hence that the defendant's consent to an order included an admission of those jurisdictional facts. Thus, where the defendant wished to consent without admitting the allegations in the complaint, the magistrate could only make an order if satisfied that the section 4 requirements were made out on facts not alleged in the complaint but at least impliedly admitted by the consent! (¶ 38–41). This decision rendered the regime of consent without admissions unworkable, until the Crimes (Family Violence) Act (1987) was amended in 2003 to overcome the effect of the decision and to provide that orders may be made by consent without the magistrate being satisfied that there are grounds for an order and without the court requiring the respondent to admit particulars of the complaint (VLRC, 2004a, p. 65). As argued previously, however, this amendment could be said to significantly weaken the effectiveness of the legislation.

Chapter 4

The Discourse of Intervention Orders

While the previous chapter focused on the process of intervention order applications, and hence mainly dealt with structural problems in the implementation of intervention order legislation, this chapter deals with the understandings of domestic violence held by registrars and magistrates, as evidenced in their comments and decisions in intervention order cases and in the opinions expressed by interviewees. Thus, it is mainly concerned with implementation problems attributable to legal culture and, specifically, the internal legal culture of the Magistrates' Courts.

The Role of the Registrar

Several commentators have described the initial interview with the clerk/registrar as being the most crucial element of women's experience in the intervention order process. For women unaccompanied by lawyers or support workers, the registrar is often their sole source of information and advice, and thus "influences the scope of the application, what information is included in it, what is provided to the magistrate, and what terms and conditions the person requests to have imposed" (VLRC, 2004a, p. 136). Moreover, the outcome of the woman's foray into the court system may largely depend upon whether the registrar is supportive or discouraging (Wearing, 1992, p. 415). In other words, clerks/registrars played an important gatekeeping role in the intervention order process. Because interviews between the applicant and the clerk/registrar generally took place "behind the scenes," however, they were not observable as part of my fieldwork. Neither did I focus on the role of the registrar in interviews with lawyers, support workers, and women who had applied for intervention orders, and only one interviewee raised the role of the registrar spontaneously. This part of the discussion, therefore, relies on other sources.

Clerks/registrars did not receive any regular or standardized training in dealing with Crimes (Family Violence) matters (Babbel, 2002, pp. 15–16; see also Chief Justice's Taskforce on Gender Bias, 1994, p. 172), and the literature suggested considerable variability in the attitudes and approaches of clerks/registrars towards intervention order applicants and in their understanding of domestic violence (Babbel, 2002, pp. 15–16; VLRC, 2004a, p. 135; Wearing, 1992, p. 16; Wearing, 2001, p. 11). The reception an applicant received could be professional, skilled, and sensitive, or arrogant, uncaring, judgemental, or hostile (VLRC, 2004a, pp. 135, 137; Wearing, 1992, pp. 17, 73–74; Wearing, 2001, p. 11). According to Wearing's study, clerks were more likely to ask questions about the most recent incident, and whether there was a physical assault and/or injuries, than to inquire about the history of abuse in the relationship (1992, pp. 48–49). The interview gave the clerk/registrar the opportunity to assess whether the application was "genuine," and to screen out "trivial" cases or applicants deemed not to be credible (VLRC, 2004a, p. 135). Some clerks/registrars would refuse to issue a complaint if they judged that there were insufficient grounds for an order (especially if there was no physical assault), or would attempt to dissuade the applicant from proceeding by advising that their case was unlikely to succeed in court (Babbel, 2002, p. 18; VLRC, 2004a, pp. 83, 124; Wearing, 1992, pp. 16–17, 54). This role was endorsed by magistrates, who said they relied on the clerks to filter cases for them (Wearing, 1992, p. 146). In one area, registrars developed a system of coloured markers on the files to convey their assessment of the applicant's credibility to the magistrate (Babbel, 2002, p. 16; VLRC, 2004a, p. 135).[1] These practices suggest a high degree of confidence by magistrates that they and their registrars shared a common understanding of domestic violence and, on that basis, would arrive at similar assessments of credibility.

For those women who were not dissuaded from proceeding, the registrar played a further role as the ultimate author of the complaint (Magistrates' Court of Victoria, 2003, ¶ 4.5). Thus, the registrar had the power to rewrite the applicant's story, to highlight and discard elements they regarded as ir/relevant, and to blanch emotion from the scene (see Wearing, 2001, p. 12). This, in turn, had an impact on magistrates' responses to applications and tended to reinforce the shared understandings of domestic violence they already held. In intervention order cases, then, it was not the applicant's lawyer but the registrar who filtered the applicant's story and produced a legally acceptable account to place before the court.

Magistrates' Understandings of Domestic Violence

The task of the magistrate in intervention order proceedings was to determine whether the legal requirements for an intervention order had been made out—that is, had there been an assault, property damage, harassment, molestation, and/or offensive behavior, and was there a likelihood of repetition of that behavior; or had there been a threat to assault or cause property damage and a likelihood of that threat being carried out? In an early (and distinctly nonfeminist) decision on the legislation, the Supreme Court had also held that intervention orders should not be made "as a matter of course." Rather, in addition to the legislative grounds for an order, the magistrate should consider

> the bases upon which all injunctions are pronounced. That is, after an arguable case is made out at a prima facie level in the case of interim orders, and also after considering the balance of convenience in the case of intervention orders. (*Fisher v. Fisher*, 1988, p. 1035)

In other words, the court assimilated the new creature called an intervention order with the familiar legal form of an injunction, and imported an additional set of criteria from the latter to the former.

The way magistrates interpreted and applied these requirements provided insights into their understandings of domestic violence. On one level, it was difficult to glean much information about magistrates' understandings of domestic violence from their statements in court, given the general brevity of intervention order proceedings and the fact that the specific allegations of violence were rarely stated or responded too. However, interview data, combined with the court observations, did yield some reasonably consistent evidence about the cognitive frameworks that magistrates brought to their adjudicative task.

The first point made by many interviewees was that there was considerable variation among magistrates in their approaches to determining intervention order applications (see also VLRC, 2004a, p. 177). Interviewees noted that the same allegations of violence would be dealt with quite differently before different magistrates (NESB Focus Group, interview, December 23, 1997; Field notes, Broadmeadows Court Support Program, October 25, 1996; see also Babbel, 2002, p. 16). Some magistrates would simply accept the veracity of the written application; some would want more detail and ask further questions; some would pass judgement—for example asking why the applicant had stayed with her abuser and not complained about his behavior previously; some were very sympathetic (F. Culpen, interview, March 17, 1997; S.1, interview, January 16, 1997; Field notes, Broadmeadows Magistrates' Court, July 11, 1997). Some magistrates were very affirming of women, while others were not (A. Palombo, interview, April 1, 1996). Some would minimize the violence they were hearing about, while others were totally supportive and helpful (S. Macgregor, interview, March 1, 1996). As a consequence, from the perspective of an individual applicant (and any support workers and/or legal representatives assisting her), the magistrate's response to her complaint would be a matter of luck (NESB Focus Group, interview, December 23, 1997; see also Conley & O'Barr, 1990, p. 111).

Among this variety, there were some themes in magistrates' understandings of violence that emerged more or less strongly from the interviews and court observations. These included participation in and endorsement of some of the social and legal narratives about violence identified in chapter 2—narratives that are at odds with feminist understandings of violence. As noted by one domestic violence worker, "Apparently there is a huge gap between what magistrates and what support workers see as evidence, as proof of violence and risk of harm" (Hall, 1999, p. 11).

Incident Focus and Emphasis on Physical Violence

Recency

First, encouraged by the terms of the legislation, magistrates tended to see violence in terms of isolated, decontextualized "incidents" rather than as a pattern of coercive behavior involving the ongoing exercise of power and control over another (see also Ptacek, 1999, p. 8; Spowart & Neil, 1997). Consequently, lawyers noted that magistrates were looking for a recent incident, the most current acts or threats, in order to grant an order, rather than wanting to hear about the history of violence in the relationship (F. Culpen, interview, March 17, 1997; D. Dawson, interview, June 5, 1996; see also Hall, 1999, p. 10; Kinports & Fischer, 1992, p. 201; Wearing, 1992, pp. 48–49).[2] Other studies have shown that there usually is a precipitating incident when women apply for intervention orders (such as an episode of violence that resulted in the police being called or the woman going to a refuge), but this episode is usually only a small part of the story (e.g., Fischer & Rose, 1995, p. 416; Trimboli & Bonney, 1997, p. 30). The focus on recent incidents and the lack of a power and control analysis created a structural problem in obtaining an order, however, as it made it more difficult to prove likely repetition. Magistrates did not see that a long history of violence (including different forms of abuse) necessarily established this element and were more likely to be persuaded by a series of recent incidents, ideally including a breach of the interim order (Spowart & Neil, 1997, p. 83).[3] On the other hand, if there had been some lapse of time between the last incident of violence and the application, there was a need to explain that gap (for example if the woman had been in a refuge), otherwise the order might not be made (K. Anderson, interview, March 8, 1996; S. Borg, interview, October 17, 1997).

Lack of Understanding of Fear

A further consequence of magistrates' focus on individual incidents rather than understanding violence in terms of power and control was that they often did not understand why women continued to be fearful of the defendant even after they had separated from him and may not have seen him for some time (Wearing, 1996, p. 152; S. Macgregor, interview, March 1, 1996; see also Scheppele, 1994, pp. 1014–1015). Commentators have noted, as a general proposition, that fear and pain are extremely difficult experiences to explain or share (Scarry, 1985, pp. 4–5). As one magistrate put it bluntly to another researcher, he wanted evidence of injury because "I can't see fear" (Wearing, 2001, p. 13). Douzinas and Warrington (1995) have written persuasively in the context of refugee cases about the double bind faced by victims of persecution in circumstances in which their fear and pain is supposed to be judged "objectively"—that is, the law claims that a judge can stand on the same footing as the refugee and can equally understand their predicament and determine the basis of their fear.

> Either he is in fear or he is not. If he is, he should be able to give facts and reasons for it which, as they belong to the genre of truth, should match up to the assessment of the judge. If they do not, the refugee is lying. If, on the other hand, he cannot give "objective" justifications for his fear the refugee is again lying. Similarly, when the refugee is inarticulate and cannot explain the "objective basis" of his fear, he is not in fear...[I]n the idiom of cognition, fear is either reasonable and can be understood by the judge or is unreasonable and therefore non-existent. (p. 208)

The same point can be made of women who have been targets of domestic violence. For example, when one of the women interviewed applied for an intervention order after suffering intimidation, emotional abuse, isolation, economic abuse, and physical assaults during a 15-year marriage, she was asked by the magistrate why she was now scared of her ex-husband. She said, "It seemed like a strange question!" (W.L.7, interview, October 28, 1997). The ex-husband of another interviewee had subjected her to the full gamut of power and control tactics in the 12 years they were married, had criminal convictions for assaults against her, and had also been convicted of rape, threats to kill, and conduct endangering life—although this conviction had been quashed on appeal and he had been acquitted at the retrial. He was still fighting her in the Family Court for access to their two children. She had had three 12-month intervention orders; however, the last of these had expired, and she was unable to obtain another one. Because her ex-husband had not breached the order or assaulted her in the last 12 months, and she was living at a secret address, he was considered no longer to be a threat to her (W.L.2, interview, December 18, 1997). A support worker in one of the focus groups also noted a case she had attended where the magistrate had decided that the applicant did not need an intervention order because she was living in a refuge. When the applicant left the refuge and went back to court, a different magistrate decided that since there was no evidence of any recent incidents of violence, she had no grounds for an order (NESB Focus Group, interview, December 23, 1997; see also Hickey & Cumines, 1999, p. 74).

Magistrates also generally failed to appreciate something that abusive men appeared to appreciate very well—that a serious physical assault had ongoing psychological effects. One severe beating could terrorize a woman for life, without the need for the perpetrator ever to lift a finger again. Yet fear arising from a long-ago incident was not sufficient to ground an intervention order (S.W.1, interview, December 23, 1997). As one interviewee put it,

> In court sometimes, if they haven't hit you, it doesn't count as violence. Mine doesn't hit me; he hasn't for 7 years. But he doesn't

> need to. What they do to your head is worse; bruises heal. (W.L.5, interview, December 19, 1997)

This woman's support worker added that if the magistrates who had heard her intervention order applications had actually sat down with her for an hour and listened to her whole story, there would be no question about her entitlement to an order. In fact, she had spoken about her experiences of violence at a magistrates' conference, and the magistrates had been very impressed and said they had not heard the issues put like that before. Yet women with similar experiences had appeared before them numerous times, and they had either not wanted to hear or had not listened (Geelong Focus Group, interview, December 19, 1997).

This failure to understand fear arising from histories of abuse was particularly evident in two of the cases I observed. In the first, a woman was applying for an interim order against her ex-boyfriend. She had not physically seen him for 4 months, but her house had been broken into and jewellery stolen, and she believed he had done it. She also believed that he would come back again to retrieve a letter that implicated him in other criminal activity. She had previously applied for an interim order against him, but had withdrawn the application following negotiations between their solicitors. The magistrate was highly skeptical of her story and questioned her closely. While she had been coherent when telling the story by herself, she was disconcerted by the magistrate's questions and had trouble getting dates and sequences of events straight. She began crying, to which the magistrate made no response. He wanted to know why she was seeking an order now, and why she thought the defendant would come back if she had had no contact with him since November. He thought it highly unlikely the defendant would return and pointed out she had suffered no physical harm. He noted that issuing an intervention order was a serious matter and he must have proper grounds for doing so, but he had not heard evidence to convince him that such grounds existed. By this stage, the applicant was sobbing and blurted out, "I'm terribly afraid," to which the magistrate responded, "I don't believe you need have any fear." The order was refused (M.C.9, March 6, 1996).

This was the only one out of 17 interim order applications in which the order was not granted.

In the second case, an interim order had been granted but had not been served because the police had been unable to locate the defendant. The allegations against him included having beaten the applicant's head against a brick wall, and it was clear that she considered him highly dangerous and was living in continuous fear that he might reappear at any time and assault her again or abduct their child. She also believed that his friends were keeping an eye on her and reporting her movements to him. The support program solicitor sought an adjournment of the final order application to allow for further efforts to serve the interim order. The magistrate granted the adjournment to a specified date, but added, "If they can't find him by then, he's not going to cause much trouble." Afterwards, in conversation with the solicitor, the magistrate said that he could not understand some women getting so worked up. In his view, if the defendant was not around, the problem was "all in their minds." Musing on what could be done to stop the fear, he considered that an intervention order might be less effective than "a good social worker" (M.C.32, July 4, 1996). In other words, the woman's well-founded fear of violence based on the defendant's previous behavior was pathologized and transformed into an individual, psychological weakness.

In a contrasting case, a woman was applying for a final order against her ex-boyfriend. They had had a 4-month relationship, during which she alleged constant physical and psychological abuse, but she had had no further trouble from him since the interim order was granted. The magistrate asked the applicant what had happened in the relationship, and she recounted a catalogue of abuse, including him locking her in a room, grabbing and bruising her arms, making death threats, and constantly demanding her attention. The magistrate promptly made an indefinite order, explaining, "You'll be better off; it's what you need" (M.C.41, October 31, 1996). Here, then, the magistrate did attend to the history of the relationship and signalled by the length of the order his view of the seriousness of the defendant's behavior and the ongoing threat posed to the applicant.

Emphasis on Physical Violence

Associated with magistrates' general focus on incidents rather than on patterns of abusive behavior was a focus on physical violence, which was considered more serious and compelling than other forms of abuse. Lawyers and support workers consistently noted that magistrates wanted to hear about (recent incidents of) physical violence, and that other forms of abuse (verbal, emotional, financial, manipulation using the children, harassment, etc.) had a lower priority and required much stronger advocacy if they were relied upon as the basis for an order (K. Anderson, interview, March 8, 1996; H. Assafiri, interview, June 24, 1997; F. Culpen, interview, March 17, 1997; NESB Focus Group, interview, December 23, 1997; A. Palombo, interview, April 1, 1996; J. Peirce, interview, August 21, 1997; S.1, interview, January 16, 1997; S.2, interview, October 28, 1997; S.W.1, interview, December 23, 1997; see also Magistrates' Court of Victoria, 2003, ¶ 4.6; VLRC, 2004a, p. 83; Wearing, 1992, pp. 49, 157–158). If incidents of abuse were seen in isolation from each other, then incidents of physical violence were easier to prove and corroborate (by means of photographs, hospital visits, or the visible evidence of a black eye, cut face, or split lip in court) (K. Anderson, interview, March 8, 1996; J. Peirce, interview, August 21, 1997; S.W.1, interview, December 23, 1997). Likewise, threats to kill would be taken seriously if there were a witness who had heard the threat (S.W.1, interview, December 23, 1997). One interviewee also observed that magistrates' focus on physical violence was reinforced by the fact that both victims and perpetrators were more likely to identify physical violence as "violence" and hence were more likely to talk about and to admit to this kind of violence. By contrast, many perpetrators did not identify verbal abuse, swearing, or social isolation as acts of violence or wrongdoing (J. Peirce, interview, August 21, 1997; see also Hickey & Cumines, 1999, p. 74; Moore, 2002, p. 9).

Relationship Conflict as the Source of Violence

A second set of understandings that magistrates frequently brought to their hearing of intervention order applications was the notion that violence was a product of spousal conflict arising from the stresses of a marriage or de facto relationship. It followed that both parties were likely to be responsible for the violence, and that the violence would stop once the parties separated (see also Carpenter, Currie & Field, 2001; Greenwood, 1996; Hickey & Cumines, 1999, p. 59). This, in turn, gave rise to something of an obligation to separate if a party no longer wished to tolerate violence in their relationship.

Dysfunctional Couples

One magistrate explained to me that intervention order cases involved "very dysfunctional people" who did not "know how to deal with their problems rationally" and used violence instead (Field notes, Broadmeadows Magistrates' Court, July 11, 1997). Another lamented,

> It's terrible all this. People never tell you the truth, that's the worst thing. They won't just say they're having a brawl. It's always "I hate him, she hates me, and only one of us is right". Sometimes you want to take people out the bush [*sic*] and make them walk home. They'd have sorted it out by the time they get there. (Field notes, Preston Magistrates' Court, July 4, 1996)

Similarly, lawyers noted that it was easier to get an intervention order in cases not involving a spousal relationship (such as parent/child cases or stalking by a stranger), as there were no assumptions or prejudgements being made by the magistrate about the relationship between the applicant and defendant, and the kinds of behavior wives and partners were expected to put up with (S. Macgregor, interview, March 1, 1996; M. Mann, interview, March 8, 1996; A. Palombo, interview, April 1, 1996). In one regional court, magistrates had adopted the practice of making intervention orders for only 3 months, to "take the heat out of the situation," on the assumption that married or de facto couples only needed to be kept apart for a brief period in order to calm down and work things out rationally (Geelong Focus Group, interview, December 19, 1997).

Again, two cases I observed illustrated this understanding. In the first, a young woman applied for a final order against her ex-boyfriend.

She alleged that he had subjected her to frequent verbal abuse, pushed her around, pushed her out of a car, harassed her parents, and pursued her. As a result, she had become fearful, had lost self-esteem and confidence, and had received counseling to try to recover from the effects of the abuse. The defendant appeared in person and refused to consent to an order because he wanted to join the police force and did not want an intervention order on his record. He was sufficiently argumentative and obstructive for the magistrate to exclaim, "What I've seen of you has convinced me that the allegations are true." Nevertheless, the magistrate allowed the defendant simply to make an undertaking not to have any further contact with the applicant, and also decided that it would be fair that the applicant should make a similar undertaking not to go near the defendant. The magistrate later explained to me that the reason for this was that the applicant had a new boyfriend and ought to be getting on with her life and not having anything more to do with the defendant (M.C.38, July 4, 1996). Thus, the magistrate converted a proven pattern of abusive conduct on the part of one party into a matter of mutual avoidance. The issue of mutual orders is discussed further later in the chapter.

In the second case, the magistrate paid more attention to the parties' bickering over which of them should have the child's toys and car seat than to the actual allegations of violence. To the observer, the parties did, in fact, appear to be merely squabbling, and this was reinforced by the fact that after making the final order by consent, the magistrate delivered a little homily about resolving their differences (M.C.98, June 27, 1997). Yet presumably there had been sufficient allegations of the defendant's violence to found an order in the applicant's favor in the first place, a point that remained invisible in the actual proceedings.

Obligation to Leave

If violence is seen as a product of relationship conflict, the obvious way to stop the violence is to end the relationship. As Merry (1997b) explains, women applying for protection orders are made into autonomous, liberal legal subjects, for whom the price of legal rights is separation and isolation (p. 304). One lawyer noted that women without children were seen as less in need of protection because they could more easily separate and relocate away from their abusive partner. In her view, this expectation was applied to gay as well as to heterosexual couples (S. Macgregor, interview, March 1, 1996).

In one of the cases I observed, the magistrate specifically stated that equivocation about her relationship would not be held against an applicant. In that case, the woman had applied for an interim order the previous week, but had withdrawn her application because the defendant undertook to change his behavior. Instead, his behavior had worsened, and she had returned to court to renew her application. The magistrate announced that he had instructed the registrars at the courts where he sat that anyone was welcome to come back to court after withdrawing an application, and no questions would be asked about that (M.C.26, July 2, 1996). This is consistent with an understanding of separation from an abusive partner as a process rather than an event, which may involve several steps over a period of time (Fischer & Rose, 1995, p. 127). By contrast, in another matter, the applicant had had a 12-month order, which had recently expired, and the defendant had taken the opportunity to assault her again. They had lived together for 5 years and he had a history of jealousy and possessiveness. As well as physical violence, his "separation assaults" had included kidnapping the children in order to persuade her to return to him, and he had been fighting her application for custody in the Family Court for 2 years. In making a new interim order, the magistrate suggested that the applicant had been indecisive about ending the relationship, ignoring both her attempts to do so and the defendant's attempts to prevent her (M.C.55, November 4, 1996).

In a third case, the woman alleged that she had been abused for 17 years, including assaults on a monthly basis. Finally, one particular incident had resulted in her going to a refuge, and she had applied for an interim order with the assistance of a refuge worker. At the return date, she was accompanied by a solicitor, a refuge worker, and an interpreter. The defendant had ignored the interim order, remained living in the house, and did not appear to contest the final order, but the magistrate was still reluctant to grant it, asking whether the applicant really needed the order. While the solicitor struggled to present the applicant's case, the magistrate took over the questioning, asking about the causes of the assaults (the defendant's drinking?) and why the applicant had returned home after 5 days in the refuge. The solicitor stated that the applicant's primary concern had been to look after her children, all of whom were of school age, and the magistrate would be aware that many women put up with domestic violence for years. The magistrate's response was that the defendant had never had an order against him, and now he had put one foot out of line and could end up in jail. The solicitor finally managed to lead evidence about an incident that had occurred in the last week, after the defendant had been served with the interim order. The applicant explained that the defendant unplugged the phone at home so that she could not call for help if she needed it. When the defendant had discovered she had a mobile phone, he had broken the battery recharger and had also smashed some plates and a glass pane in a door. The magistrate was unmoved by the defendant's isolation and intimidation of the applicant, but reluctantly agreed to make the final order on the basis of the defendant's breach of the interim order. As discussed further later in the chapter, he was also extremely reluctant to include a term in the order requiring the defendant to move out of the house (M.C.42, October 31, 1997). His view seemed to be that if the applicant had put up with the violence for 17 years, she could either put up with it further, or end it by taking the initiative to move away herself.

Encouragement of Reconciliation

At the same time (and illustrating the sometimes contradictory discourses in which applicants found themselves enmeshed), some magistrates appeared very keen on the idea of couples overcoming their "differences" and keeping their families intact, or, if they had separated, reconciling. Although none of my observations involved refusals of orders on the basis that the order might prevent parties addressing the "real problems" in their marriage (Busch, 1994, p. 107; Scutt, 1990,

p. 249) or might "break up families" (Ptacek, 1999, p. 55), applications for variations and revocations of orders frequently elicited comments from magistrates that tended to privilege "family values" over applicants' safety (see also Busch, 1994, p. 106; Chief Justice's Taskforce on Gender Bias, 1994, p. 178; Hickey & Cumines, 1999, p. 17).

In one matter, the applicant wanted her order varied so that she could facilitate greater contact between the defendant and their child. She noted that the defendant had been attending counseling and that this had been very beneficial. The magistrate granted the variation, observing that the relationship seemed to be improving, and that that was good for their son. She further asked whether there was a prospect of reconciliation, but the applicant was not going that far (M.C.13, June 11, 1996). Similarly, in another case, the applicant sought a variation of the order so the parties could discuss the welfare of their child. The magistrate responded that of course they could talk about matters relating to the welfare of their child, and exhorted the parties to see if they could resolve their troubles and keep away from the courts (M.C.39, October 31, 1996).

A third matter was an application for a final order, involving serious allegations of assault. The applicant had suffered occasional physical assaults in 7 years of marriage, but alleged that over the last 7–8 months, the violence had become more frequent, including pushing, punching, threats to kill, destruction of property, and hitting their son. Both the applicant and the defendant were from a non-English speaking background and were not fluent in English, but did not have interpreters. The applicant was very tearful and emotional, but was also at pains to stress that the defendant was not a criminal, and she did not want him charged (perhaps reflecting a lack of familiarity with the operation of civil courts in Australia).[4] However, she was clear that she could no longer cope with the defendant's behavior, that her son had become fearful of his father, that she did not want her son to see his father behaving aggressively and to copy that behavior, and that the defendant needed to deal with his behavior problem. At the magistrate's suggestion, the defendant consented to an order for 2 months, while denying the allegations.

The applicant had asked for the order to include a ban on contact by phone, but the magistrate removed that clause, explaining that "you two need to talk to each other, you need counseling, help with your marriage" (M.C.18, June 18, 1996). Thus, the magistrate constructed the "problem" as being the marriage rather than the defendant's behavior, which could be remedied by a brief, physical separation accompanied by discussion and counseling, rather than by the defendant taking responsibility for and changing his behavior.

In relation to applications for revocation of intervention orders, the Supervising Magistrate for Family Law in Victoria had asserted,

> In some family violence cases an urgent complaint is made for an ex parte order with, at times, horrendous allegations being made. After the defendant has been served it is not infrequent for the parties to arrive back at Court, hand-in-hand, seeking a revocation of the order. If the Court is not satisfied that the revocation is entirely voluntary, it may elect to continue with a clause prohibiting the defendant from assaulting, harassing, molesting, threatening or intimidating the complainant. It is rare for such a complainant to refuse to have such an order remain in place, even if there has been a reconciliation. Indeed, there is often a sigh of relief by the complainant when such a suggestion is made. (Blashki, 1997, pp. 7–8)

Regrettably, my own observations did not bear out this concern for the safety of applicants and the voluntariness of revocations. Indeed, one of the shortest cases I observed ran like this (M.C.17, June 18, 1996):

> [Case is called; applicant and defendant come to the front of the court together.]
> MAGISTRATE: [To applicant] What's your relationship with the defendant?
> APPLICANT: He's my husband.
> MAGISTRATE: Have you had a reconciliation or something?
> APPLICANT: I want to give him a chance.
> MAGISTRATE: OK, fine, the order is removed. That's it.

In a slightly longer variant of a revocation case, the magistrate did not ignore the issue of the applicant's safety, but was more interested in promoting harmonious relationships (M.C.64, February 21, 1997):

MAGISTRATE: [To applicant] You have an order in place?
APPLICANT: Yes.
MAGISTRATE: And now you want to revoke it? Why?
APPLICANT: We've tried to reconcile. My husband has decided to go to counseling, and we want to get back together.
MAGISTRATE: [To defendant] Is that the situation?
DEFENDANT: Yes.
MAGISTRATE: I haven't gone into the evidence, I only have this [the interim order application] before me, but if the allegations are true, you musn't repeat…
DEFENDANT: I haven't seen any documents, I've got no documents.
MAGISTRATE: Haven't you been served with the order?
DEFENDANT: No.
MAGISTRATE: OK, well I don't know if there's any truth in the allegations, but if you have been unpleasant to your wife, you should go to counseling with her, see if you can sort out your differences.
DEFENDANT: I'm 100% behind that.
MAGISTRATE: By consent, I revoke the order.

In only one revocation case observed did the magistrate act to protect the applicant from potential future violence. In this case, when the matter came on, the magistrate asked for the original file to see what the allegations had been. These included harassment, violent destruction of property, threats to the children, and irrational behavior by the defendant. In the last incident, just over a month previously, the defendant had scratched his keys along the side of the applicant's car. The magistrate explained that the courts were cautious about revoking orders, especially since in this case the order had been made only a month ago, and she asked what had changed so dramatically in that time. The applicant responded that she and the defendant were living apart and would probably stay that way, but she wanted to be able to see his young daughter, who lived in Perth and came to visit once a year, without having any trouble from her family. They did not like the defendant and would use the order as an excuse to interfere and complain to the police if they could. The magistrate sought an assurance that no one had coerced or threatened the applicant to apply for a revocation. She then revoked the clauses of the order that would prevent contact with the defendant and his daughter, but left in place the clauses prohibiting the defendant from harassing or molesting the applicant or damaging her property (M.C.86, June 27, 1997).

Denial and Minimization of Violence

Much of the feminist literature on violent men observes their tendency to minimize and deny their violent actions, to deny responsibility and blame their victims for those actions, and to see themselves as victims (see chapter 2, and also Ptacek, 1999, p. 71; Simon, 1995). Rather than confronting defendants' neutralization techniques, magistrates tended to take men's accounts of violence at face value. Consequently, they only contingently accepted the evidence given by women in interim order applications, and when faced with conflicting accounts from defendants on return dates, tended to conclude that women were lying, or at least exaggerating. This was put to me with some force in discussions with several magistrates. One stated that often the story given at the interim order stage "turns out to be completely false" when the other side gave their version on the return date (Field notes, Broadmeadows Magistrates' Court, July 11, 1997). The possibility that the other side's story might be false was not mentioned. Another argued that women do not understand the difference when they return for the final order and are required to produce some evidence to support their story. They think they are not being believed. They simply want to get their order stamped at the counter. They do not see why they have to go into court and cannot see why the defendant has to be notified and given a chance to give his version. They expect magistrates to just take their word for it (Field notes, Broadmeadows Magistrates' Court, February 21, 1997; Moonee Ponds Magistrates' Court, November 1, 1996). While this observation accurately captures some of the concerns women expressed about defendants lying in court and getting away with it, it ascribes an entirely different motive to those concerns. Rather than understanding that defendants may seek to minimize, deny, and shift blame, this magistrate had concluded that women do not want to give men a "fair go" in the legal process—a conclusion damaging to women's credibility.

At the same time, magistrates themselves sometimes participated in the minimization and denial of violence, and the shifting of blame, through their reactions to women's stories. A study of protection order applications in the Northern Territory observed magistrates ascribing defendants' behavior to emotional difficulties experienced after separation from their wives, and urging women to take responsibility for defendants' behavior and to handle them better (Spowart & Neil, 1997, p. 82; see also Gilchrist & Blisset, 2002, p. 359). A domestic violence worker interviewed noted that magistrates' theories of violence often included a prominent role for alcohol, so they tended to ask questions of applicants about whether alcohol was involved in the defendant's behavior (S.W.1, interview, December 23, 1997).

One of the interim order applications observed provided a good illustration of minimization. The magistrate only wanted to hear about the most recent incident, but the applicant wanted to tell much more. Eventually, she succeeded in speaking about the defendant's abuse around access to the children and about his threats made by telephone to abduct the children, something he had done before in a previous relationship. He had also assaulted her during their relationship, including pushing and choking her while she was pregnant. He had a history of violence when drinking, and on one occasion her friends had called the police, but he had forced her out of the house before the police arrived. The magistrate granted an interim order for 2 weeks, limited to prohibiting the defendant from coming within 100 meters of the applicant's house (M.C.6, February 27, 1996). The abusive phone calls and risk of child abduction were not addressed at all.

Another case involved a curious mixture of empathy and potential blame shifting. This was an application for an interim order, in which it was alleged that the defendant had been violent and aggressive for the last 3 years of the parties' 6-year relationship. The violence included physical abuse, rape, and threats to kill the applicant, their children, and himself; the applicant was very fearful that the defendant would perpetrate further violence or carry out his threats. The magistrate tried to put the applicant at ease, was very sympathetic, elicited further details of the allegations, made suggestions about ensuring her safety ("have you thought about going to a refuge?"—"be careful!"), understood why she wanted to keep her address confidential, and offered support and validation ("no woman has to put up with what you have"). But at the same time, he asked questions such as, "why did he hit you?" "was it connected with alcohol?" and "have you got someone else in your life?" (M.C.109, July 11, 1997). Through these questions, the magistrate appeared to be searching for supposed reasons (or excuses) for the defendant's violence. As it turned out, the answers removed any sympathy the magistrate might have had for the defendant (the defendant blamed the applicant for his violence, hit her first thing in the morning, and had formed another relationship while she had not), and the order was granted.

The Influence of Ethnicity and Class

A more collective form of minimization and blame shifting is found in the notion that violence is a feature of certain ethnic communities (and by implication, not of others). Assafiri and Dimopoulos (1995), drawing on the experiences of Refuge Ethnic Workers Program (REWP) workers in Melbourne, argue that when "ethnic" women apply for intervention orders, "the victim's behaviour and her culture [are positioned] as the appropriate arena for scrutiny, rather than the adjudication of the violence of the perpetrator" (p. 20). The belief that culture causes violence meant that some magistrates were all too willing to believe stories of violence told by women from particular cultures, especially those from the Middle East and former Yugoslavia (p. 21). For example, magistrates explained to me in conversation that some Muslim women are "terrified" of their husbands. They "creep into court" and slowly tell a "horrendous story." These men are "frightening, primitive peasants." It is "ingrained in them that women are to be treated like packhorses," and if they do not obey, they get beaten. And despite terrible abuse, the women are still reluctant to leave their husbands because of their upbringing (Field notes, Broadmeadows Magistrates' Court, July 11, 1997). A lawyer noted that if she could get into evidence the fact that the defendant was Muslim, Turkish, or Yugoslav, she knew this would help to get the order (S. Macgregor, interview, March 1, 1996), while a support worker also observed that it was possible to play on magistrates' desire to rescue women from patriarchal men (H. Assafiri, interview, June 24, 1997).

"Cultural" arguments could cut both ways, however, and represented an uncertain and unreliable source of protection for immigrant women who were victims of violence. Magistrates could decide that since violence was a "natural" part of their culture, they should put up with it, or work within their community to address its patriarchal elements (Assafiri & Dimopoulos, 1995, p. 21; NESB Focus Group, interview, December 23, 1997; M.C.42, October 31, 1997). While some cultures were seen as violent, women from Asian backgrounds had difficulty convincing magistrates of their need for protection, because of the physical stereotype of Asian men as relatively small and weak (S. Macgregor, interview, March 1, 1996), and/or because of the stereotype of Asian women as passive and compliant, and thus seeking legal intervention when they should be doing more to help themselves (Assafiri & Dimopoulos, 1995, p. 21). Further, men from some cultures might be excused on the basis that protection for women against domestic violence was not a familiar concept in their countries of origin, and thus they were unaware of the implications of their behavior in Australia (Assafiri & Dimopoulos, 1995, p. 22). In these circumstances, the magistrate appeared to believe that a lecture to the defendant would be sufficient protection for the applicant, rather than the order that she sought. Alternatively, defendant lawyers might argue that given his cultural background, the defendant had in fact been very restrained in limiting the extent of his violence towards the applicant, and thus should be given credit for that. Finally, immigrant women sometimes faced accusations that they were only seeking an intervention order in order to be able to stay in the country after leaving their husbands. Whether or not this was factually correct, or even legally plausible, it was an effective way of undermining the applicant's position (H. Assafiri, interview, June 24, 1997).[5] Magistrates tended to take suggestions of ulterior motives in applying for intervention orders very seriously. This point is discussed further in chapter 7, in the context of the more commonly expressed concern that women only sought intervention orders to gain an advantage in Family Court disputes.

Ethnic/cultural stereotypes in the disposition of intervention order applications were also accompanied by class stereotypes. While, as one interviewee put it, magistrates tended to expect that "working-class women should be roughed up a bit," they were less likely to accept stories of domestic violence in middle-class families (H. Assafiri, interview, June 24, 1997; M. Mann, interview, March 8, 1996). Again, though, class position could cut both ways. It might be easier to establish violence by a man who was unemployed, or an unskilled labourer, than by a professional man (S. Macgregor, interview, March 1, 1996), but a working-class woman might also be expected to put up with more, or be considered more likely to have provoked or deserved the violence (K. Anderson, interview, March 8, 1996). Violence against middle-class women might be considered more shocking, but, on the other hand, a lawyer noted that it was difficult to get an intervention order for a well-dressed, articulate, well-presented woman in full-time employment, since there was an expectation that such a woman should be able to look after herself rather than turning to the courts for assistance (S. Macgregor, interview, March 1, 1996). In the intervention order applications observed, class played a particular role in contested matters, as discussed in the next section.

In summary, while individual magistrates' understandings of violence—and hence what they "heard" when deciding intervention order applications—varied widely, they did share a tendency to be incident focused and to privilege physical violence, rather than understanding violence as a pattern of abusive behaviors designed to exercise power and control over another. This meant, in practice, that they wanted to "hear" very little, placed little emphasis on power dynamics in relationships, had difficulty understanding women's ongoing fears of violence, and assumed that violence would stop once parties separated. Women could be caught in a bind between encouragement to try to sort out differences in their relationships and expectations that they should exercise self-help in removing themselves from proximity with perpetrators. Some magistrates were more concerned with giving the defendant a "fair go" than with ensuring women's safety, and could participate in denial, minimization, and blame shifting in relation to men's violence. Cultural and class "differences" added an extra layer of complication to these responses, but not in any consistent or predictable way.

Contested Matters

As noted in chapter 3, only 14 of the cases observed were contested. Of these, 12 were contests of final orders by the defendant. The remaining 2 were applications for variation and revocation of orders against them by the defendant, both of which were contested by the applicant (or on her behalf) and ultimately refused.[6] Among the 12 contests of final orders, 2 involved family relationships rather than intimate relationships and are not considered here. Three were adjourned to a later date, so that the actual contest was not observed. In a fourth case, the contest was not observed due to the fact that as soon as the case began, the applicant raised strenuous objections to anyone being present in court, and the court was closed. The features of the remaining 6 cases are set out in table 10.

Table 10. Contested intervention order applications observed.

Case	Applicant	Applicant's Represent'n	Defendant	Defendant's Represent'n	Outcome
M.C.21	female	barrister	husband	barrister	order refused
M.C.45	male	self	ex-wife	self	limited order
M.C.52	female	barrister	husband	self	order made as sought
M.C.63	female	barrister	husband	barrister	order refused
M.C.101	female	barrister	husband	self	limited order
M.C.108	female	self	ex-husband	self	order made as sought

It can be seen that when applications were contested, success for the applicant was by no means guaranteed—in fact, quite the opposite (see also Kinports & Fischer, 1992, pp. 201–202). Of the 6 contested cases observed in full, the applicant was completely successful in only 2 cases. In neither of these cases did the defendant have legal representation. In a further 2 cases, the applicant was partially successful, and, again, the defendant in those 2 cases was not legally represented. In the 2 cases in which the defendant was legally represented, no order was made, despite the fact that the applicant was also legally represented.

Contested hearings provided greater scope than interim hearings or uncontested final dispositions for defendants and their legal representatives to offer denials and excuses, to attempt to shift blame, and to minimize the defendant's violence, and for the infusion of judicial views about violence in relationships. In all of the contested cases observed, there appeared, on the balance of probabilities, to be grounds for the making of an intervention order in terms of the legislative requirements for a physical assault, property damage, or harassing or offensive behavior, and the likelihood of its recurrence. In 5 of the 6 cases, however, the question of whether or not to make an order came down to an exercise of the magistrate's discretion, and it was in this context that social narratives about domestic violence came into play, helping to account for defendants' relative success in these cases.

The Nature of the Relationship

All of the parties in the 6 contested cases had been married and separated, although in 3 of the cases, the separation had been quite recent, there were ongoing disputes as to who should retain possession of the matrimonial home pending the final disposition of the parties' property, and the application included a request for sole occupancy. In 5 of the cases, there was clear evidence of a history of abusive and controlling behavior on the part of the husband, both before and after separation. For example, in M.C.21 (June 27, 1996), the defendant had assaulted the applicant several times during the marriage, including attacking her in the car and attempting to choke her when she refused to have sex with him. There was also evidence of constant verbal abuse and sexual jealousy. The parties were currently separated but both continued to live in the matrimonial home. Although it appeared that the husband did not accept that the marriage was over and still hoped for a reconciliation, he had also engaged in a campaign of harassment in an attempt to force the applicant to move out of the house, consisting of many small, annoying actions that were individually minor but cumulatively exhausting. There was also a recent incident of physical violence, in which the defendant had tried to stop the applicant from going out by taking her handbag. When she tried to retrieve it, he had bitten her arm and drawn blood.

In M.C.45 (October 31, 1996), the woman (who was the defendant) alleged that her ex-husband had assulted her repeatedly during their 14 years of marriage, including during her pregnancies, and now refused to abide by Family Court orders regarding contact with their son. Rather, he exercised contact only at times of his own choosing, making it impossible for her to organize her own life.[7] In M.C.52 (November 4, 1996), the defendant had subjected the applicant and their children to frequent, shouted verbal abuse during the marriage, including a threat to burn down the house. The parties had separated and "reconciled" on a number of occasions. After the first separation, the defendant had abducted two of the children, and the applicant had agreed to resume living with him if he brought the children back. In the most recent incident, the defendant had kicked in the front door of their house, and the police had been called.

In M.C.63 (February 21 & 25, 1997), the husband had moved out of the matrimonial home but came to the house, entered, and stayed at will. On these occasions, he had threatened and verbally abused the applicant in front of the children, seriously physically assaulted her, and walked through the house carrying two guns. He had also made statements to their daughters involving both direct and implied threats to kill the applicant and her new partner. In M.C.101 (June 27, 1997), the defendant had assaulted the applicant when she was pregnant and, more recently, had dragged her out of bed and severely bruised her arms, kicked in the door of her new partner's car, been verbally abusive and made abusive phone calls to the applicant, set rules that the applicant was supposed to observe, and again let himself in and out of the house as he pleased after he had moved out, tampering with window locks and leaving notes to signal his presence. The defendant made it abundantly clear that he was planning to move back into the family home, and into the master bedroom, because he had a "right" to do so. The applicant argued that she would not be safe if this occurred.

In response, only one of the defendants admitted the allegations against him. In M.C.108 (July 11, 1997), it was alleged that the defendant had sent and was continuing to send his family harassing and abusive letters several times a week. The defendant did not deny that he had sent the letters (which were also in breach of Family Court orders), but instead stubbornly insisted on his right to do so and on the unfairness of his treatment by the legal system. This was one of the 2 cases in which the applicant was wholly successful in gaining the intervention order she sought.

The defendants in the other 5 contested cases denied or minimized their violence and/or sought to shift blame for the violence to the wife. In M.C.63 (February 21 & 25, 1997), the defendant denied most of the allegations, in particular, that he had ever physically assaulted the applicant or made most of the statements alleged to have been made to his daughters. He also argued provocation on the applicant's part—that she had yelled and screamed at him—and tried to present himself as the aggrieved party: while he was being reasonable in trying to negotiate with her, she refused to discuss matters with him; while he just wanted to maintain contact with his children, she was trying to push him out of her life. This strategy of denial and blame shifting had evidently worked successfully on previous occasions, as this was the applicant's third attempt in 8 months to obtain an intervention order against the defendant. On both previous occasions he had contested the matter, and orders had not been made due to insufficient evidence, as it was simply "her word against his." On this occasion, in order to get beyond "her word against his," the applicant called her two daughters as witnesses. They largely corroborated their mother's story and provided further evidence of the defendant using his contact with them to maintain power and control over the applicant. As explained subsequently, however, this corroborating evidence did not tip the balance in the applicant's favor.

In M.C.52 (November 4, 1996), the unrepresented defendant attempted to deny and minimize his behavior, to establish that the applicant was the one who started the "arguments," and to demonstrate that the applicant did not take his threats seriously. In this case, the applicant was seeking sole occupancy of the matrimonial home for a short period pending the availability of public housing for herself and the children. She argued that it would be unsafe for the defendant to remain living with them, while the defendant argued that he should be able to stay in the house until they moved out and that he posed no threat to them in doing so. In M.C.101 (June 27, 1997), the defendant denied some of the applicant's allegations and sought to minimize others, arguing that he was emotional and upset about the breakup of their marriage and about the applicant's new relationship, and had done things he did not really intend. He also gave evidence of "provocative" acts by the applicant, including destroying the marriage, failing to obey his "rules," allegedly abusing and intimidating him, removing his clothes and possessions from the house, and changing the locks.

In M.C.21 (June 27, 1996), the defendant's barrister focused closely on the alleged incidents of physical violence and worked to minimize these so that the defendant's physical violence all but disappeared. He also set out to portray the applicant as provocative and at least as violent towards the defendant as he had been towards her. In relation to the incidents of physical violence, the defendant's barrister first objected to the applicant's evidence of assaults during the marriage on the basis that they were irrelevant history, and in cross-examining the applicant, the barrister was at pains to establish that she was relying on only one allegation of assault (the biting incident) as the basis of her application for an intervention order. He then sought to establish that it was the applicant who had initiated physical contact in that incident: she had attacked the defendant because he had her handbag, so that when the defendant had bitten her, he was only acting in self-defense.

The barrister's picture of the applicant as provocative and violent was built up through cross-examination of the applicant and through evidence in chief given by the defendant, his brother, and his sister-in-law. All of the forms of harassment that the applicant alleged as breaches of the interim order were claimed to have been provoked or justified in some way. Evidence was also elicited of the applicant in the past slapping the defendant's face twice in public, making threats against him, punching him, and subjecting him to other, unprovoked physical and verbal violence during the marriage. The applicant's barrister did not seek to object to this evidence on the basis that the incidents were irrelevant history. Rather, he sought to object that the evidence was irrelevant since the defendant was not seeking an intervention order against the applicant. The magistrate ruled, however, that the applicant's alleged assaults on the defendant went to the question of her credit. The applicant admitted that she had hit the defendant on one occasion after he had taunted her about her working-class origins, telling her that she "should go back to the Housing Commission estate." In Australia, Housing Commission estates signify poverty and disorder, with implications of violence and lawlessness. The identification of the applicant as being from a Housing Commission estate thus bolstered the claims about her propensity for violence.

In the 3 cases in which the parties were still in the process of separation (M.C.21, M.C.52 and M.C.101), the magistrate analysed the violence in terms of "relationship stress and conflict," involving mutual responsibility and provocation, rather than in terms of the husband exercising power and control over the wife, and the wife reacting to that. In M.C.52 (November 4, 1996), the magistrate described the relationship between the parties as "turbulent" and concluded that most of the trouble was caused by lack of money. He specifically noted that it was not a physically violent relationship. However, he accepted that there had been violent verbal confrontations and that the defendant did lose his temper "out of frustration." His primary concern was the effect of the verbal violence and the defendant's angry outbursts on the four children (as opposed to their mother), and this was his major reason for making a sole occupancy order for a period of 3 weeks until alternative accommodation became available for the applicant and the children.

In M.C.101 (June 27, 1997), the magistrate excused the incident in which the defendant had dragged the applicant out of bed on the basis of the defendant's "remorse." She thus found there had been no recent physical violence. In relation to harassing or offensive behavior, she found there was emotional volatility on both sides. In response to the applicant's request for a sole occupancy order, therefore, she concluded that "separation under one roof may be no more stressful than the current situation." Consequently, while she did believe it was appropriate to make an order restraining the defendant from assaulting, harassing, molesting, threatening, or intimidating the applicant for 12 months, she refused to make the sole occupancy order. She also urged the parties to attend mediation, reach a property settlement, and go their separate ways, so there would be no need for further orders after the 12-month period had elapsed.

In M.C.21 (June 27, 1996), the magistrate found that the parties' relationship was volatile and marked by animosity, and considered that it was not in the interests of the children for the parties to remain together but, ultimately, that was a matter for them. He found that in biting the applicant, the defendant had been acting in reasonable self-defense and had in fact shown restraint, being bigger and stronger than her, and it was to his credit that he had left the house rather than continuing to assault her. Nevertheless, he found there were sufficient grounds to make an order under the legislation, but he was also satisfied on the basis of the evidence of unprovoked assaults that the applicant had greater propensity for violence than the defendant in this case. He therefore concluded that it would be improper for him to exercise his discretion in favor of the more violent of the two parties and refused to make any order.[8]

The remaining 2 cases were not susceptible to a "relationship stress and conflict" analysis, as the parties had been separated for a longer period. They could arguably have been analysed in terms of the husband's exercise of power and control and/or separation assaults. However, the two magistrates also eschewed such an interpretation in favor of other considerations.

"Fright" Narratives: The Bad Mother and the Vindictive Ex-Wife

As noted in chapter 2, social narratives involving feared feminine characters may be invoked against victims of violence who attempt to claim or defend themselves against their former partners in court. In the contested intervention order proceedings observed, women complaining about domestic violence were sometimes constructed as bad mothers or vindictive ex-wives, either as an alternative to a "relationship stress and conflict" analysis, or in conjunction with it.

In M.C.63 (February 21 & 25, 1997), in which the applicant sought to counter the defendant's denials by calling her two daughters as witnesses, the magistrate was absolutely scathing about the applicant having put the children into the witness box and having subjected them to cross-examination. Rather than recognizing the applicant's dilemma in relation to the production of corroborating evidence of the defendant's behavior and threats, he saw the case as one of two bickering people trying to use their children against each other. While he described the outcome as "line ball," he decided not to grant the order sought by the applicant. In M.C.45 (October 31, 1996), when the female defendant attempted to counter her ex-husband's allegations of violence against her by cataloguing the abuse she had experienced during their marriage, the magistrate did not consider whether the applicant had a greater propensity for violence than the defendant (as in M.C.21), but rather described the defendant as "a very bitter woman" who was "prepared to exaggerate things."

Further, in M.C.101 (June 27, 1997), the defendant supported his opposition to the wife's application for a sole occupancy order with the argument that the applicant was a bad mother and he was concerned for the welfare of the children. He cited two instances in which the applicant had allegedly left one or other of their teenage children unsupervised for a period of time. She disputed his account of one of these incidents and gave a different version of events. At the same time, the applicant provided evidence of the effect on the children of the defendant's campaign of terrorization against her since he had moved out of the house. In deciding not to grant the sole occupancy order, the magistrate gave considerable weight to the evidence of the applicant's supposedly negligent parenting, but appeared to ignore the evidence of the effect on the children of the defendant's behavior.

The Influence of Class

Finally, while all of the parties to the contested matters were Anglo-Australian, and thus there was no issue of ethnicity involved in any of the cases, class issues did appear to operate in some of them. In M.C.52 (November 4, 1996), the working-class status of both parties enabled the magistrate to conclude that most of their "disputes" had been about money. It was also assumed that the applicant would be given priority for public housing, so that her need to stay with her children in the matrimonial home was only temporary. By contrast, the middle-class wife who applied for a sole occupancy order in M.C.101 (June 27, 1997) was unsuccessful, and the defendant was simply asked to wait 3 days before moving back in to the house so the applicant could make a decision about what she wanted to do and make arrangements to move out if necessary. It appears to have been assumed that she would have the resources to make alternative living arrangments. In this case, too, the parties' middle-class status appears to have contributed both to an understanding of the defendant's dogged attachment to what he perceived to be *his* property (in fact the house was jointly owned and the applicant was currently paying the bills) and to the very high standard of parenting to which the applicant was held, given that the evidence only established one real lapse of judgement, rather than any need for ongoing supervision of the children by the defendant.

In M.C.21 and M.C.45, there was a class disparity between the parties, which worked to the benefit of the (middle-class) husband in each case. As noted earlier, the applicant's working-class origins were made manifest in M.C.21 (June 27, 1996). In the witness box, she appeared tough and hard bitten, while the defendant came across as plausible and innocent. In M.C.45 (October 31, 1996), too, the applicant's credibility was boosted by his genteel manner. He appeared as upright, bemused, regretful, unhappy, and reluctant to repeat the swear words allegedly left by the applicant on his answer machine—quite different from the picture painted of him by the applicant. By contrast, she was somewhat forceful and self-righteous, making it easier to believe in her violence than in his.

In making findings of fact and exercising their discretion whether or not to grant the orders sought in these contested cases, magistrates appeared to refer neither to an understanding of domestic violence in terms of the exercise of power and control in a relationship, nor to the underlying intention of the legislation to ensure the safety of victims of violence. Rather, the magistrates' focus appeared to be on whether the women coming before them fit into the category of "real," "deserving" victims of domestic violence. As Römkens (2001) has observed,

> The representation of...the domestic violence victim, regularly shifts from a group category of "deserving victims" during the stage of lawmaking, to a category of potentially flawed, unreliable, irresponsible, exaggerating, and undeserving individuals in its day-to-day legal implementation of laws that were originally intended to protect and support women. (p. 286)

The contested cases discussed here also set troublesome precedents. They perpetuated nonfeminist social and legal narratives about domestic violence, and they tended to give a misleading impression of the frequency with which women's applications for intervention orders turn out to be unfounded.

THE TERMS OF ORDERS

As indicated in the previous section, legal understandings of domestic violence were sometimes evident not just in the decision whether or not to grant an order, but also in the decision as to what orders to grant.

This section explores this point further, in relation to three problematic elements of intervention orders: the duration of orders, sole occupancy orders, and mutual orders.

The Duration of Orders

Final orders were made in 54 of the cases observed, for the durations set out in table 11.

The orders made for less than 12 months were for 2 months, 6 months, and 8 months, respectively. While some magistrates asked applicants how long they wanted their order to last (though without giving them any idea of the options available), others indicated their view of the seriousness of the case or the merits of the application by means of the duration of the order (12 months or longer), while others simply would not make orders for more than a limited period, regardless of the evidence presented to them. Consistent with magistrates' views of the causes of violence and the dynamics of violent relationships, a 12-month order seems to have been considered an appropriate length of time for the parties to sort out their differences and/or to go their separate ways (see Wearing, 1992, pp. 108–109, 178–179).

Yet as Klein and Orloff (1993) have noted, given the evidence of long-term stalking, harassment, and physical abuse engaged in by some men, "courts cannot presume that a batterer's attempts to control and injure the abuse victim will end in a month, a year, or ten years" (pp. 1086–1087). Women interviewed complained about the problem of having to go back

TABLE 11. Duration of final intervention orders made.

Duration of Order	No.	Percentage
< 12 months	3	5.6
12 months	21	38.9
2 years	9	16.7
2.5–5 years	5	9.3
Until further order	16	29.6
Total	54	100.0

to court to renew their orders every year, and, as discussed earlier, some were deterred from doing so or were told they no longer had grounds for an order (NESB Focus Group, interview, December 23, 1997). It is notable that none of the 100 cases observed involved an application for extension of an order. One of the women interviewed had been unable to get an order for any longer than 5 months, despite multiple breaches by the defendant. She had at one stage requested an indefinite order, but the magistrate had said he did not feel he had the power to restrict the defendant to that extent. Yet, she pointed out, her life was completely restricted by the defendant's ongoing harassment of her and by the need to go back to court continually to seek renewed protection (W.L.5, interview, December 19, 1997).

As noted in the previous chapter, the Crimes (Family Violence) Act (1987) was amended in mid-1997 to clarify that magistrates could make orders of unlimited duration, which would obviate the problem of continual returns to court, further contact with the defendant, and adjudication by a series of different magistrates. Yet this provision seems to have been little relied upon. In contrast to my observation sample, only 16.3% of final orders were made for more than 10 years or indefinitely in 1999–2000, and this figure declined to 11.5% in 2002–2003. By contrast, in 2002–2003, 57.3% of final orders were made for 12 months or less, and 17.2% were made for 1–2 years (VLRC, 2004a, pp. 107–108). The larger proportion of indefinite orders in my sample may be attributable to differences between metropolitan and statewide practices, but even so it appears that magistrates' preference for orders of limited duration may have hardened over the years.

Sole Occupancy Orders

In cases in which the parties were not yet living separately, magistrates were very reluctant to grant intervention orders that would involve the eviction of the defendant from the matrimonial home (see also Edwards, 2004; Hickey & Cumines, 1999, p. 42; Nunn, 2001, p. 35; VLRC, 2004a, p. 162; Wearing, 1992, pp. 25–26, 105–108, 167; Wearing, 1996, p. 152). In this, they were encouraged by the legislation, which made a particular issue of orders restricting access to premises. As noted in the previous chapter, the Crimes (Family Violence) Act (1987) provided that

> [b]efore making an order which restricts the defendant's access to any premises, the court must take into account—
>
> (a) the need to ensure that the aggrieved family member is protected from violence; and
> (b) the welfare of any children who may be affected by the order; and
> (c) the accommodation needs of all persons who may be affected by the order—
>
> and give paramount consideration to the matters in paragraph (a). (s. 5(2))

However, it was clear that magistrates did not give paramount consideration to the matters in paragraph (a), or much consideration to the matters in paragraph (b) (see also Babbel, 2002, p. 14; Edwards, 2004, p. 10). As seen in the previous section, the magistrate in one of the contested cases observed granted a sole occupancy order for a limited period primarily in order to protect the children from the defendant's angry outbursts and verbal violence (M.C.52, November 4, 1996); however, in my observations, magistrates dealing with sole occupancy applications never adverted to the effects of forced relocation on children, including disrupted schooling, loss of contact with friends, loss of toys and belongings, and feelings of insecurity (see also Edwards, 2004, pp. 3, 11). Rather, magistrates hearing such cases gave paramount consideration to the matters in paragraph (c). And in this context, it was apparently expected that women and children would leave home, perhaps spending some time in a refuge and then moving on to other (often public) housing, while the notion that "a man's home is his castle" seemed to prevail in relation to defendants (see also Wearing, 1992, pp. 167, 171; Nunn & D'Arcy, 2001, p. 20).

I was informed that magistrates would not remove a man from the house on an interim basis, although there was some suggestion that this might occur if the applicant came to court with visible injuries (Field notes, Sunshine Magistrates' Court Support Program, July 2, 1996; see also Alexander, 2002, p. 170; Field, Carpenter, & Currie, 2001, p. 9; Hickey & Cumines, 1999, p. 74; Kinports & Fischer, 1992, p. 195; Nunn, 2001, p. 35; Nunn & D'Arcy, 2001, p. 20; Wearing, 1992, pp. 105–108, 167–168). In practice, it appeared that magistrates imposed an extralegal requirement of "exceptional circumstances" in order to make a sole occupancy order on an interim basis. In my observation sample, 2 of the 17 interim orders made gave the applicant sole occupancy. In one, the exceptional circumstance was the fact that the applicant was pregnant (M.C.8, March 6, 1996). In the other, there did not appear to be anything particularly exceptional about either the applicant or the nature of the alleged violence (persistent violence by the defendant, escalating over the last few months, and a threat to kill the applicant), but the magistrate specifically stated that he was "satisfied" that this was an "exceptional case" (M.C.60, February 21, 1997). Possibly the exceptionality related to the fact that the couple lived in public housing, and there was therefore no suggestion that the defendant was being evicted from "his" property.

In relation to final orders, as already seen, the possibility of a sole occupancy order appeared to be a significant reason for defendants contesting applications, often successfully. In all 3 contested matters observed involving sole occupancy applications, the abusive husband was ultimately allowed to remain in the house while the wife either intended to move out or was expected to do so if she did not wish to remain under the same roof as him (M.C.21, June 27, 1996; M.C.52, November 4, 1996; M.C.101, June 27, 1997). Although the defendant in M.C.52 was excluded temporarily, the difficulty of achieving such a result on a long-term basis no doubt contributed to the applicant's strategy of seeking sole occupancy only for a limited period. Indeed, the applicant's barrister stressed at the commencement of the hearing that the applicant wished to leave the matrimonial home and would make no claim on it, but needed time to find alternative accommodation for herself and the children.

Even when the defendant did not appear on the return date, applicants faced a high standard of proof to obtain a sole occupancy order, including the need to address alternative accommodation arrangements for the defendant (see also Babbel, 2002, p. 14; Edwards, 2004, pp. 8–9, 14; Nunn, 2001, p. 35; VLRC, 2004a, p. 163). For example, in the first interim order application mentioned previously, the magistrate quizzed the applicant on where the defendant would live if he were ordered out of the house, and on why she could not move out (M.C.8, March 6, 1996). One interviewee observed that magistrates were particularly loathe to put older men out of the house, thus making it more difficult for older women to succeed in their applications (S.W.1, interview, December 23, 1997). This point was well illustrated in the case discussed earlier, in which, despite the defendant's nonappearance, the magistrate effectively contested the application for a sole occupancy order on the basis that the defendant had abused the applicant for 17 years, was well established in the home, and was unemployed, and now the applicant had the temerity to want to remove him. Although the magistrate considered the option of making a limited order (i.e., one not including sole occupancy) to "see how it goes," he did, belatedly, recall that his primary concern in deciding the matter was to protect the applicant and her children from violence and so agreed to make the order. But he did so only for a period of 12 months, rather than making the indefinite order the applicant had sought (M.C.42, October 31, 1997).

In total, only 6 of the cases observed explicitly raised the issue of sole occupancy, and the applicant was successful in only 4 of those cases.[9] The relative scarcity of sole occupancy applications may have been due to the fact that parties had already separated in many instances, but other contributing factors may have included clerks/registrars discouraging applicants from asking for sole occupancy or refusing to include a request for sole occupancy in complaints (VLRC, 2004a, p. 163; Wearing, 1992, pp. 105–108), and the fact that sole occupancy is not included as a discrete category of order in the legislation or on the application form, so unrepresented applicants may have been unaware that they could ask for such a thing (Edwards, 2004, p. 8; Field et al., 2001, p. 10; Southwell, 2002, pp. 5–6).[10] A New South Wales study noted that the arguments made by the police prosecutor could make or break an application for sole occupancy, suggesting that unrepresented applicants would have even greater difficulties in gaining sole occupancy (Edwards, 2004, p. 13). In my observation sample, 3 of the 4 successful applicants had legal representation, together with both unsuccessful applicants. By contrast, a recent program instituted by a domestic violence outreach service in Melbourne, which provided a support worker to assist women to apply for and obtain sole occupancy orders, experienced a greater degree of success from a much larger number of applications, even though 40% of applications were contested by the defendant (VLRC, 2004a, pp. 164–165). In the absence of concerted (feminist) advice or advocacy, however, it appears that the expectation that the victim should leave and the sanctity of male property ownership prevail in magistrates' minds.

Mutual Orders

Finally, this chapter considers the widely observed practice of making mutual intervention orders, in which both parties are restrained from assaulting, harassing, molesting, and so forth, the other. Mutual consent orders, like consent orders without admissions, are a way of speeding up the process (C. McNamara, interview, June 14, 1996; Field notes, Broadmeadows Court Support Program, October 25, 1996; Broadmeadows Magistrates' Court, February 21, 1997; Sunshine Court Support Program, July 2, 1996), obtaining an order for the victim without a potentially traumatic hearing (K. Anderson, interview, March 8, 1996; M. Mann, interview, March 8, 1996; A. Palombo, interview, April 1, 1996; S.1, interview, January 16, 1997) and allowing the perpetrator to save face (and for this reason are often favored by defense lawyers) (Field notes, Broadmeadows Court Support Program, October 25, 1996; Broadmeadows Magistrates' Court, February 21, 1997; Sunshine Court Support Program, July 2, 1996). But like orders by consent without admissions, they come at a high price. Mutual orders stem from and reinforce the view that violence is caused by conflict and stress in relationships, with both parties being equally capable of violence against the other and each party bearing equal responsibility for the violence. This ignores power differentials in the relationship

(Spowart & Neil, 1997, pp. 82–83; Walker, 1995, pp. 124–125); the difference between attack or aggression and self-defense or retaliation (Pence & Paymar, 1993, pp. 5–6; Spowart & Neil, 1997, pp. 82–83; Walker, 1995, pp. 124–125); the differential strength of men and women, along with the fact that men's violence inflicts far more severe injuries on women than vice versa (Spowart & Neil, 1997, pp. 82–83; Walker, 1995, pp. 124–125); and the differential effects of violence (creating fear and compliance or attacking the woman's autonomy, as opposed to creating annoyance or supposed "provocation") (Mahoney, 1991, p. 65; Pence & Paymar, 1993, pp. 5–6).[11]

Moreover, mutual orders trivialize women's suffering because the grounds on which orders are granted against them (if, indeed, any exist at all) are usually far more minor than the grounds they have for obtaining an order against the defendant (Babbel, 2002, p. 14; F. Culpen, interview, March 17, 1997; Spowart & Neil, 1997, p. 83; S.W.1, interview, December 23, 1997). In circumstances where the defendant consents to an order against him only on the basis that the applicant agrees to a tit-for-tat order against her, he effectively obtains an order without making a formal complaint and without producing any substantiating evidence (Blashki, 1997, p. 8; A. Palombo, interview, April 1, 1996; see also Kinports & Fischer, 1992, pp. 202–203; Nunn & D'Arcy, 2001, p. 20). Orders are never made in favor of women on this basis. Mutual orders also have serious repercussions if the police are called to a subsequent domestic violence incident, as they are likely to find both parties to be in breach of their orders and thus to be equally at fault (C. McNamara, interview, June 14, 1996; Spowart & Neil, 1997, p. 84), or the defendant may allege or engineer breaches on the part of the applicant as a further form of harassment (S. Borg, interview, October 17, 1997; S.W.1, interview, December 23, 1997). In effect, obtaining mutual orders fails to ensure the applicant's safety (F. Culpen, interview, March 17, 1997; Nunn & D'Arcy, 2001, p. 20) and continues and reinforces the defendant's power and control over her (S.1, interview, January 16, 1997; Spowart & Neil, 1997, p. 84; S.W.1, interview, December 23, 1997; Walker, 1995, p. 125).

Despite interviewees' trenchant criticisms of mutual orders, they occurred relatively infrequently in my observation sample. Mutual consent orders were made in only 3 of the cases I observed. In addition, there were 3 cases in which the defendant consented to an order without admissions and the applicant also made an undertaking to the court, and 2 further cases in which the parties made mutual undertakings to the court without an order being made. Although undertakings by the victim of violence not to be violent towards the perpetrator have the same damaging, symbolic effect of suggesting equal propensities to violence, they do not give rise to the risk of criminal prosecution for alleged breach (see also Kewley, 1996, pp. 3–4). Where mutual undertakings are made, however, clearly the victim of violence goes away from the court unprotected (see also Babbel, 2002, p. 14; Nunn & D'Arcy, 2001, p. 21; VLRC, 2004a, p. 105).[12]

A notable feature of all of the cases involving mutual orders or undertakings was that they involved legal representation, with the most usual pattern being a self-represented applicant opposing a legally represented defendant (in 5 of the 8 cases). This is consistent with interviewees' observations that parties are pushed into mutual orders by particular barristers and solicitors, and especially by means of informal "bargaining" between defense lawyers and applicants (H. Assafiri, interview, June 24, 1997; S.W.1, interview, December 23, 1997). It appears that defense lawyers "persuaded" unrepresented applicants to make undertakings—and, in one case, mutual consent orders—as the price for the defendant consenting to an order or undertaking, even though there was no cross-application by the defendant (M.C.53, November 4, 1996; M.C.85, June 17, 1997; M.C.91, June 27, 1997; M.C.98, June 27, 1997; M.C.110, June 27, 1997). In 3 of the 5 cases in which this occurred, the lawyers concerned were Legal Aid duty lawyers, representing the defendant at no cost, when the applicant had no representation. In one of these cases, the allegations of violence against the defendant were sufficiently serious for the applicant to have police protection present, but the applicant was still coerced by the duty lawyer into agreeing to mutual orders (M.C.85, June 17, 1997).

In the 3 cases involving mutual orders or undertakings in which the applicant was represented, 2 were assisted by the court support program while the defendant was self-represented, and one involved private representation for both parties. In one of the 2 involving a court support program lawyer, as discussed earlier, there was only a single application for an order against the defendant, but the magistrate insisted that both parties make undertakings to the court not to harass or approach each other (M.C.38, July 4, 1996). Cross-applications by both parties had been filed in the other 2 cases, and in those circumstances, the only way to avoid a contested hearing was for mutual consent orders to be made (M.C.70, March 20, 1997; M.C.82, June 17, 1997). In addition, one of the women interviewed said she had been bullied by the court into consenting to mutual orders when the defendant appeared at court on the return date (W.L.5, interview, December 19, 1997).

It appears, then, that mutual orders or insisting on reciprocal undertakings from the applicant were largely a defense tactic, achieved either through a cross-application on the part of the defendant, or out of court "negotiations." Even though the defendant was represented and the applicant unrepresented in most of the cases involving mutual orders or undertakings, there was never any interrogation by the magistrate of the freedom or fairness of the applicant's consent. Nor, in cases where there was no cross-application, did the magistrate seek to determine whether there was any evidence to support an order or undertaking for the benefit of the defendant. Although I would argue that consent without admissions was more problematic because it occurred more frequently, the courts' willingness to grant mutual orders and accept unnecessary undertakings by the applicant was a further illustration of the distance between magistrates' and feminist understandings of domestic violence, and the extent to which the aim of ensuring women's safety had been left behind.

Conclusion

Intervention order proceedings have both material and cultural or communicative effects. In her study of the management of domestic violence in a small town in Hawaii, Sally Merry (1997b) observed, in relation to protection order proceedings,

> While men are presented with the [punitive] side of the law, women experience it as supportive and are encouraged to use it for help. The court becomes a place for women to turn for protection rather than a place that reinforces male authority. For men, it is a place of alienation, a disruption of their sense of the social support for male authority. (p. 275)

Indeed, Merry argues that in relation to domestic violence, law is more successful in its cultural effects than in the material sanctions it imposes (1997a, p. 263). Likewise, Fischer and Rose (1995) note the important communicative role of the legal system in providing reassurance and support for battered women that they do not have to tolerate violence and emotional abuse in their lives, and in sending a message to abusers about society's intolerance of domestic violence and the need for them to change their behavior (p. 127; see also Fenton, 1998, p. 30). The intervention order proceedings observed in my study, however, generally failed to fulfil this cultural/communicative role, more often remaining embedded within, and contributing to, nonfeminist narratives about women and violence.

One strategy adopted in other jurisdictions in order to overcome such problems has been to remove the adjudication of intervention order or similar applications from the mainstream court system and to establish specialist domestic violence courts with committed personnel, often as part of an integrated violence control program incorporating support services for women, men's programs, and police (see Busch & Robertson, 1994, p. 34; Epstein, 1999, p. 28; Fischer & Rose, 1995, p. 291; Kahan, 2000, p. 629; Kinports & Fischer, 1992, pp. 239–242; Stewart, 2005, pp. 20–33; Tsai, 2000). Such an initiative has now been launched in Victoria, with the first two Domestic Violence Courts being piloted from 2005–2009. These courts operate as a "one stop shop" for domestic violence matters, hearing intervention order and summary criminal matters as well as victims' compensation applications and family law matters relating to family violence, and bringing together specialist magistrates, registrars and court staff, a range of support services for victims, and court-directed counseling/behavioral change programs to which male perpetrators of violence may be referred to help stop their violent behavior. The courts also coordinate with local police and community family violence services (Attorney General for Victoria, 2004; VLRC, 2004a, p. 5). The model includes professional development, education, and training for magistrates, registrars, and court staff in the dynamics of family violence and cultural diversity issues.[13]

This would appear to be a considerable improvement on the current system and should go some way to addressing the various implementation problems raised in this and the previous chapter. The provisions for specialization of personnel, professional development, education and training, and greater coordination with support services are likely to increase the influence of feminist understandings of domestic violence, including those sensitive to class, racial, and other differences. Importantly, the trained personnel available include lawyers and defendant support workers. In her review of specialist domestic/family violence courts in Australia and overseas, Stewart (2005) notes that the personnel who make a difference in such courts include "defendants' legal representatives who are sympathetic to and prepared to support the aims of the court" (p. 9; see also Mirchandani, 2005, pp. 397–400). This point is borne out in particular in the discussion in this chapter of the role of defense lawyers in contested cases and mutual orders.

The structural factors identified in the previous chapter are less obviously addressed. In terms of the overload of cases and the routinized and bureaucratic approach to intervention orders, Rekha Mirchandani (2005) demonstrates in a recent article on the Salt Lake City domestic violence court that is it possible to deal quickly with a large caseload while also meeting substantive goals and commitments—hearing battered women, making violent men take responsibility for their actions, and sending appropriate messages to the community—by having regular, specialized personnel collectively focused on achieving those substantive goals in the most efficient way (pp. 397–407). But such an outcome presumably needs to be consciously worked at, not assumed. In addition, the legislation needs redrafting to state clearly its objectives, to reformulate the grounds for an intervention order, to deal with the question of judicial discretion, to require defendants to give notice of their intentions to consent to or contest the order ahead of the return date, and to abolish the option of consent without admissions. Courtrooms and waiting areas need to be designed with victims of violence in mind. Reliable, sensitive interpreting services need to be available.[14] And all regular players need to be mindful of the possibility that the maintenance of their good relationships may be privileged over the interests and needs of individual applicants, although, where all personnel share substantive rather than simply procedural goals, this may be less likely to occur.

The other potential drawback with specialized courts is that they let other courts off the hook. This suggests either that access to a specialized court must be realistically available to all survivors of domestic violence within the jurisdiction, or that the kinds of changes identified need to be adopted more widely.[15]

Endnotes

1. The Magistrates' Court of Victoria *Family Violence and Stalking Protocols* (2003, ¶ 4.7) now provide that if a registrar forms the view after interview that a complaint should not be issued because of insufficient evidence, but the applicant insists on proceeding, the matter should be placed before the court.
2. The *Family Violence and Stalking Protocols* now encourage registrars to include in the complaint a "brief description of [the] past relationship" and a description of the "incident that brought the person to the Court for an order" (Magistrates' Court of Victoria, 2003, ¶ 4.6). The form that applicants are asked to complete prior to their interview with the registrar (Form 1) asks them to provide details of the most recent incident, including the date on which and the place at which it occurred, and also asks, "have there been other incidents in the past, if so when and where?" Seven lines are provided for the most recent incident, and only six lines are provided for previous incidents. Notably, too, the form asks about previous *incidents* rather than the history of the relationship.
3. The *Family Violence and Stalking Protocols* require registrars to include in a complaint "stated reasons why there are concerns the behaviour would continue unless an order is made" (Magistrates' Court of Victoria, 2003, ¶ 4.5) and suggest that registrars should note "[w]hat concerns the [applicant] has for future behaviour by [the] defendant" (¶ 4.6). Form 1 asks the applicant to specify, "Why do you fear such incidents are likely to occur again? Explain and give details"—but provides only four lines for this purpose. In both cases, fears for the defendant's future behavior are structurally disconnected from the account of the defendant's past behavior.
4. Keys Young (1994) noted that "NESB women commonly believe that [a domestic violence protection order] is a serious criminal matter which will automatically result in their partner going to gaol" (p. 56).
5. In order for a woman to obtain permanent residence in Australia on the basis of marriage to an Australian citizen or permanent resident, she was required to remain in a genuine and continuous relationship with her husband for 2 years. If the marriage broke down during that 2-year period, the woman was likely to be deported unless she could provide proof of domestic violence. This could be proved by means of an intervention order, a proven charge or conviction of the husband for assault against his wife, or a statutory declaration that violence had occurred supported by statements from

community workers. Given the existence of the third option (which had been introduced into the migration legislation in the mid-1990s), it could not be said that a woman in this situation would need to obtain an intervention order in order to avoid deportation (Blazejowska, 1996, p. 114; VLRC, 2004a, p. 79).

6. In one of these cases, M.C.11 (July 11, 1996), the defendant had a long history of attempting to have the order against him revoked, and the proceedings were ultimately stayed pending payment of previous orders for costs and security for costs. Many years later, the same defendant was still trying to obtain leave to apply to revoke or vary the intervention order against him (*Kay v. McIntosh*, 2003).
7. This scenario of a violent marriage followed by ongoing problems in relation to child contact, with the abuser continuing to exercise power and control over his ex-wife by abusing her at handovers and having contact when he chooses to do so, is familiar from a number of Australian studies. See, for example, Kaye, Stubbs, & Tolmie (2003); Rendell et al. (2000); Sheehan et al. (2005). This issue is also discussed further in chapter 7.
8. In the New Zealand context, Ruth Busch (1994) has also noted judges' tendency to impose extra criteria when the statutory criteria for an order are actually met, such as the perceived reasonableness of the defendant's actions, or some undeserving behavior on the part of the applicant (p. 111).
9. All discussed previously: 2 interim order applications, and 4 final order applications, in 1 of which the defendant did not appear, while the other 3 were contested. Southwell (2002) has observed that no data is kept on the frequency with which sole occupancy orders are made; there is only anecdotal evidence that they are made *very* infrequently (p. 8). In Edwards' (2004) study, which examined apprehended domestic violence order applications in two large Local Courts in Sydney (each making around 80 orders per week) over a 6-month period, only 32 sole occupancy applications were identified, of which 22 were successful, although the majority (14) were made by consent (pp. 7, 14).
10. The current Form 1 provides a series of possible orders for the applicant to tick, including prohibiting the defendant from "[b]eing at or within 200 metres of the aggrieved family member's residence" but it is not made clear that this can include the defendant's current residence when that is shared with the aggrieved family member.
11. Vickers (1996) argues that because these distinctions are even less likely to be drawn in cases involving same sex partners, same-sex domestic violence is always conceived of as "mutual violence" (1996, ¶ 47). However, in

Stewart's (2000) study, respondents to cross-applications were more likely to be married or to have been married than other respondents, suggesting that cross-applications may often be a further power and control tactic used by the abuser (p. 85).

12. The *Family Violence and Stalking Protocols* (Magistrates' Court of Victoria, 2003, ¶ 19.1) now provide that while there is no legislative provision in the Crimes (Family Violence) Act for the taking of undertakings, they may be "accommodated" by the court if the applicant and defendant wish to consider them, and the magistrate considers they may be an appropriate resolution as an alternative to an intervention order "(for example no physical violence)." This formulation completely ignores the power relations involved in cases where undertakings are "suggested," and perpetuates magistrates' emphasis on physical violence to the exclusion of other forms of controlling behavior, by implying that undertakings are an appropriate alternative to an intervention order where no physical violence is alleged (presumably in the most recent incident). The protocols also state that the complaint can be reinstated on written notice to the court of the defendant's breach of the undertaking, but this seems unlikely to be followed through, and also does not deal with the situation where the undertaking is made by the applicant herself, often in the absence of a complaint by the defendant.
13. The courts are known as the Family Violence Division of the Magistrates' Court of Victoria, and were established by the Magistrates' Court (Family Violence) Act (2004).
14. Many of these recommendations were echoed by the VLRC in the final report of its *Review of Domestic Violence Laws* (2006, pp. xxvii–xlv). In response, the Victorian government has introduced the Family Violence Protection Bill (2008), which, among other things, proposes to set out the rationale and objectives of the legislation, expand the definition of "family violence," amend the grounds for making an intervention order, considerably strengthen the provision for making sole occupancy ("exclusion") orders, and ensure that where the final order is contested, both parties have the opportunity to obtain appropriate legal advice and representation. In this respect, the Bill stops short of implementing the VLRC's recommendation that the defendant be required to give notice in advance of his intention to contest the order. It also continues to allow for consent without admissions (while stipulating that both parties must consent to this), and continues to specify that once the grounds for an order are made out, the grant of an order is discretionary rather than mandatory.

15. In addition to the family violence court pilots, the Victorian government has also funded court-based specialist family violence services, involving police prosecutors, magistrates, family violence registrars, and support workers, at an additional four Magistrates' Courts in the Melbourne metropolitan area. These services offer enhanced assistance and support for women applying for intervention orders, but do not go so far as to provide a "one stop shop" for domestic violence matters, and are still available in only a limited number of locations.

Chapter 5

Family Court Proceedings

Introduction

In Australia, legislative jurisdiction over divorce, and the custody and guardianship of children in relation to divorce, are vested in the federal parliament (Australian Constitution 1901, s. 51(xxii)). The federal government did not initially exercise this jurisdiction until 1959, when it enacted the Matrimonial Causes Act, which consolidated and extended existing State legislation governing the dissolution of marriage. The Matrimonial Causes Act (1959) prescribed a range of grounds on which marriage could be dissolved, all of which were fault based. In 1975, however, the federal government enacted a new Family Law Act, which swept away all of the former fault-based grounds and introduced a single, no-fault ground for divorce: irretrievable breakdown of marriage, evidenced by 12 months' separation (s. 48). Whereas under the Matrimonial Causes Act (1959), the focus of divorce litigation was on whether a ground for divorce was established, under the Family Law Act (1975), divorce became virtually an administrative procedure, with the focus of litigation shifting to the division of matrimonial property, and to custody of and access to children of the marriage. In 1987 the States ceded to the Commonwealth their power over "ex-nuptial children" (i.e., the children of unmarried couples), so that all matters concerning arrangements for children following the separation of their parents could be dealt with under the Family Law Act (1975). De facto property division, however, remained an area of State legislative responsibility.

The Family Law Act (1975) also established a new, specialist federal court, the Family Court of Australia, to hear cases under the Act. It was intended that the court would take a more conciliatory approach than other civil and criminal courts. As well as its hearing functions, it also had a counseling service, and litigants were encouraged to attend counseling before lodging formal proceedings and were also required to engage in other dispute resolution processes in the course of proceedings—in particular, counseling in children's matters and conciliation conferences in property matters. By means of such court processes and negotiations between solicitors, the overwhelming majority of cases filed in the court were settled between the parties. As a court established under Chapter III of the Australian Constitution (1901), however, the Family Court is bound to act "judicially" and in accordance with the rules of evidence, in cases that do proceed to hearing (*R v. Watson; ex parte Armstrong*, 1976).

In line with the Act's no-fault ethos and the court's conciliatory approach, the issue of domestic violence during the course of the marriage or relationship was considered to be irrelevant to the determination of post–divorce/separation arrangements, with one writer describing the court as being "philosophically ill-attuned to domestic violence cases" (Seddon, 1993, p. 75; see also Graycar, 1996a, p. 88; Nicholson, 1995, p. 2). This position began to change in the early 1990s, with recognition by the court that violence could be relevant in both children's and property proceedings, although the jurisprudence concerning the impact of violence on children developed to a much greater extent than did that concerning the impact of violence on property division.

The Family Law Reform Act (1995) introduced extensive amendments to the Family Law Act in relation to dispute resolution, children's matters, and domestic violence. The emphasis on alternative dispute resolution rather than litigation as the preferred means of dealing with family law disputes was further strengthened, with alternative dispute resolution being relabelled "primary dispute resolution" (PDR) in the Act (Part III). An amendment to section 43 of the Act added the new requirement that in exercising its jurisdiction, the Family Court must have regard to "the need to ensure safety from family violence" (s. 43(ca)). A new Part VII of the Act introduced new guiding principles governing the court's resolution of matters relating to children (s. 60B), and changed the language of "custody" and "access" to that of "residence" and "contact" in an attempt to replace concepts of parental rights with an emphasis on children's rights and parents' responsibilities. The Act also introduced additional factors to be taken into account by the court in determining questions of residence and contact, including the issue of family violence affecting the child (s. 68F(2)(i)). The Family Law Reform Act (1995) came into force on June 11, 1996. The court had also, by that time, adopted a set of guidelines on the management of cases involving domestic violence, aimed at ensuring the safety of court clients who might be subject to ongoing violence by their partners (Family Court of Australia, 1993; and see now Family Court of Australia, 2004).

At the time of the fieldwork, the other relevant legislation in force was the Jurisdiction of Courts (Cross-vesting) Act (1987). This Act sought to facilitate the pursuit of civil proceedings that fell under both federal and State jurisdiction, by vesting State courts with federal jurisdiction and federal courts with State jurisdiction to the extent necessary to enable proceedings to be consolidated. In the family law context, the cross-vesting legislation gave rise to the possibility that women who had suffered injuries as a result of domestic violence could bring a tort claim for compensation concurrently with their family law property proceedings, so that any tort damages awarded to the wife could be paid out of the share of the property awarded to the husband.[1] Such proceedings brought the issue of domestic violence squarely and unavoidably before the Family Court. In 1999, however, the cross-vesting legislation was struck down by the High Court as unconstitutional (*Re Wakim; ex parte*

McNally), bringing to an end the short-lived experiment with cross-vested tort proceedings in the Family Court.

PROCEDURE

Unlike the requirements for an intervention order, it was not necessary to give oral evidence before a judge, or even to appear in court, to obtain a Family Court order concerning children or property. If parties had agreed on the outcome they wanted in negotiations prior to approaching the court, they could file an initial application for consent orders (Form 12A), which would be dealt with in chambers, without any need for the parties to appear in person. Alternatively, a party could file an application for final orders (Form 7). The other party would then file a response and/or a cross-application, and the court process would provide ample encouragement and opportunities for dispute resolution through directions hearings, interim hearings and orders, counseling appointments, conciliation conferences, and pretrial conferences, before a full adversarial hearing before a judge could occur. At any stage during this process—including during the final hearing—the parties could hand up minutes of consent orders embodying the agreement they had reached, which would usually be endorsed by the court without question (see Family Law Act (1975), s. 68F(3)). Consequently, only about 6% of cases filed ultimately received a judicial determination (Bordow, 1994, p. 254; Hunter, 1999, pp. 153, 157, 160; Hunter, Genovese, Melville, & Chrzanowski, 2000, pp. 339–340).

Observations of trials in the Family Court thus represented only the tip of the iceberg of matters commenced in the court. It was a very particular tip, however. Cases that went to trial were those that had proved intractable to multiple efforts at dispute resolution. They involved serious conflict between the parties, were highly contested, and often involved multiple applications and hearings before different judges.

Many of the children's matters proceeding to trial included a child's representative.[2] Children's representatives were lawyers appointed to represent the welfare/best interests of the child in circumstances where it was considered that those interests required independent representation. In *Re K* (1994, pp. 555–558), the Full Court of the Family Court had specified circumstances calling for the appointment of a child's representative, including where the case involved allegations of child abuse; an apparently intractable conflict between the parents; alleged antisocial conduct by either or both of the parents that seriously impinged on the child's welfare; a proposal by one of the parties that the child be relocated to a place where the other party's access to the child would be greatly restricted or, for all practical purposes, excluded; or neither of the parties being legally represented. In cases involving a child's representative, the court would also usually commission a child expert (either a Family Court counsellor or private counsellor or child psychologist) to write a Family Report giving their recommendations as to the most appropriate postseparation arrangements for the child or children. The Family Report writer based their opinions on time spent with the children, observations of the children's interactions with each parent, interviews with the parents, and their own training and expertise in the area. As discussed in the next chapter, the court generally saw the Family Report, its writer, and the child's representative as nonpartisan and "objective" in the adversarial proceedings between the parents, and thus accorded considerable weight to their views and proposals.

By the time a matter was ready for trial, a large number of documents had been filed, including the parties' applications for final orders and responses, applications for interim orders, and any interim orders made. The parties' evidence in chief and that of their witnesses was contained in affidavits. In a children's matter there might also be a Family Report, while in a property matter, there would be the parties' financial statements and, in some cases, competing valuations of the property in dispute. Each party was also required to file a chronology of what they considered to be significant events during the relationship and up to the time of the trial, an outline of argument in support of the orders sought, and minutes of the final orders sought.

Despite its conciliatory elements, the court's basic procedure was adversarial and predicated on the involvement of solicitors and, at trial, of counsel. Most parties had legal representation, although at the time the fieldwork was conducted, this was beginning to change, with unrepresented litigants appearing increasingly in children's matters in particular (see Hunter, Genovese, Chrzanowski, & Morris, 2002). There were several reasons for this emerging phenomenon, including the abolition of pleadings by the court in January 1996, which had encouraged some litigants to believe that they could handle their cases themselves (Hunter et al., 2002, pp. 32–33); the rise of the fathers' rights movement, which promoted a distrust of solicitors and considered that the only way men could pursue their true wishes in the Family Court was to represent themselves (Berns, 2000, p. 17; Kaye & Tolmie, 1998b, p. 64); and cutbacks to legal aid, which had created a growing group of litigants who were ineligible for legal aid but who could not afford to pay for legal representation (see Fleming, 2000; Giddings, 1998; Hunter, Giddings & Chrzanowski, 2003; Noone, 2001). In order to be eligible for legal aid in family law, applicants had to satisfy both means and merit tests. In addition, at the time of the fieldwork, the Victorian Legal Aid Commission had imposed a cap on the amount of funding available in any one case, and was applying the cap retrospectively to cases that were already on foot, resulting in the termination of funding in some long-running cases. All of these issues relating to legal aid and self-representation arose in my observation sample.

FILES AND OBSERVATIONS

Since my interest was in the way in which women's stories about violence were dealt with *in court*, it was necessary to identify cases going to trial that involved allegations of violence against women. In order to do this, I was granted access by the court to the files of matters listed for defending hearings in the months of June–August 1996, and December 1996–April 1997. Since cases tended to run for between 1 and 5 days, the choice of these months was dictated by my practical ability to sit in court for extended periods. The court suggested, and I agreed, that I should focus on files involving children's matters or joint children's and property matters, on the basis that these matters were far more likely to include allegations of violence than were matters involving property only. Accordingly, I only read property-only files where there was some indication that violence might be involved, such as an application by the wife for sole occupancy of the matrimonial home, or a cross-vested application for damages attached to a property claim. Although my primary interest was in violence against women, I also determined in each case whether there were any cross-allegations or separate allegations that the wife/mother had been violent towards the husband/father.

From the files containing allegations of domestic violence, I then selected cases to observe. Not all of these cases actually ran: some settled at the door of the court, and others were adjourned. In November–December 1997, I went back to the files to determine the outcomes in cases I had been unable to observe, and also to see whether there had been any subsequent proceedings in the group of cases. Not all files of cases going to hearing (initially) or cases identified as containing allegations of violence (subsequently) were available for viewing at the times I wanted, resulting in some gaps in coverage. The results of the process of reading files are set out in table 12.

It can be seen that a high proportion (around two thirds) of (mainly children's) cases listed for hearing involved allegations of domestic violence. Although there are no accurate figures available on the proportion of all children's or property matters filed in the Family Court that include domestic violence allegations, the high incidence of violence allegations in children's cases listed for hearing is consistent with the fact that cases that reach this stage of the Family Court process are the most serious and involve the highest level of conflict between the parties (see also Brown, Frederico, Hewitt, & Sheehan, 1998; Family Court of Australia, 2004, p. 3; Kaspiew, 2005, p. 117). Consistent also with this was the fact that subsequent proceedings occurred in at least 30% of the files viewed that included allegations of domestic violence. In some instances, this was because the scheduled hearing had been for interim orders, so that subsequent proceedings for final orders were always envisaged. But in the majority of cases, the subsequent proceedings arose because the orders

TABLE 12. Family Court files.

Category	Details	No.
Files read	Children-only or joint matters	117
	Property-only matters	7
	Total	124
Files including allegations of domestic violence	Alleged violence by husband towards wife	79
	—cross-allegations of violence by wife towards husband	(21)
	—cross-allegations of child abuse by wife	(8)
	—cross-allegations of violence between wife and new partner	(2)
	Alleged violence by new partner towards wife	1
	Total	80 (64.5% of files read)
Cases observed	Contested hearings	12
	Undefended hearing (no appearance by husband)	1
	Settled at door of court	6
	Adjourned	1
	Total	20 (25% of files with allegations)
Outcomes	Judicial decision	23 (28.8%)
	Consent orders	37 (46.3%)
	Adjourned	3 (3.8%)
	Unknown	17 (21.3%)
	Total	80
Subsequent proceedings	Involved subsequent proceedings	24 (30.0%)
	No subsequent proceedings	33 (41.3%)
	Unknown	23 (23.8%)
	Total	80

made by the court or the consent orders agreed by the parties had broken down (see also Logan, Walker, Horvath, & Leukefeld, 2003, p. 276; Rendell et al., 2000, p. 83; Rhoades, 2002, 85–87; Rhoades, Graycar, & Harrison, 2000, pp.72–73). One party did not comply with the orders and the other party sought enforcement in the court, a party appealed against the trial judge's decision, or a party sought variation of the orders made or to reopen the case altogether due to an alleged change of circumstances. These subsequent proceedings thus indicate ongoing conflict between the parties and, in some instances, ongoing harassment of a survivor of violence through Family Court processes by their abusive former spouse (see also Kaye, Stubbs, & Tolmie, 2003, p. 143; Kaspiew, 2005, p. 114; Rhoades, 2002, p. 77).

It is notable that in none of the files viewed was it alleged that the wife/mother had been the only violent party in the marriage (see also Family Court of Australia, Research and Evaluation Unit, 1992, p. 10). Where allegations were made against wives/mothers, they were always accompanied by (usually more serious) allegations of violence on the part of the husband/father. In almost three quarters of the files involving allegations of domestic violence, the allegations were made against the husband/father alone. Also notable was the high proportion of these matters (where the outcome was known) that were settled by consent orders. As discussed subsequently, it is questionable what kind of "consent" can be given by a woman who has been subjected to sometimes extremely serious violence, and who continues to be afraid of her former partner.

Details of the 20 cases observed are set out in table 13. The children's matters included applications by the wife/mother for residence of or contact with the children ($n = 5$), applications by the husband/father for contact with the child/ren ($n = 5$), applications by the wife/mother to relocate to another city with the children ($n = 3$), and applications by the husband/father for sole or joint residence of the children ($n = 3$), together with one application by a wife to vary her ex-husband's contact regime and one application by a husband for the enforcement of contact orders against his ex-wife. These represent a reasonable spectrum of family law disputes regarding postseparation arrangements for children. The 4 property matters in the observation sample were less representative: 2 were applications by husbands, one for division of the parties' property, and the other for sole use and occupation of the matrimonial home. The other 2 were applications by wives, one for leave to institute proceedings for property division and maintenance out of time

TABLE 13. Details of Family Court observation sample.

Category	Details	No.
Matter	Children only	16
	Children and property	3
	Property only	1
Applicant	Wife/mother	10
	Husband/father	9
	Unclear	1
Wife's representation	Represented	19
	In person	1
Husband's representation	Represented	15
	In person	4
	No appearance	1
Child's representative	Appointed	12
	Previously appointed but discharged	2
	None	3
	Unknown	3
Wife's language	English first language	13
	Non-English speaking background	7
	—required interpreter	(4)
Husband's language	English first language	15
	Non-English speaking background	5
	—required interpreter	(3)
How resolved	Contested decision	8
	Undefended decision	1
	Part settled, part contested decision	1
	—in favor of wife/mother	(7)
	—in favor of husband/father	(3)
	Consent orders	10
	—interim	(3)
	—final	(7)

(this was the property-only matter) and the other for property division, maintenance, and a cross-vested claim for damages for personal injury against the husband.

Wives/mothers were more likely to have legal representation than husbands/fathers, so that while only one mother appeared in person, 4 fathers did so. As a general proposition, mothers were more likely than fathers to qualify for legal aid in family law proceedings, since they were more likely to be welfare dependent after divorce and hence to pass the legal aid means test, and were also somewhat less likely to bring unrealistic applications that had insufficient prospects of success to pass the merit test. Although the financial position of the mother was not evident in all of the 20 cases, in the 9 cases where this information was available, the mother was a sole parent welfare recipient engaged in home duties in 5 of them. Of the remaining 4 mothers, one was supported financially by her ex-husband and property investments, one was supported financially by her new husband and part-time work, and 2 supported themselves, one with part-time work and one with full-time work.

The mother in full-time employment was the only wife/mother to appear unrepresented. The father in that case also appeared unrepresented and also worked full-time. Both would have had incomes in excess of the means threshold for legal aid and they either were unwilling or unable to pay for their own lawyers, or took the view that they could adequately represent themselves. That was the only case in which both parties appeared unrepresented (F.C.7, January 8–10, 1997). Of the other 3 unrepresented fathers, 2 had applied for legal aid and been rejected. One had clearly been rejected on the basis of merit, while in the other case, it was unclear whether the reason for rejection was means, merit, or the operation of the funding cap. The third was unrepresented by choice. He felt he had been given poor advice and been manipulated by his previous solicitor, and now distrusted any legal representatives and insisted that the only way he could get his point across to the court was to do so in person.

All of the cases involving self-represented litigants proceeded to hearing and judgment rather than settling before or during the hearing. This is unsurprising, since self-represented litigants do not expect and rarely possess the skills to engage in pretrial negotiations in the way that lawyers are used to doing, and may resist any attempts at settlement initiated by the opposing lawyer or the child's representative. The consequences of self-representation at trial are discussed subsequently.

The high proportion of cases involving a child's representative is also indicative of the high level of conflict between the parties and the seriousness of the allegations made of violence and child abuse. The proportion of all matters filed in the Family Court in which a child's representative is appointed is much lower, at around 13% (Hunter, 1999, p. 173). The two cases in which the child's representative had been discharged had been affected by lack of funding. When the court appoints a child's representative, self-funding parties are required to share the cost, while if the parties are legally aided, the court requests the Legal Aid Commission to fund the child's representative.[3] In F.C.7 (January 8–10, 1997), the case in which both parties were self-represented, the mother had refused to continue contributing to the cost of the child's representative, which resulted in their withdrawal some time before the matter reached a hearing. In F.C.16, the case had been decided in November 1996, subject to hearing the evidence of one further witness. That witness was scheduled to be heard in early January 1997, which is when the case came into my observation sample (January 6, 1997). However, at the trial in November, the child's representative had been funded by Legal Aid only for 1 day, and had withdrawn after the first day of the hearing, even though the matter ran for a further 2 days. Thus, although the court had considered that a child's representative was required in these cases, in neither of them did the child's representative have the opportunity to cross-examine both of the parties and their witnesses, to call their own witnesses, or to put to the court in final submissions their view of the child's best interests.

One quarter of husbands/fathers and one third of wives/mothers in the observation sample were from a non-English speaking background. This is broadly indicative of the multicultural population in the catchment area of the Melbourne Registry of the Family Court. In most cases, both parties were immigrants from the same country (eastern or southern Europe or east or southeast Asia), although in 2 cases, the husband was Anglo-Australian while the wife was from overseas (east Asia and the Pacific). Not all of these parties required an interpreter, but several did. Women's experience of giving evidence and following proceedings through an interpreter is discussed further later in the chapter.

Finally, as with the broader file sample, it is notable that in over half of the cases in the observation sample, all or some of the matters in dispute were resolved by means of consent orders. Again, this gives rise to the question of the nature of consent in the context of domestic violence and to the kinds of orders to which survivors of violence may have consented.

Going to Court

Safety Issues in Court

As with applicants for domestic violence orders, women attending for a final hearing in the Family Court spent a considerable amount of time waiting, either during door-of-the-court settlement negotiations between their lawyers, or before the case was called on. Although cases were technically scheduled for between 1 and 5 consecutive days' hearing, commencing at 10:00 a.m. on the first day, this did not always occur in practice. In June–August 1996, in the Melbourne Registry of the Family Court, a number of cases would be scheduled before the same judge at the same time, on the assumption that most would settle wholly or in part, leaving only a few actually running for the full length of time. From December 1996 onwards, the listing practice changed so that only one case was listed before a judge at any one time, but there was also a reserve list of cases that would be prepared and ready for hearing in the expected event that some of those listed would settle. And of course, since the listed duration of each case was only an estimate, many ran over time. Consequently, cases that ran often started late, as the judge disposed of the previous case and dealt with minutes of consent orders in matters that had settled.

The approximate waiting time involved in the cases I observed (including time spent at court in negotiations between lawyers and time spent waiting for judgment to be delivered) is set out in table 14. Waiting time was calculated from 10:00 a.m. each day, although, of course, parties would have been present at court well before 10:00 a.m., so the times given in the table are underestimates.

Parties to cases that went to hearing spent longer waiting in court on average than those whose cases settled, although the total waiting time for the former was often spread over several days, while that for the latter occurred on a single occasion.

TABLE 14. Waiting times in Family Court cases observed.[a]

Waiting Time (hrs)	Settled by Consent (n = 8)	Proceeded to Hearing (n = 8)
Minimum	0:00	0:00
Median	2:03	3:17
Maximum	5:63	9:00

[a]The time spent in negotiations was not recorded in 3 of the cases that settled, or in the case that was dealt with on an undefended basis.

While general waiting areas outside the various courtrooms in the Family Court were more extensive and spacious than those available in Magistrates' Courts, they were also not visibly policed, and offered ample scope for an abusive husband/father to threaten, intimidate, or even assault his former partner (see also Kaye et al., 2003, p. 51; Rhoades et al., 2000, p. 73; Zorza, 1995, pp. 308–311). The court was well aware of this possibility, with the Chief Justice's Practice Direction on the Management of Cases Involving Family Violence stating unequivocally,

> It must be recognised that in cases where there are allegations of family violence...the very presence of the person at the Court's premises may place her or him in jeopardy, if the allegations are well founded. Equally, a person's fear may be severe and disabling even though others may think that the allegations are not well founded. (Family Court of Australia, 1993, p. 1)[4]

The practice direction went on to specify that "members of the legal profession are encouraged to advise court staff of cases where they have fears of family violence," and "Australian Federal Police officers are to be informed of cases where family violence is involved on the occasions when the persons associated with the case are likely to be on court premises" (Family Court of Australia, 1993, p. 3). Views differed among the lawyers and women interviewed, however, as to the effectiveness of the safety measures available in the court.

Five of the lawyers thought that security in the Family Court was good and noted the availability and effectiveness of Federal Police protection for frightened or vulnerable clients (D. Dawson, interview, June 5, 1996; M. Lee, interview, June 3, 1996; M. Mann, interview, March 8, 1996; B. Phelan, interview, October 29, 1997; S.2, interview, October 28, 1997). Two other lawyers mentioned the availability of Federal Police protection, but placed more emphasis on other forms of security, such as support workers, friends, court networkers, and the lawyer herself, who collectively could present a "strong front" (B.1, interview, October 17, 1997; B.2, interview, October 22, 1997). Two lawyers also pointed out that while the Federal Police were good, they were also few, which meant that large areas of the court remained unpoliced (B.2, interview, October 22, 1997; J. Trickey, interview, March 20, 1996). On the other hand, one lawyer was adamant that there was no safety at the Family Court and that court facilities were inadequate. She noted in particular that as there was no X-ray machine or scanner at the entrance to the court, there was no restriction on weapons being brought into the court. She concluded that if anyone thought they were safe in the court, it was only because they had not yet been attacked (S.1, interview, January 16, 1997). Another lawyer further observed that anyone could walk into the court with anything, and concluded, on balance, that she did not think it was particularly safe in the court for either clients or practitioners (B.2, interview, October 22, 1997).

Four of the 6 women interviewed who spoke about their experiences in the Family Court said they had had significant fears for their safety in the court (see also Kaye et al., 2003, p. 51). Two had had Federal Police protection, but this had not entirely alleviated their fears. The first had had a police officer sit with her in the waiting area because her ex-husband kept walking past and harassing her, but inside the courtroom, with her ex-husband sitting and glaring at her, she still did not feel completely safe, despite assurances (W.L.3, interview, August 18, 1997). The second had had Federal Police protection on several occasions, but not, apparently, all of the time. She said that the Family Court definitely needed more security. Having two Federal Police in the building was not much use if three women needed protection. On one occasion, her ex-husband had come to court with a large bag, the contents of which were never checked, and she was concerned that he was carrying a weapon. On other occasions, he would try to block the entrance to the courtroom when she was walking in or out. She placed more trust in having support workers or other friends accompany her to court, so she would have someone watching her back, but this was not always possible. Every time she attended court she was afraid he would do something, because she knew he had no fear of the law (W.L.2, interview, December 18, 1997). The third interviewee had also relied on a support worker for security. Because she had an intervention order, she had been kept in an interview room while waiting before her hearing; however, because she was very nervous, she frequently had to go out to the toilet and had been "protected" by her support worker on these trips (W.L.12, interview, December 19, 1997). The fourth interviewee commented that the waiting area in the Family Court at Melbourne was a huge, big room with no security. You could not get away, and a perpetrator of violence could do what he liked (W.L.9, interview, December 19, 1997).

The cases observed did suggest a lack of recourse to or limited availability of Federal Police officers, as they were evident in only 2 of the 20 cases. In 6 of the cases—3 that went to hearing (F.C.1, June 20–21 & 24, 1996; F.C.7, January 8–10, 1997; F.C.11, February 10–14 & March 3–4, 1997) and 3 that resulted in consent orders (F.C.6, December 16, 1996; F.C.17, January 20, 1997; F.C.18, April 9, 1997)—no measures whatever appear to have been taken for the safety of the wife/mother. One of these was the case in which both parties were unrepresented. Since the Chief Justice's Practice Direction placed responsibility on parties' legal representatives to notify the court of any apprehended violence, it was unclear how a self-representing litigant could obtain protection if she needed it, other than by asking a court officer for assistance once she arrived at the court. In 4 cases, rather than requesting Federal Police protection, lawyers simply sequestered their clients in an interview room for the period they were required to spend waiting out of court, and then physically escorted them into the courtroom (F.C.2, June 25–26, 1996; F.C.8,

January 17, 1997; F.C.9, January 20–24, February 10–11, & February 14, 1997; F.C.19, April 17, 1997). Most commonly, however, parties simply waited as far away as possible from each other in the large, open waiting areas, sometimes, but not always, "protected" by their new partners and/or friends (e.g., F.C.3, July 15–18 & 23, 1996; F.C.9, January 20–24, February 10–11, & February 14, 1997; F.C.10, February 7, 1997). In one of these cases, the file indicated that since separating, the father had harassed, assaulted, and verbally abused the mother, and that she had obtained two intervention orders and gone into a refuge for a period as a result of his abuse and irrational behavior. However, the mother's barrister informed me that there was "no violence" in this case—it was simply a matter of the father having a psychiatric illness and behaving inappropriately at times. She clearly had faith that he would not behave inappropriately while waiting unsupervised in court, and hence did not see any need for protection of the mother (F.C.4, July 29, 1996). In another matter, where the mother was obviously in great distress, there had been no request for protection. At one stage, the court officer sought assistance for the mother from a court networker, although this was more for the provision of comfort than of safety. This was a case in which the father broke a spring at the top of the courtroom door while slamming it open after the second day's hearing, and in which the judge ultimately decided that the mother was so fearful of the father that he should not have contact with their son (F.C.3, July 15–18 & 23, 1996).

The 2 cases observed in which Federal Police officers were present were quite distinctive in that there had been some history of the father posing a threat to the court or the court's processes rather than (just) to the mother. It is not clear whether in these instances the Federal Police presence was the initiative of the mother's lawyers or of the court itself (see also Stewart, 2005, p. 24). In one, the father had seriously assaulted the mother during a joint counseling session at the Family Court, for which he had been criminally charged and convicted (F.C.16, January 6, 1997). In the other, the husband was a repeat litigant with a well-known and frequently expressed animosity towards the Family Court, and it appeared that the two Federal Police officers who spent a considerable amount of time in the courtroom during the hearing were there more to protect the court than to protect the wife. During breaks in proceedings, the wife and her mother sat in the open waiting area, not in an interview room and not, apparently, subject to any particular concerns for their safety (F.C.5, December 2–6, 1996).

Clearly, too, women came to court for steps prior to the final hearing of their case in the absence of appropriate protection against violence (see, e.g., the Family Court Lobby Group, 1990, p. 21). While I was waiting one morning before a scheduled hearing, an incident occurred in the waiting area for that morning's duty list. The father had not seen the mother for several months and had taken the opportunity to confront her outside the courtroom. She felt she was being intimidated and burst into tears. Her solicitor ushered her into a vacant courtroom and went to call security. Drawing on defense tactics familiar from the Magistrates' Courts, the father's barrister warned him that if the mother sought a restraining order from the court, he should only consent to the making of mutual orders, without admitting the need for an order against him (Field notes, Family Court of Australia, Melbourne Registry, April 17, 1997).

The Court Setting

Courtrooms in the Melbourne Registry were medium sized and traditionally configured, with a raised bench for the judge, a lower bench for the court officer, a bar table facing the bench, a witness box to the side, and the gallery behind. Judges and barristers wore robes and wigs, while instructing solicitors, if present, wore business suits and sat at the bar table opposite the barrister with their backs to the judge. Litigants sat in the first row of the gallery, behind their barristers.

Lawyers described how they prepared women for court so as to try to avoid "malfunctions" in the witness box. They would take them to court to observe other cases (B. Phelan, interview, October 29, 1997; S.2, interview, October 28, 1997), make sure they met the barrister early so they got to know her or him (S.1, interview, January 16, 1997; S.2, interview, October 28, 1997), explain the roles of the various actors and the order of proceedings (B.1, interview, October 17, 1997; S.1, interview, January 16, 1997), tell them just to answer each question during cross-examination and not to try to give a monologue (S.2, interview, October 28, 1997), and make them aware that while lies would be caught out (S.1, interview, January 16, 1997), judges would listen to the truth and were very good at discerning the "ring of truth" in a person's evidence (B.1, interview, October 17, 1997). Since witnesses were not allowed to come into court until they had given evidence, the woman might be advised to bring someone else with her who was not a witness for moral support (S.1, interview, January 16, 1997). A barrister said that she tried to prepare women so that they felt able and confident to reveal their feelings and expose their emotions, and although women might feel shame or be reluctant to speak about the violence they had endured, this should not impede their right to be heard (B.1, interview, October 17, 1997).

Despite such preparation, however, at least one solicitor acknowledged that most women were petrified of the court setting (S.1, interview, January 16, 1997), and this seemed to be borne out in my fieldwork data. One of the women interviewed said that she did not see much of a difference between the Magistrates' Court and the Family Court. While the lawyers and judicial officers wore different clothes, both were just as frightening to begin with (W.L.3, interview, August 18, 1997). And although another said she had found the actual hearing in the Family Court to be fairly straightforward, she described the court as very stuffy, pompous, traditional, and intimidating (W.L.2, interview, December 18, 1997).

Two of the women in the cases observed also expressed how difficult they found it to be in court. One told me at one point during a break in the hearing that she was no longer *very* nervous in court, as she had been there so often and was getting used to it, but she still could not eat very much during the (5-day) hearing (F.C.5, December 2–6, 1996). The other, who was from a non-English speaking background, spent part of a 2-week break in the hearing back in court observing other cases. She explained that she was afraid because she could not understand everything that was going on in court, so she had attempted to conquer that fear by coming to sit in court to try to understand more about it. On the resumption of the hearing, she was cross-examined about this self-help exercise: Why were you here in court all day for 3 days last week, while your children were left in after-school care? What were you doing? The wife replied that she was frightened of being in court, but the hearing was so important, and she did not want to lose her children just because she was scared and unable to answer questions properly. The husband's barrister then pointed out that witnesses had observed her sitting in courtrooms where no evidence was being heard, deliberately missing the point that her unfamiliarity with court procedures might extend to not knowing which court to go to or what to look for (F.C.9, January 20–24, February 10–11, & February 14, 1997).

Court Proceedings as a Form of Harassment

As suggested earlier, it was clear that some men were using the Family Court process as a means of continuing to harass their ex-wives, both in bringing repeated applications and in exploiting the court's concern to assist self-representing litigants (see also Kaye et al., 2003, p. 91). There was no equivalent category of women litigants. For example, while one of the women interviewed was now representing herself, she said she had not yet found any advantages of being a litigant in person. She felt, however, that her ex-husband had enjoyed advantages when she had a lawyer and he did not. Her perception was that the court had bent over backwards for him, even when he had, at one stage, picked up a chair and threatened her with it. She thought that if she had done that she would have been charged with contempt (W.L.2, interview, December 18, 1997). Likewise, another said that her ex-husband had no respect for the court. He treated it with contempt and got away with it, whereas anyone else would be penalized. After her first hearing in the court, the judge had ordered that her ex-husband should have no access to the children and that he should not lodge any fresh applications for 9 months. He had appeared on her doorstep wanting to see the children the very next day, and made a new application to the court, which resulted in a 6-day hearing during which he again represented himself and made lengthy speeches of self-justification. He was again unsuccessful in gaining access and was declared a vexatious litigant, meaning that he could not make any further applications without leave of the court. With the support of a men's group, he had appealed this decision unsuccessfully to the Full Court and then to the High Court. He then went back to the Family Court and obtained leave to file a new application. As she put it, a squeaky wheel gets oiled. He had been given a great deal of leeway because he was unrepresented, while she was harassed by being brought back to court again and again (W.L.3, interview, August 18, 1997).

The husband in F.C.5 (December 2–6, 1996) also fit this profile. The parties had made consent orders 3 years previously that gave custody to the wife and access to the husband. The husband had subsequently applied unsuccessfully to the court to restrain the wife from changing the children's school. He then applied for joint residence of the children, and the matter had been listed before one of the women judges in Melbourne. During that hearing, the husband formed the view that this judge was biased against him, and he made an application for her to remove herself from hearing the matter. This application was dismissed, but the husband then appealed to the Full Court, which upheld the decision. He was ordered to pay the wife's costs of the appeal, but had refused to do so on the basis that he did not agree with the Full Court's decision or order for costs, and maintained his view that the trial judge was biased against him. The matter then came on before a different judge and fell into my observation sample.

The husband's protests about the Family Court's decisions had gone as far as a large sign criticizing the court that he had painted on the side of his shop, and plans to publish and distribute a magazine called *Men's Voice*, which he said would also expose the court's iniquities. He was fixated on the idea that he should have equal time with his children and agreed in cross-examination that he would never give up trying to achieve this. In his closing address, he asserted that everyone in court was "blinded by the matriarchal family law system" and that the system would eventually have to "pay for the crimes" that were "killing families." The barrister for the children's representative described him in her closing address as obsessive, overbearing, aggressive, and intolerant of different views. The wife had reached the limit of available legal aid funds in defending his applications, and the Legal Aid Commission had also placed a caveat over her home. In his decision, the judge refused the husband's application for joint residence and also acceded to the wife's application for costs and request to restrain the husband from making any further applications without leave, finding that the husband had no understanding of the destructive effects of his repeated applications, of the hardship they caused, or of their effect on the wife's peace of mind and financial position. He also found that in making repeated applications, the husband was not attempting to promote the welfare of the children and was hindering the court's processes. The husband stormed out of the court shouting, "I don't know how you can all live with yourselves." And he would undoubtedly be back.

CONSENT ORDERS

As previously noted, a significant proportion of cases in which the files indicated quite a serious history of domestic violence resulted in settlement by consent orders prior to or during the final hearing. The Chief Justice's Practice Direction on the Management of Cases Involving Family Violence stated the principle that "[t]he well-being and safety of people using the Court's services will not be compromised by attempts to arrive at negotiated resolution of their disputes" (Family Court of Australia, 1993, p. 2)—but this principle appears to have been considered relevant only to the court's counseling and mediation services, and not to the process of arriving at consent orders (see also Family Court of Australia, 2004). Likewise, while there is a well-developed literature on the unsuitability of mediation and other forms of ADR between parties to violent relationships (e.g., Alexander, 1992; Astor, 1994a, 1994b; Cobb, 1997; Hunter, 2003; Keys Young, 1996), there has been little corresponding concern with the appropriateness of lawyer-led settlement negotiations in cases involving such relationships (see also Family Law Council & Law Council of Australia, Family Law Section, 2004).

The Prevalence of (Failed) Consent Orders

A series of studies have pointed both to the prevalence of consent orders in family law cases involving violence (e.g., Hore, Gibson & Bordow, 1996, pp. 20–23; Logan et al., 2003, p. 276) and to the strikingly "non-stick" nature of the agreements reached (e.g., Kaye et al., 2003, pp. 100–101; Rhoades, 2002, p. 85). As previously noted, at least 30% of the files read involving domestic violence resulted in subsequent proceedings, and at least half of these had been "resolved" by means of consent orders. One of the women interviewed described being coerced by her barrister into signing consent orders giving access to her two children to her ex-husband; however, her ex-husband ignored the conditions imposed in the orders, and she subsequently suspended access after he threatened to kill her. When he was sent to jail for assaulting her, he agreed to have no contact with the children so long as she sent him photos from time to time, but as soon as he was released, he commenced new proceedings, and the matter had still not been finally resolved (W.L.2, interview, December 18, 1997). Of the 13 cases observed in which it was possible to determine the fate of consent orders made either during the observation period or at an earlier stage, only two agreements had held, and these were both agreements that had supported the position and attempted to ensure the safety of the mother. Consent orders in the other 11 cases had all broken down because the wife/mother could not realistically comply with what she had "agreed" to, because the husband/father chose not to comply with the orders, and/or because the husband/father was not satisfied with the compromise he had made and pressed for a more complete victory.

The same phenomenon has been observed in other studies (e.g., Hewitt, Brown, Frederico, & Martyn, 1996, p. 24; Logan et al., 2003, p. 276; Rendell et al., 2000, p. 83). Women who have been targets of violence agree to arrangements that they know to be unsafe and unworkable (e.g., Kaye et al., 2003, pp. 108–109, 112; Rhoades, 2002, p. 86; Rhoades et al., 2000, p. 71). Not surprisingly, then, these agreements break down, resulting in further applications for final orders, for variation of the consent orders, or for enforcement proceedings against the mother. In her study of contravention applications in the Family Court, Rhoades (2002) found that 88% of applications concerned alleged contraventions of consent orders and that a common outcome of these applications was an investigation of the circumstances by means of a Family Report and subsequent variation of the orders to provide more appropriate arrangements for the children and the mother (pp. 76, 87)—surely an inefficient, dangerous, and traumatic method of achieving a satisfactory outcome.

Reasons for "Consent"

The reasons why settlement occurred in cases involving domestic violence were a combination of clients' circumstances, the court's expectations, the state of the law in whose shadow bargaining took place, and lawyers' practices.

Cost Considerations

The advantages of settlement for clients were seen to be that it was much less costly than running a case to hearing (J. Peirce, interview, August 21, 1997; S.2, interview, October 28, 1997), quicker (S.2, interview, October 28, 1997), avoided the need for the client to speak in court if they were frightened of doing so (M. Mann, interview, March 8, 1996; S.2, interview, October 28, 1997), and avoided the client being subjected to cross-examination (J. Peirce, interview, August 21, 1997; S.2, interview, October 28, 1997). Cost considerations were a particular issue for legally aided clients. The imposition of funding caps on legally aided cases meant that victims of violence who had exhausted the funding available from legal aid were forced to settle in preference to continuing unrepresented (J. Peirce, interview, August 21, 1997; S.1, interview, January 16, 1997). The women interviewed also referred to financial considerations as the strongest reason for settling. One had made an application for property division in the Family Court that included a cross-vested tort claim for damages. However, she had agreed to drop this claim as part of the settlement as she did not have the funds to pursue it. In a context in which she would have to spend

$10,000 and risk losing in order to gain only $40,000, the cost benefit of continuing to hearing did not add up (W.L.12, interview, December 19, 1997). Another had settled her property case at the door of the court. When asked whether she was happy with the outcome she replied, "Yes and no." If she had gone to trial, she would have had to get valuations, and the exercise would have cost twice as much for a not very different result. Nevertheless, she felt she had lost a lot of money and ended up with less than she had put into the matrimonial home (W.L.9, interview, December 19, 1997). A third similarly said she did not have a choice about settlement because she could not afford to go to trial. In her pithy summation, "You take as much justice as you can afford to get" (W.L.5, interview, December 19, 1997; see also Erlanger, Chambliss & Melli, 1987, p. 592).

Bullying and Appeasement

Other studies have noted the use of fear, coercion, and bullying by violent men, with women agreeing to unfair property settlements and unsatisfactory contact arrangements in the hope of preventing further violence (Family Law Council, 1998, p. 29; Kaye et al., 2003, p. 109; Women's Coalition Against Family Violence, 1994, p. 95). One woman quoted by Kaye et al. (2003) said, "I consented so hey lady, you're happy with everything. By consenting that means you're happy—wrong. By consenting you're just buying peace. It's got nothing to do with whether you were happy about the arrangements or not" (p. 110; see also Rhoades et al., 2000, p. 72).

In my own study, there was also ample evidence of coercion in the process of arriving at consent orders. In 5 of the cases observed, the consent orders agreed to suggested that the mother had at best been badly advised given the context of violence, or at worst completely overborne. In 2 of these cases, the appalling history of violence in the relationship, the ongoing dangerousness of the father, and the damaged and terrified state that the mother was in would have amply justified orders for no contact. Indeed, the violence and level of fear in these cases was considerably worse than in one of the cases observed that went to hearing and in which a no-contact order was made. Nevertheless, the women in both of these cases consented to contact orders. In one, the mother's tort claim for damages for ongoing physical injuries and sexual and emotional abuse was also dismissed as part of the property settlement (F.C.15, December 5, 1996). In the other, the mother eventually did seek an order for no contact, and was successful in the Full Court of the Family Court (F.C.16, January 6, 1997).

In one of the other cases in which the bully succeeded, it was alleged that the father had subjected the mother to every form of violence imaginable and continued to harass and intimidate her. The mother sought variation of the contact arrangements to better suit the children's activities, and orders for the father to sign passport applications for the children, as she wished to take them on a visit to her parents overseas. The consent orders resolving this application, however, made absolutely no concession to the children's activities in the contact arrangements and restrained the mother from removing the children from the country (F.C.18, April 9, 1997). In a fourth case, the mother had been forced to leave the child with the father and was applying for orders for more extensive contact than the father would allow. Late in the morning, it was reported to the judge that the parties were preparing minutes of consent orders, but the child's representative did not agree to the terms currently proposed. The child's representative was very concerned that the agreement proposed to leave the child with the father, as there was evidence that the father and his family were turning the child against the mother, and in the process subjecting the child to severe emotional abuse. However, the child's representative could see that the mother was being worn down by the insistence on the father's side that the child stay with them. By the middle of the afternoon, the judge was told that the parties had "resolved" the matter, along the lines earlier indicated, while the child's representative looked very unhappy (F.C.17, January 20, 1997). Clearly, in these cases, the woman's "consent" was merely a product of her continued subordination to the perpetrator of violence (B.1, interview, October 17, 1997).

The Court's Promotion of Settlement

At the same time, the court's "settlement culture" (see, e.g., Armstrong, 2001, p. 151; Hunter et al., 2000, ch. 7; Rhoades, 2002, pp. 83, 87), reinforced by the Family Law Reform Act (1995), exerted strong pressure towards resolution by means of consent orders. One solicitor, for example, advised all of her clients before going to court that they would be required to try to settle the case (S.1, interview, January 16, 1997), and a barrister referred to the statistical inevitability that "95.6% of cases settle" (B. Phelan, interview, October 29, 1997). In one of the cases observed, which had involved serious incidents of physical violence and the husband threatening the wife with a gun, the judge encouraged the parties to engage in settlement discussions and gave them a lecture on the importance of talking to each other and reaching agreement, since they had many years of joint parenting ahead of them (F.C.1, June 20–21 & 24, 1996).

The court's encouragement of settlement was also manifested in the process of approving consent orders. Judges usually congratulated the parties on reaching agreement and commended them for acting so cooperatively in relation to their future parenting, thus sending a strong message that this was what the court hoped for and expected (e.g., F.C.4, July 29, 1996; F.C.6, December 16, 1996; F.C.10, February 7, 1997; F.C.12, April 7, 1997; F.C.14, August 9, 1996). One of the women interviewed had found this little speech utterly galling. She said her ex-husband had strung out the process of settlement (in relation to property issues) all day, mucking around, playing games, and wearing her down, so that by the time they got into court to have the orders approved, she was very angry. She wanted to ask for costs, but her solicitor said the Family Court does not like to blame anybody. Then the judge commended them for reaching an amicable agreement, and she had to sit there and say nothing (W.L.5, interview, December 19, 1997).

The Role of Lawyers

Lawyers were an integral part of the court's settlement culture and played a crucial role in achieving settlements (Hunter et al., 2000, ch. 7).

For example, one of the solicitors I interviewed noted that all of his cases settled well before they reached a final hearing, and he also briefed barristers who were good settlers (S.2, interview, October 28, 1997). Solicitors did acknowledge certain drawbacks of consent orders: parties had a sense that they were selling out and could have done better, and many were unhappy with the compromise outcome achieved (S.1, interview, January 16, 1997; S.2, interview, October 28, 1997). Some women were also disappointed that they had not had the opportunity to tell their story to the court (S. Macgregor, interview, March 1, 1996; J. Peirce, interview, August 21, 1997; S.1, interview, January 16, 1997; S.2, interview, October 28, 1997) and that there was no official affirmation of what they had been through (J. Peirce, interview, August 21, 1997; S.2, interview, October 28, 1997) or public censuring of their abuser (B. Phelan, interview, October 29, 1997)—although lawyers observed that clients who went to hearing expecting affirmation or vindication would be likely to be disappointed anyway, since the Family Court rarely made crushing moral judgements about any of the parties before it (B. Phelan, interview, October 29, 1997; S.2, interview, October 28, 1997). As noted earlier, too, the hearing process itself might be an even less desirable alternative.

Clients who did not see the "sense" in settling were often pressured by their lawyers to do so (see also Erlanger et al., 1987, p. 593; Rhoades et al., 2000, p. 72; The Family Court Lobby Group, 1990, p. 22). One interviewee noted that "you see women in the waiting area of the Family Court being pressured every day" (C. McNamara, interview, June 14, 1996), and this was certainly true of my observations. In one of the cases I observed that ultimately settled, there were clearly some sticking points along the way, and the barristers on both sides worked very hard to get their clients to reach an agreement (F.C.19, April 17, 1997). In another case, the barristers negotiated the final terms of consent orders between themselves at the bar table, in consultation with the judge but with almost no reference to their clients (F.C.6, December 16, 1996), while in a third case, the matter was "resolved" between the barristers and solicitors, who then proceeded to have the minutes of consent orders translated to the non-English speaking mother (F.C.20, April 24, 1997). Her participation in actually reaching the agreement appears to have been minimal.

Legal Uncertainty

As well as the court's emphasis on settlement, women who had been targets of violence also faced the changing doctrinal contours of the Family Law Act (1975). As discussed in the next chapter, the period of the fieldwork was one of doctrinal uncertainty in relation to domestic violence, as old and new paradigms contested for dominance. In this somewhat unpredictable climate, women felt compelled to consent to agreements because it was by no means guaranteed they would achieve any better result by going to court (see also Mnookin & Kornhauser, 1979). For example, the barrister of one of the women interviewed had persuaded her to sign consent orders on the basis that the judge was going to grant access to her ex-husband anyway, and consent orders would give her greater control over the conditions of access. She later felt that she had been "shafted" (W.L.2, interview, December 18, 1997). The argument that consent orders provided the client with greater certainty and control over the outcome than they would have if the matter was to be decided by a judge was frequently used by solicitors as a means of persuasion to settle, telling clients that they were taking a big risk and anything could happen if they went before a judge rather than reaching an agreement (B. Phelan, interview, October 29, 1997; S.1, interview, January 16, 1997; S.2, interview, October 28, 1997). One barrister interviewed disagreed with this rationale, considering that solicitors might have less understanding of why particular results eventuated in court, whereas she had more faith in the judges, believing that if the matter went to hearing, a result would be arrived at that was appropriate for the case (B.1, interview, October 17, 1997). Both of these positions reinforced the point made by Erlanger et al. (1987) that "the shadow of the law is…cast by lawyers, who declare their expectations of judicial behavior" (p. 599). At the time of the fieldwork, the dominant account of judicial behavior purveyed by family lawyers was that it was unpredictable, and hence, settlement was a safer option.

The Results of Consent Processes

Given the various pressures towards consensual rather than adjudicated outcomes in family law cases, including those involving a history of and sometimes ongoing domestic violence, to what extent did consent processes incorporate concerns to ensure the safety of the women and children affected by them? As noted earlier, the evidence from other studies suggests that unsafe and unworkable agreements are often made in cases where violence is an issue, and that such agreements have a high rate of breakdown. On the other hand, there is also some evidence to suggest that consent orders that protect the woman and children against further violence might be more durable than those that do not (see previous discussion in this chapter, p. 177).

Some of the lawyers interviewed said that they attempted to protect and empower women who had been victims of violence in the settlement process, for example, by demonstrating their understanding of the client's position, acknowledging the limited capacity of some clients to make independent decisions, not exploiting the client's dependence and vulnerability, and ensuring the client was emotionally supported and given enough time to think (e.g., B.1, interview, October 17, 1997; B. Phelan, interview, October 29, 1997). I also observed 2 cases in which the husband's lawyer appeared to be "crunching" him to agree to a settlement that respected the position of the wife to a far greater degree than the husband's instructions would have conceded (F.C.10, February 7, 1997; F.C.12, April 7, 1997). At the other end of the spectrum, though, there were many lawyers who appeared to be quite prepared to prey on the vulnerability of abused clients or to ignore their needs in order to achieve a settlement (as previously discussed, and S.1, interview, January 16, 1997). Women in Kaye et al.'s (2003) study also reported many examples of negative experiences with lawyers, including not acceding to their concerns, not following their instructions in negotiations, and pressuring them to agree to arrangements that were not in accordance with their wishes (pp. 74–75).[5]

While I observed consent orders being made in 11 cases, the orders in only 4 of those cases incorporated protections for the safety of the wife/mother and children in the context of the husband/father's past and continuing violence. These orders supported the wife's position (maintaining residence of the children, allowing her to relocate interstate, withdrawing the husband's application to penalize the wife for breaching contact orders) and minimized the need for contact between the parties (by allowing the wife to relocate, temporarily suspending the husband's contact with the children, providing for contact only at the child's request, or providing handover arrangements that kept the parties well apart), thereby reducing the capacity for the husband to engage in ongoing harassment and abuse of the wife. In the other 7 cases, as previously discussed, the orders at best made no concessions to safety, and at worst perpetuated the husband's/father's abuse and control.

In addition, and consistent with its encouragement of settlement, the court in the course of approving minutes of consent orders generally failed to scrutinize the nature of the "consent" that had been given or the safety of the proposed orders. Margaret Harrison (1996) has observed that the court's role is "most commonly reduced to a forum which ratifies lawyer-negotiated agreements" (p. 243). Registrars interviewed by Rhoades et al. (2000) also said that if minutes of consent orders were presented to them, they would generally make the orders without inquiry (pp. 97–98; see also Erlanger et al., 1987, p. 598). In my observations, although judges did sometimes scrutinize consent orders to ensure that they did not present unacceptable risks to the child (e.g., F.C.4, July 29, 1996),[6] they never queried consent orders on the basis that they failed to ensure the mother's safety or perpetuated abuse against her, and never invoked section 68K, which required the court, as far as possible, to ensure that orders did not expose a person to an unacceptable risk of family violence.

Finally, I observed how an earlier instance of "consent" could be used as evidence that the woman's allegations of violence lacked either credibility, seriousness, or relevance. In one of the cases that went to hearing, the husband's barrister made much of the fact that soon after an incident in which the husband had allegedly assaulted and tried to strangle the wife, and she had stabbed him with a knife in self-defense, the parties had been "able" to reach a "consent" agreement for shared custody. In his argument, this demonstrated that despite a high level of hostility between the parties, they were still able to agree about the best interests of the children and to make successful shared arrangements. This argument invoked the nonfeminist understanding that violence by one parent towards the other had no bearing on the first parent's relationship with the children, and sought to challenge the received wisdom in psychology and social work circles that shared parenting was only a practicable arrangement in cases where there was a high level of cooperation between the parties. The judge seized on this argument, finding that although there was a deep degree of hostility between the parties, they had nevertheless made arrangements for shared parenting (F.C.1, June 20–21 & 24, 1996). In other words, rather than questioning the validity of the consent in the context of violence, it was the claims about violence and its effects that were questioned in the context of supposed consent.

Speaking in Court

Only 2 of the women interviewed had been to a defended hearing in the Family Court. Both of these were facing former partners who made repeated applications to the court, so that both had attended more than one final hearing on different applications (W.L.2, interview, December 18, 1997; W.L.3, interview, August 18, 1997). Most of those interviewed, however, were still in the interlocutory stages of proceedings, or had settled their cases before trial. For these women, then, the Family Court was a place where other people spoke for and about them, but they did *not* speak. While one was relieved that she had not had to say anything in court (W.L.8, interview, November 7, 1997), 2 others felt silenced and frustrated during the interlocutory stages of their Family Court proceedings.

One complained that too many registrars had not given her a chance to say anything because her ex-husband was the applicant and she was the respondent; she certainly had not been given equal time to speak (W.L.2, interview, December 18, 1997). The other was even more adamant that in the Family Court, "you don't have your own voice." "You're invisible in the courtroom," "you're just there as a spectator," and you were powerless to do anything about it. While she had had an opportunity to tell her story in the Magistrates' Court when applying for an intervention order, in the Family Court, she was never allowed to speak about the violence she had experienced, and never felt heard (W.L.5, interview, December 19, 1997; see also Kaye et al., 2003, p. 46).

Evidence in Chief

One of the structural features contributing to this feeling of not being heard was that evidence in chief was given primarily by way of affidavit. Thus, although the woman might have had the chance to present a written narrative, which would be read by the court and the other side, there was little or no opportunity for her to tell her story orally and for the court to be seen to be listening, especially if the matter settled before trial (K. Anderson, interview, March 8, 1996; S. Macgregor, interview, March 1, 1996; M. Mann, interview, March 8, 1996). One of the lawyers interviewed recounted the case of a client who had been unhappy with the amount of affidavit space devoted to the history of violence in the relationship and had insisted on filing a further affidavit with more detail about the violence she had experienced. This had cost her money, but she wanted the details on the record (K. Anderson, interview, March 8, 1996). It appears that most women, however, did not see or were not satisfied with affidavits as the primary means of telling their story, particularly since, in the form in which it was presented, the affidavit tended to be a narrative of legally relevant material written by the woman's solicitor rather than a full account of the client's position from her own perspective.

When matters went to trial, it was typical for evidence in chief to consist of an affirmation of the contents of the Order 30 affidavit (the affidavit of evidence in chief submitted before trial), plus some fairly brief reiteration of the main points of the party's evidence and supplementary questioning in relation to any events that had occurred after the affidavit was filed. While from the court's perspective this saved time, and one of the barristers interviewed saw it as a relatively easy way to get the woman's story out (B.2, interview, October 22, 1997), the consequence was that the main speaking role given to parties in court was in responding to questions asked in cross-examination by the other party's barrister. As one of the women interviewed explained, at the hearing of her case, she was not really able to tell her story. She responded to questions in cross-examination, but she was never given the opportunity to sit in the witness box and give her own narrative (W.L.3, interview, August 18, 1997).

Cross-Examination

The relative amounts of time parties spent giving evidence and being cross-examined in the 8 defended hearings observed is shown in table 15.

It can be seen that the median amount of time spent in the witness box did not differ greatly between wives/mothers and husbands/fathers, other than the fact that wives/mothers were cross-examined for 20 min longer on average than husbands/fathers. The main reason for this difference appears to be that in 3 of the cases, the husband/father was self-representing, and these parties tended to subject their former

TABLE 15. Times giving evidence in Family Court cases observed.

Type of Evidence	No.	*Mdn* Wife/Mother	*Mdn* Husband/Father
Evidence in chief	8	10 min	12.5 min
Cross-examination by other side	8[a]	82 min	62.5 min
Cross-examination by child's rep.	6[a]	45 min	49.5 min
Reexamination	8	2 min	4.5 min

[a]In F.C.11 (February 10–14 & March 3–4, 1997), 1.5 days of the wife's case were not observed, during which the wife gave her evidence in chief and was cross-examined by the husband and partly by the child representative. Thus, the precise times for these components of the mother's evidence are not available.

partners to more lengthy cross-examination than did barristers. In the cases in which cross-examination of the other party was undertaken by a barrister, the median time for wives/mothers to be cross-examined was 67.5 min, while the median time for husbands/fathers to be cross-examined was 68 min.

The table also clearly shows that the vast majority of the parties' time in the witness box was spent being cross-examined, at least by the other side, and often by the child's representative as well. Consequently, not only did women who had been victims of violence not get the opportunity to tell their own story in a coherent way, they were compelled to spend most of their time in the witness box attempting to un-tell the other side's story through one-word answers, while being subjected to a verbal battering by their former partner or his barrister. As already noted, a (well-founded) fear of cross-examination was one of the reasons why women might decide to settle for less than they could otherwise obtain.

The Traumas of Cross-Examination

One of the barristers interviewed conceded that "being cross-examined is never pleasant" and said that if she was representing a violent man, she would "fight hard and admit nothing" (B.2, interview, October 22, 1997). All of the barristers representing husbands/fathers in the cases observed adopted some version of this strategy. A solicitor noted that some women who had been targets of violence came out of court having experienced a double abuse (J. Peirce, interview, August 21, 1997). Most of the wives/mothers in the cases observed were reduced to tears at some point during cross-examination, and displayed other signs of distress, as well as obvious relief when their time in the witness box was over (F.C.1, June 20–21 & 24, 1996; F.C.2, June 25–26, 1996; F.C.3, July 15–18 & 23, 1996; F.C.7, January 8–10, 1997; F.C.9, January 20–24, February 10–11 & February 14, 1997). Those who were cross-examined by counsel had their motives for wanting to relocate closely questioned (F.C.1, June 20–21 & 24, 1996), and their credibility attacked, particularly in relation to their claims of violence (F.C.2, June 25–26, 1996; F.C.8, January 17, 1997). In one case, the husband's barrister sought to construct the wife as terminally incapable of punctuality in collecting her children and, therefore, as undeserving of the varied contact arrangements that she sought (F.C.2, June 25–26, 1996), while in another, the wife was constructed as mad, out of control, and abusive to the children and the husband, while the husband's own violence towards the wife was minimized (F.C.9, January 20–24, February 10–11 & February 14, 1997). In this latter case, the husband's barrister played real "hardball," arguing with, verbally bullying, and interrupting the wife, the wife's barrister, and even the judge. The wife, who was accompanied by an interpreter, was cross-examined for a total of 5 hr 40 min.

The lawyers interviewed tended to downplay the trauma of cross-examination for women who had been targets of violence, so long as their case was ultimately successful. One noted that even women who were grilled nastily usually still had their stories accepted by the court (S.2, interview, October 28, 1997). Another said that if women felt empowered to speak about their experience and were able to describe their situation with dignity and give the judge access to their experience, the results could be very therapeutic. Giving evidence, naming the behavior, standing up to cross-examination, and being heard and believed by the judge could be a fantastic experience and very effective in helping the victim to move forward. On the other hand, she also noted that the process of emerging from being a victim of violence could be a long and slow one, and if the woman was not sufficiently recovered, she could be a disaster in the witness box and be more damaged by having gone to court (B.1, interview, October 27, 1997; see also Kaye et al., 2003, p. 90).

Direct Cross-Examination by a Self-Represented Ex-Partner

If a perpetrator of violence was self-represented in the Family Court, he was entitled to directly cross-examine his former partner. As Rendell et al. (2000) have observed, "Being cross-examined by a former partner is demeaning and terrifying for many women" (p. 110). Among other things, the former partner may use "meaningful" body language to intimidate the woman, which will not be observable to others in the court.

The ex-husbands of two of the women interviewed were repeat litigants who represented themselves in the Family Court. One had been told by her barrister that if her ex-husband's latest application went to a hearing, it would be like a mini rape trial, as he could ask her any questions he liked. This prospect in fact held fewer terrors for her than it might have, since she had already been through two rape trials in the County Court with him as the defendant (W.L.2, interview, December 18, 1997). The other had endured several stints in the witness box being cross-examined by her ex-husband, with, as she said, her stomach turning over. During one 4-day hearing she had been in the witness box for more than a day, with him intimidating and trying to humiliate her. Her solicitor had advised her not to get into an argument with him, just to answer his questions, but she considered it very unfair that the woman had to get up and have everything thrown at her (W.L.3, interview, August 18, 1997).

One of the barristers interviewed also referred to a recent case that she described as "shocking," which had run for 9 days with a "very clever and mean" self-represented father. The only strategy available in this situation was to try to position the woman in the witness box so that her abuser was out of her line of vision, and she did not have to look at him at all during the cross-examination (B. Phelan, interview, October 29, 1997).

Four of the cases observed involved an allegedly violent, self-represented husband/father directly cross-examining his ex-partner, although in one of these cases, I was unable to observe most of the cross-examination (F.C.11, February 10–14 & March 3–4, 1997). In another, the cross-examination was relatively short, although the wife sat facing away from the husband and looking at the judge for the duration (F.C.5, December 2–6, 1996). In the third, the very distressed mother was protected by the judge rather than by her own barrister. It was the judge who seated the mother in the witness box so that she was looking directly at her and could not see the father. During cross-examination, the judge asked the father to tell her each question he wanted to ask, and the judge would then rephrase it and put it to the mother. She prevented the father from getting aggressive with the mother, stopped them from arguing, and also prevented the mother from going off on long, tangential explanations and giving hearsay evidence. The mother spent almost her entire time in the witness box weeping. She was cross-examined by the father for 1.5 hr (F.C.3, July 15–18 & 23, 1996).

In the fourth case, the mother was much more robust, but was also in person, and no attempts were made to shield her during cross-examination. The father's cross-examination was lengthy, running for just over 3 hr. The judge initially intervened only occasionally to stop the father from interrupting the mother's replies, to clarify her answers, or to add questions of his own. However, as time went on, he clearly became impatient with the level of detail the father was going into and what he perceived as irrelevant lines of inquiry, and he made greater efforts to limit the father's questioning. When it came to the mother's turn, she did not return the favor, declining to cross-examine the father at all (F.C.7, January 8–10, 1997).

Reliance on Interpreters

The difficulties of speaking in court and of cross-examination were particularly acute for women whose access to the court was mediated by an interpreter. Only one of the lawyers interviewed, however, spoke about the impact of needing an interpreter on the client. She observed that needing an interpreter made the case longer and more difficult for the client, as she would probably not be able to understand everything that was happening when others were giving evidence. Needing an interpreter was also an added expense for the client (B.2, interview, October 22, 1997). Although the court would arrange and pay for an interpreter for the final hearing, the client themselves had to pay if they wished to have an interpreter at the interlocutory stages in the court, and for meetings with their solicitor, reading affidavits and correspondence, and so on (M. Mann, interview, March 8, 1996). If the client was legally aided, out-of-court expenditure on interpreters meant that they were likely to reach the legal aid funding limit more quickly than English-speaking clients (B.2, interview, October 22, 1997; S.1, interview, January 16, 1997).

Lawyers more often spoke about the court's attitude to working with interpreters (no problems were raised in this regard) (B.2, interview, October 22, 1997; D. Dawson, interview, June 5, 1996; S. Macgregor, interview, March 1, 1996) and the role of the interpreter in translating the client's words to the court. Only one of the lawyers expressed no reservations about the quality and effectiveness of the interpretation services provided (B.1, interview, October 17, 1997). The others all had some concerns, ranging from perceived failures to convey the woman's exact meaning, including nuances and cultural conventions (D. Dawson, interview, June 5, 1996; S. Macgregor, interview, March 1, 1996; B. Phelan, interview, October 29, 1997; S.1, interview, January 16 1997; J. Trickey, interview, March 20, 1996), to acknowledgement that the impact of the woman's story is always diminished, and her emotions attenuated, when she is speaking through another person (B.2, interview, October 22, 1997; S.1, interview, January 16, 1997; S.2, interview, October 28, 1997). Two of the lawyers referred particularly to the fact that the difficulties of talking about violence were compounded by the language barrier, especially with a male interpreter, and noted their practice of specifically requesting a female interpreter in such cases (B. Phelan, interview, October 29, 1997; J. Trickey, interview, March 20, 1996).

Two of the women in the cases observed were accompanied by interpreters, while a third from a non-English speaking background had reasonably good English and did not request an interpreter, although some language problems did emerge during her cross-examination. For example, when being questioned about the various times the parties had separated and resumed cohabitation prior to their divorce, it became clear that the wife did not understand the meaning of the word "reconcile," even though it was written in her affidavit (F.C.8, January 17, 1997).

In F.C.9 (January 20–24, February 10–11 & February 14, 1997), the wife's conversational English was somewhat limited, and she had difficulty reading English. The husband's barrister indicated at the beginning that he intended to establish that the wife's English was good enough for her to give her evidence in English rather than via an interpreter, which would save time for the court. The judge cut him short, however, pointing out that the court's time was not the issue. If the wife felt more comfortable speaking about the delicate issues in the case through an interpreter, she would be allowed to do so.

In fact, the wife did give most of her evidence in English, with the interpreter limited to translating to her some of the general proceedings, some words and concepts that she needed explained during examination in chief and cross-examination, and conversations between the barristers and judge regarding interjections and objections to particular questions on cross-examination. During examination in chief, the wife's barrister attempted to modify his language so as to ask questions in plain English rather than legalese, though when the questions got too long, the wife looked to the interpreter. When answering in English the wife sometimes spoke very fast, and her accent and grammatical constructions made it difficult to understand what she was saying. During cross-examination, the husband's barrister spoke to the wife very loudly and slowly, as if speaking to a deaf person of limited intelligence. The barrister's success in dispensing with the interpreter backfired, however, as there was clearly a great deal of misunderstanding between him and the wife. Some of her answers were very unclear and it was not evident that she had understood some of the questions, and his attempts to pick fine points and highlight supposed inconsistencies in various documents were doomed to failure, as she could not read the documents in English and his points were quite literally lost in translation. Thus, it was the barrister's effort in attacking the wife's credibility, rather than the wife's own story, that was muted as a result of the language barrier.

In case F.C.11 (February 10–14 & March 3–4, 1997), both parties had interpreters, and the interpreters did translate the whole of the proceedings to the respective parties and acted as the conduit for the parties' evidence. The exception was when the husband, who was self-representing, cross-examined the wife. At this point, the husband and wife conversed together in their own language, and the interpreters translated their conversation for the court. More difficulties arose when the wife was cross-examined by the barrister for the children's representative. The questions he asked were very convoluted, and it was not at all clear that the sense of the questions was being conveyed to the wife, or that her answers were responsive. This was important, as the husband was accusing the wife of child abuse, including sexual interference with their two young sons. The fact that the children's representative was unable to elicit clear evidence from the wife on these factual questions (in a context in which the husband was unrepresented, so the court was relying particularly heavily on the children's representative) could have been detrimental to her case.

This chapter has focused mainly on the structural features of Family Court proceedings that might prevent women from speaking in court about their experiences of violence and having those experiences appropriately heard and responded to. The next chapter focuses on doctrinal and cultural impediments to implementation of the family violence provisions of the Family Law Act.

ENDNOTES

1. Note that the Family Law Act (1975), section 119, abolished the doctrine of interspousal tort immunity. The cross-vesting legislation also enabled de facto property proceedings to be brought in the Family Court concurrently with Family Court proceedings concerning arrangements for children following the breakdown of the relationship (Family Law Council, 1998, p. 41). In addition, some damages claims were brought by children against their father or stepfather in conjunction with property proceedings between their parents. Cases involving tort claims dealt with by the Family Court are discussed in chapter 6.
2. These are now known as "independent children's lawyers," but in the following discussion, I have maintained the terminology as it was at the time of the fieldwork.
3. Note, however, that the court has no power to compel the Legal Aid Commission to provide the requisite funding if it refuses to do so: *Re JJT; ex parte Victoria Legal Aid* (1998). Private parties may be compelled by means of contravention or contempt proceedings, but in practical terms, such action would rarely if ever occur.
4. See now the court's *Family Violence Strategy 2004–2005* (Family Court of Australia, 2004), whose eight Guiding Principles include "1. All who attend the Court...should be safe," and which commits the court to review all court premises and security measures and to "develop and adopt effective and consistent measures to identify and document potential security concerns before and during Court events" (pp. 6, 9).
5. It is notable that the only reference to the need for lawyers to protect clients who are victims of violence in settlement negotiations in the current *Best Practice Guidelines for Lawyers Doing Family Law Work* (Family Law Council & Law Council of Australia, Family Law Section, 2004), is that such clients should not be forced into face-to-face meetings with the other party in the course of "door of the court" settlement discussions. The guidelines do not mention any need to ensure that agreements reached prioritize the safety of the client and the children.
6. See also *T v. N* (2003), in which the trial judge refused to make the consent orders presented by the parties, which provided for the father to have unsupervised contact with the child, on the basis that they posed an unacceptable risk to the welfare of the child, due to the evidence of the father's violence towards one of the children.

Chapter 6

Family Law, Legal Culture, and Domestic Violence

The Legislation and Case Law Relating to Domestic Violence

Unlike the Crimes (Family Violence) Act (1987), the Family Law Act (1975) was the subject of frequent appeals to the Full Court of the Family Court, and occasionally to the High Court of Australia. An extensive jurisprudence had been established around the Act, which needs to be considered alongside the legislative provisions. This section gives an account of the legislation and jurisprudence prior to the Family Law Reform Act (1995), the changes introduced by the Reform Act, and their interpretation by lawyers and judges.

Children's Matters Before the Family Law Reform Act

The Influence of "No-Fault"

As originally enacted, the Family Law Act (1975) simply specified that "[i]n proceedings with respect to the custody or guardianship of, or access to, a child, the court shall regard the welfare of the child as the paramount consideration" (s. 64(1)(a)). The Act was amended in 1983 and again in 1991 to specify a list of factors that the court was required to take into account in determining the welfare of the child, including "the need to protect the child from abuse, ill treatment, or exposure or subjection to behaviour which psychologically harms the child" (s. 64(1)(bb)(va)). The 1991 amendment was accompanied by a new Division 12A in Part VII of the Act, which made special provision for cases involving allegations of child abuse, including provision for the involvement of child welfare authorities in such cases.

But while direct abuse of a child by a parent was clearly considered relevant to the welfare of the child, the court refused to entertain allegations of abuse of one parent by the other parent, on the basis that any such consideration of marital conduct would involve a reintroduction of "fault" in divorce by another guise (Nicholson, 1995, p. 2). Graycar (1995) argued,

> The no-fault philosophy...permeated so deeply that instead of being seen as a change in the way we deal with divorce—a progressive response to the bad old days when proof of adultery, desertion, cruelty, etc were required before people were allowed to end their relationships—it...[came] to be seen as the central tenet of all issues involved in family law. (p. 66)

Thus, in a string of early cases under the Family Law Act (1975), the court excluded evidence about the husband's violence towards the wife, refused to take that evidence into account, or refused to make findings about the existence of spousal violence in determining the question of custody and access, on the basis that the only relevant conduct was that relating to a party's parenting capacity (e.g., *In the Marriage of Chandler*, 1981; *In the Marriage of Heidt*, 1976; *In the Marriage of Lythow*, 1976; *In the Marriage of Schenck*, 1981; *In the Marriage of Smythe*, 1983; see also ALRC, 1994, pp. 174–175; Graycar, 1995, pp. 62–63; Murray, 1995, pp. 36–37; Parkinson, 1995, pp. 41–42). These decisions rested on two assumptions noted in chapter 2: first, that men's behavior as husbands bore no relation to their behavior as fathers, and second, that children were unaffected by violence occurring between the adults in their household.

The Emerging Jurisprudence of the Early to Mid-1990s

Assumptions about the irrelevance of domestic violence in children's matters began to be questioned in the 1994 case of *Jaeger*. In that case, the trial judge had excluded evidence sought to be submitted on behalf of the husband that the wife had suffered serious domestic violence at the hands of her new partner. The wife and her partner denied the existence of violence. The husband wanted to argue that the wife should not be awarded custody because of the violence occurring in her new home, but the judge stated that he was "not really interested in whether the home is a peaceful haven or…a bit rougher than that." The Full Court overturned the decision on the basis that the evidence should have been admitted, but did not give specific reasons as to why it thought the evidence of violence was relevant to the welfare of the child. It is ironic that this "breakthrough" case was one in which the victim of violence did not wish to speak about the violence, but rather the fact of her victimization was being used against her in an attempt to remove the child from her care.

Subsequent cases began to spell out how evidence of violence in the parents' relationship was relevant to the welfare of the child. For example, children were likely to be frightened and distressed if they witnessed violence against their mother, which went to the question of the perpetrator's fitness as a parent. Further, even if the children were not directly exposed to the violence, a history of violence and consequent fear of the perpetrator could impact on the survivor's parenting capacity if she was compelled to maintain contact with the perpetrator, with a resulting impact on the children (e.g., *JG and BG*, 1994; *In the Marriage of Grant*, 1994). Moreover, a father's violent behavior went to the issues of his suitability as a role model for the children, and his capacity to promote the children's relationship with their mother and to contribute positively to their development (*In the Marriage of Patsalou*, 1995, p. 429).

Yet, as various commentators noted, these decisions did not go very far. They did not fully respond to the growing research evidence about the impact on children of domestic violence (ALRC, 1994, pp. 175–176; Parkinson, 1995). There was still a tendency to discount a history of violence in the belief that custody and access in the future would be unaffected by violence once the parties had separated (Parkinson, 1995, p. 43; Women's Coalition Against Family Violence, 1994, p. 91). Moreover, the court's well-known views on the irrelevance of domestic violence had resulted in practitioners being reluctant to raise issues of violence in evidence (Nicholson, 1995, p. 2). And when women did attempt to introduce such issues, they found their credibility attacked by lawyers, Family Court counsellors, and judges, who tended to suspect women of ulterior motives (attempting to deny access to the father out of vindictiveness) or to believe that the violence could not have been as bad as women claimed, otherwise they would have left the relationship long before they did (ALRC, 1994, p. 171; Graycar, 1995, pp. 58–59, 65–66; Nicholson, 1995, p. 2). In other words, many of the nonfeminist understandings of domestic violence identified previously were deployed to minimize the impact of violence in Family Court proceedings relating to children.

The ALRC held an inquiry into equality before the law for women in 1993–1994, as part of the federal government's New National Agenda for Women. Among other things, it received many submissions expressing concern about the Family Court's approach to domestic violence, and its report recommended amendments to the Family Law Act (1975) to make express reference to domestic violence as a factor affecting the welfare of the child (ALRC, 1994, chap. 9, pp. 181, 187; see also Graycar, 1995). A national feminist lobby group, the Women's Justice Coalition, was formed to promote the implementation of the recommendations in the ALRC's report on equality before the law, and its efforts and those of the National Network of Women's Legal Services resulted in the inclusion of the violence provisions in the Family Law Reform Act (1995).

Children's Matters After the Family Law Reform Act

The Legislative Amendments

The new Part VII of the Family Law Act (1975) introduced by the Family Law Reform Act (1995) continued to specify that "[i]n deciding whether to make a particular parenting order in relation to a child, a court must regard the best interests of the child as the paramount consideration" (s. 65E). However, the list of factors to be considered by the court in determining what was in the child's best interests was expanded to include

(g) the need to protect the child from physical or psychological harm caused, or that may be caused, by:

  (i) being subjected or exposed to abuse, ill-treatment, violence or other behaviour; or
  (ii) being directly or indirectly exposed to abuse, ill-treatment, violence or other behaviour that is directed towards, or may affect, another person;

(i) any family violence involving the child or a member of the child's family;
(j) any family violence order that applies to the child or a member of the child's family. (s. 68F(2))

"Family violence" was defined to mean

> conduct, whether actual or threatened, by a person towards, or towards the property of, a member of the person's family that causes that or any other member of the person's family to fear for, or to be apprehensive about, his or her personal well being or safety. (s. 60D(1))

Thus, the definition of family violence, unlike that in the Crimes (Family Violence) Act (1987), did not focus on particular types of actions by the perpetrator (incidents or threats of physical violence or property damage), but rather concentrated on the effect of the perpetrator's behavior on family members—putting them in fear for their personal well being or safety, however caused.

A "family violence order" was defined to mean a domestic violence protection order issued by a State court, however named. The new Part VII further required parties to proceedings concerning children in the Family Court to inform the court of any family violence order applying to those children (s. 68J). And in all children's cases,

> In considering what order to make, the court must, to the extent that it is possible to do so consistently with the child's best interests being the paramount consideration, ensure that the order:
>
> (a) is consistent with any family violence order; and
> (b) does not expose a person to an unacceptable risk of family violence. (s. 68K(1))

In order to ensure that no person was exposed to an unacceptable risk of family violence, the court was also empowered to include in the order any safeguards that it considered necessary for the safety of those affected by the order (s. 68K(2)). Significantly, this section directed attention not just to the child's need for safety and protection from family violence, but also to the need to protect and ensure the safety of other persons, including—presumably—mothers who had been targets of violence.

The violence provisions were not the only amendments made by the Family Law Reform Act (1995), however, and other amendments were not necessarily consistent with them. Chief among these new provisions was section 60B(2), which set out for the first time the principles underlying Part VII of the Act. Section 60B(2) stated that

> ...except when it is or would be contrary to the child's best interests:
>
> (a) children have the right to know and be cared for by both their parents...; and
> (b) children have a right of contact, on a regular basis, with both their parents and with other people significant to their care, welfare and development; and
> (c) parents share duties and responsibilities concerning the care, welfare and development of their children; and
> (d) parents should agree about the future parenting of their children.

The children's "rights" set out in section 60B(2) were derived from the United Nations Convention on the Rights of the Child (1989)

(UNCROC, arts. 7.1, 9.3, 18.1); however, as Behrens has pointed out, the rights included were selective. There was no mention, for example, of a child's right to protection from physical or mental violence, injury, or abuse while in the care of their parent(s) (UNCROC, art. 19.1; Behrens, 1996, p. 44). Rhoades (2000) has also observed that the notion of a child's right of contact with both parents was

> not supported by any uncontested research. The studies of this issue had established that a number of interacting variables, rather than contact per se, affect children's long term adjustment, and that poverty and parental conflict are more significant predictors of negative outcomes for children than loss of contact. (p. 151)

The principles of ongoing shared responsibility for and care of children by both parents after separation, and the child's right of regular contact with both parents, clearly had the potential to conflict with—and to override—the need to protect children from being exposed to family violence, and certainly to override any concern to protect a parent who had been subjected to violence from ongoing contact with their abusive former partner (see, e.g., Behrens, 1996; Troup, 1995). While the introductory words in section 60B(2) did suggest that giving effect to the principles might sometimes be contrary to the child's best interests, the overall structure and force of section 60B suggested that, at least in the vast majority of cases, giving effect to the principles would *by definition* be in the best interests of the child.

Post–Reform Act Case Law and Legal Culture

The relationship between sections 60B, 65E (best interests of the child as the paramount consideration) and 68F (factors the court must take into account), and how they were to be applied in practice, was examined in a series of cases concerning the issue of relocation—that is, where the parent with residence of the child proposed to relocate a significant distance away from the contact parent. In the first of these cases, *B and B* (1997), it was argued that the principles in section 60B(2) represented a fundamental change in the law and required the court to take a new approach to relocation cases in order to give effect to the principle of the child's right of regular contact with both parents. The Full Court noted, however, that the best interests of the child remained the paramount consideration and needed to be determined in the circumstances of each case. In determining the best interests of the child, the Full Court and subsequently the High Court held that a trial judge should consider all relevant factors stated in section 68F(2), section 60B(2), and elsewhere in the Act (*B and B*, 1997, pp. 733–774; *U v. U*, 2002, p. 260). In other words, the courts placed sections 60B(2) and 68F(2) alongside each other, rather than according a primary or "trumping" role to section 60B(2) in the determination of the child's best interests.

Several empirical studies on the implementation of the Family Law Reform Act (1995) demonstrated, however, that regardless of these decisions, the section 60B(2) principles in practice came to dominate the approach taken to children's matters after the Reform Act, resulting in the development of a "pro contact [legal] culture," to which the issue of domestic violence and the family violence provisions of Part VII were firmly subordinated (e.g., Armstrong, 2001; Dewar & Parker, 1999, p. 104; Dick, 1998; Kaspiew, 2005, pp. 112–113; Kaye et al., 2003, pp. 101–105; Rhoades, 2000, p. 158; Rhoades et al., 2000).[1] Thus, for example, lawyers gave greater priority than previously to maintaining contact between children and their nonresident parents in accordance with section 60B(2) (Dewar & Parker, 1999, p. 102), and advised their clients who had escaped violent relationships that it would be very difficult or impossible to prevent or even restrict their former partner's contact with the children (Kaye et al., 2003, pp. 74, 106; Rendell et al., 2000, p. 79; Rhoades, 2000, p. 145; Rhoades et al., 2000, pp. 72, 74). Fathers were more likely to seek equal time with their children and to insist on contact even if they had a history of violence (Rhoades et al., 2000, pp. 39, 44, 71). Judges were more reluctant to suspend contact, and the number of interim orders made by the court providing for no contact with the father declined dramatically (Dewar & Parker, 1999, p. 103; Rhoades et al., 2000, pp. 47, 70, 79), while interim orders for unsupervised contact in cases involving allegations of violence increased (Rhoades et al., 2000, pp. 47, 70, 79). And it became more difficult for resident mothers to relocate away from the vicinity of the father's home (Dewar & Parker, 1999, p. 103; Rhoades et al., 2000, pp. 86–87). Indeed, Dewar and Parker (1999) referred to the "reverse effect" of *B and B* (1997): while the court refused to give paramount consideration to section 60B(2) in relocation cases, the practical effect of the Reform Act was that nonresident parents were more likely to contest their former partner's plans to relocate, and resident parents were advised by their lawyers that they must accept restrictions on their freedom of movement in order to ensure the maintenance of contact between their children and the other parent (p. 103). More generally, solicitors interviewed by Rhoades et al. (2000) expressed the view that in children's cases involving allegations of domestic violence, the right to contact principle had turned the clock back to the position prior to the mid-1990s case law on family violence, when allegations of violence were considered irrelevant and ignored (p. 74).

There has, in fact, been very little reported case law following the Family Law Reform Act (1995) specifically considering the provisions relating to family violence in sections 68F(2) and 68K. The two leading post–Reform Act cases involving family violence are *In the marriage of Blanch* (1998) and *T v. S* (2001); however, both of these cases concerned the failure to apply section 68F(2)(g) or (i), and section 68K due to the trial judge's failure properly to consider the mother's evidence of the violence to which she had been subjected. In both cases, the matter was remitted for rehearing. The empirical studies suggest, however, that where family violence was found, it was only in exceptional cases that it would result in suspension of contact, and could be accorded very little weight overall (Kaspiew, 2005, pp. 114, 122–123, 132, 136, 143; Rhoades et al., 2000, p. 74).[2] For example, according to Rhoades et al. (2000), "In some instances, orders for unsupervised contact were made because of assumptions about the long-term benefits of contact to the child's welfare, and that this outweighed the present detrimental effects of the father's violent behaviour" (p. 81).

Similarly, writing in a practitioner journal in 1998, Altobelli agreed with the extracurial views of one of the Family Court judges that domestic violence should be considered a *relevant*, but not the *prevalent*, consideration in children's matters (pp. 8–10). Thus, there was a need to consider first whether violence was relevant to the orders sought, and to avoid making allegations in affidavit material that "unnecessarily inflame the litigation" (p. 8). In Altobelli's opinion, for example, violence would be less relevant in contact than in residence disputes, and would have little impact on very young children.[3] If violence could be shown to be relevant, then there was the question of the weight or significance that should be given to that factor as opposed to all of the other section 68F(2) factors, recalling that "[t]he court has, at the back of its mind, a concern not to unnecessarily interfere with the relationship between the child and the perpetrator of violence" (p. 10). This approach clearly did not accord with feminist understandings of domestic violence and contrasted sharply with the "best practice" position advocated by Jaffe et al. (2003) that domestic violence should be considered not just "relevant" but "it should be a fundamental consideration in determining the best interests of the child postseparation" (p. 29). Jaffe et al. argue that in family law disputes involving allegations of domestic violence, the central issue, issues for assessment, focus of the court hearing, planning for the future, and resources required should be quite different from those in disputes that do not involve such allegations. Thus, for example, the central issue in children's matters not involving violence is the promotion of the child's relationship with the nonresidence parent, while the central issue in disputes that do involve domestic violence allegations must be the safety of the mother and children (p. 52).

Property Matters

Property Division Under the Family Law Act

There is no presumption in the Family Law Act (1975) that property acquired during the marriage will be divided equally between the parties. Rather, the Act establishes a discretionary regime, enabling the court to make such orders as it thinks fit, altering the interests of the parties in the total property pool held between them. The Act specifies factors in section 79(4) for the court to take into account in determining whether—and if so, what—orders should be made. These include (a) parties' financial contributions to the acquisition, conservation, or improvement of any property during the marriage; (b) parties' nonfinancial contributions to the acquisition, conservation, or improvement of any property during the marriage; (c) parties' contributions to the welfare of the family, including any contribution made in the capacity of homemaker or parent; and (e) the matters referred to in subsection 75(2) so far as they are relevant. While section 79(4) focuses on past contributions to property and family welfare, section 75(2) focuses on future needs. The specified factors include (a) the parties' age and state of health; (b) the parties' income, property, and financial resources, and their capacity for gainful employment; (c) parties' responsibilities for the care and control of minor children; (e) other support responsibilities; (k) the duration of the marriage and its effect on parties' earning capacities; (l) "the need to protect a party who wishes to continue that party's role as a parent"; (m) the financial circumstances relating to either party's cohabitation with another person; and (o) "any fact or circumstance which, in the opinion of the court, the justice of the case requires to be taken into account."

As was the case with children's matters, the Family Court moved quickly to assert the no-fault principle and to exclude consideration of marital conduct in property proceedings. Initially, the court clarified that section 75(2)(o) did not provide an avenue for the introduction of evidence about violence in the marriage. Rather, the paragraph had to be read consistently with the rest of section 75(2), so that "any fact or circumstance" referred only to facts or circumstances having an economic significance (*In the Marriage of Ferguson*, 1978; *In the Marriage of Soblusky*, 1976). The court conceded that matrimonial "fault" might be relevant under section 79(4), to the extent that the behavior of a party had resulted in the value of the parties' property being diminished or destroyed; however, the objective in such a (rare) case was not to punish a party's behavior or to revive claims for compensation for marital misconduct, but to assess the parties' relative contributions as part of determining what order to make for property division (*In the Marriage of Ferguson*, 1978; *In the Marriage of Mead*, 1983; *In the Marriage of*

Sheedy, 1979). Likewise, under section 75(2), allegations of violence would have to be tied to specific financial needs that were alleged to have arisen as a result of the violence, and in such a case, it was the needs themselves that were relevant, not their cause (*In the Marriage of Fisher*, 1990).

In an influential 1993 article, Juliet Behrens argued that domestic violence by a husband towards his wife ought to be analysed as a negative contribution to the welfare of the family under section 79(4)(c). This reasoning was implicitly approved by the Full Court in *Doherty* (1996), but in the subsequent case of *Kennon* (1997), a majority of the Full Court preferred to express the issue not in terms of negative contributions by the abuser, but in terms of the victim's contributions to the marriage having been made "significantly more arduous than they ought to have been" as a result of the abuse (p. 24). The court in that case also expressed concern about opening the floodgates to allegations about marital conduct, and stressed that the notion of more arduous contributions should only be applied in "exceptional cases" or in the "relatively narrow band of cases" in which one party's conduct in the course of the marriage had had a "discernible impact" on the other party's contributions (p. 24).

The Full Court's insistence in *Kennon* (1997) on the exceptionality of domestic violence cases in which property contributions could be considered to have been affected does appear to have limited the scope for arguments about the relevance of domestic violence in property matters. Reviews of Family Court property judgments in the years following *Doherty* (1996) and *Kennon* (1997) found only a very small proportion involving claims of negative or more arduous contributions by reason of the husband's violence, and even fewer that were successful (Dessau, 2000; Middleton, 2001, p. 259). Claims failed because the allegations of violence were not linked to contributions, there was insufficient evidence of domestic violence in the marriage, or the violence established was not sufficiently serious to satisfy the more onerous contributions test (Middleton, 2001, pp. 234–236). Successful claims tended to involve "longstanding and significant" abuse, almost invariably including physical violence (Middleton, 2001, p. 236). Moreover, even when arguments about domestic violence were accepted, they had little impact on the overall outcome of the property division (Dessau, 2000; Middleton, 2001, p. 243).

Given the limitations of the jurisprudence on domestic violence in property cases, the Family Law Council recommended in 2001 that both sections 79(4) and 75(2) of the Family Law Act (1975) be amended to direct courts to have regard to the effects of family violence on the contributions and future needs of both parties,[4] in order to clarify the law, overcome the restrictions imposed by *Kennon* (1997), and provide women who had been targets of violence with an extra bargaining chip in settlement processes. This advice was the result of a long-running consultation by the Family Law Council about violence and the Family Law Act, commenced in the mid-1990s under the previous federal government (see, e.g., Family Law Council, 1998, p. 8). By the time the advice was provided, however, there was a new federal government whose family law policy agenda did not prioritize domestic violence. Consequently, the advice was never implemented.

Tort Claims Under the Cross-Vesting Legislation

In the 1980 case of *Hack*, the husband had injured his wife so severely as to render her a quadriplegic. The trial judge awarded maintenance to the wife, but refused to increase the share of the property awarded to her above 50%, on the basis that her cause of action for damages against the husband was still alive and could be pursued in the State courts. Bringing tort proceedings in a State District or Supreme Court, however, can be a costly and time-consuming exercise, and is not one contemplated by many survivors of domestic violence (Behrens, 1995, p. 74).

As noted in the previous chapter, the advent of the Jurisdiction of Courts (Cross-vesting) Act (1987) opened the possibility for tort claims for damages to be run in conjunction with Family Court property proceedings. The first reported case to pursue this option was *Marsh v. Marsh* (1993). The trial judge found on the balance of probabilities that the husband had assaulted and beaten the wife. Although she suffered no economic loss, he awarded her $2,000 general damages, $3,000 exemplary damages, and $2,000 aggravated damages. The husband was ordered to pay the damages from his share of the property division.

Cross-vested claims for damages, however, were no panacea for victims of domestic violence in Family Court proceedings, and no substitute for the court taking violence into account more directly in making decisions about property division. For example, tort claims relied on the existence of at least one reasonably serious physical assault in order for the plaintiff to succeed and to obtain more than trivial damages. Compensation could not be awarded for emotional distress or economic abuse alone (Family Law Council, 1998, p. 46). Tort claims also focused on an individual incident or incidents, which had to be separately identified and proved, and did not "adequately capture the dynamic of ongoing domestic violence" (Behrens, 1995, p. 75; see also *In the Marriage of Kennon*, 1997, pp. 8, 60). Such claims were also fruitless where the limitation period had expired (Behrens & Bolas, 1997; Family Law Council, 1998, p. 46), where there was little or no matrimonial property available for distribution (Gordon Clark, 1997), or where the potential plaintiff could not afford the legal representation required to handle a combined property and tort case in a context in which legal aid was not available for such proceedings.[5] Moreover, claims could only be brought if the parties had been married, unless there were concurrent proceedings involving ex-nuptial children (Family Law Council, 1998, p. 41). And there were also problems with the relationship between the two proceedings, including the impact of the damages award on the assessment of the wife's future needs (Family Law Council, 1998, pp. 43–44).

In *Kennon* (1997) the Full Court also made clear its distaste for cross-vested damages claims. Fogarty and Lindenmayer JJ referred to the court's traditional reluctance to deal with issues of matrimonial fault and stated that "[t]here is not, we think, any legitimate basis for concluding that the Family Court is uniquely suited to the adjudication of domestic violence damages claims" (p. 11), while Baker J thought it preferable that issues of domestic violence be considered as part of the assessment of contributions under section 79(4), rather than in pursuit of damages claims in cross-vested proceedings (p. 67). The court also made it clear that it would not automatically entertain such claims, but would decide in each case whether it should do so or whether the matter should be transferred to a State court (pp. 9, 12).[6] Thus, even before the brief period of cross-vested claims came to an end with the invalidation of the cross-vesting legislation, the Family Court had already moved to discourage the bringing of claims for damages for domestic violence in conjunction with property proceedings.

Competing Understandings of Domestic Violence

At the time of the fieldwork for this study, in 1996–1997, family law in Australia relating to domestic violence was undergoing a paradigm shift. For that brief period, rather than there being a clear and widely accepted doctrinal approach to violence, a range of competing positions contended for domination. The legacy of the "no-fault" approach still held considerable sway. This was challenged by the rather weak, early to mid-1990s jurisprudence on the relevance of violence in children's and property cases, supported by feminist academic writing and by the feminist-inspired family violence provisions of the Family Law Reform Act (1995). At the same time, the "right to contact" provisions of the Family Law Reform Act had also been introduced, and there was considerable uncertainty as to whether the provisions relating to violence or those relating to the child's right of contact would prevail. The cases observed as part of the fieldwork had generally been initiated prior to the passage of the Reform Act, but were being decided in a post–Reform Act but pre–*B and B* (1997) and pre-*Kennon* (1997) environment. This was a state of relative sympathy to arguments about the impact of domestic violence (perhaps, indeed, the high point of such sympathy in the Family Court's history; see, e.g., Rhoades, 2002, p. 82), but it was also a state of relative uncertainty and unpredictability.

Family Lawyers' Understandings of Domestic Violence

The discussion in the previous chapter concerning waiting at court and consent orders highlights the crucial role played by legal representatives in either prioritizing the safety of clients whose former partners had been violent towards them, or failing to do so. Solicitors also determined the legal framing of applications or responses and the extent to which a history of violence in the parties' relationship would be incorporated into their client's claims. Thus, long before the matter came to court for a hearing, lawyers acted as arbiters of violence in their clients' cases. If the case did reach a hearing, counsel would almost always be briefed to conduct door-of-the-court settlement negotiations and/or to run the hearing, which introduced a second arbiter into the proceedings (B.1, interview, October 17, 1997).

In line with the development of family law doctrine at the time, interviewees generally considered that while there was a growing level of awareness and understanding of the issue of domestic violence amongst family lawyers, there was still some way to go in this regard. For example, one solicitor thought that while there was a high level of understanding of violence among lawyers working in community legal services, this was not reflected in large city firms, where the issue was less likely to be discussed, and hence lawyers lacked experience in dealing with it (J. Peirce, interview, August 21, 1997). Another solicitor noted cases in which practitioners had failed to see evidence of violence as significant and had consequently recommended joint counseling, round table conferences, and continued, unrestricted contact between children and abusive fathers (S.1, interview, January 16, 1997; see also Dewar & Parker, 1999, p. 105). Two barristers pointed out that they and other lawyers had received no formal training in relation to domestic violence. They had learned variously from hearing experts in court, reading professional literature, a background in another discipline, and life experience (B.1, interview, October 17, 1997; B. Phelan, interview, October 29, 1997). One barrister noted that lawyers were trained in logic, clear thinking, and rationality, and since domestic violence did not fit that paradigm, their initial response was to disbelieve or disregard women's stories of violence (B.1, interview, October 17, 1997; see also Kaye et al., 2003, p. 41; Rendell et al., 2000, p. 80; Valente, 1995, p. 190). She thought there was a need for seminars and lectures to inform lawyers of issues such as the ongoing fear experienced by women who had been targets of violence, and she also considered that reported cases dealing with violence could be very educational, with the court's jurisprudence in this area building up over time (B.1, interview, October 17, 1997).

The Relevance of Violence

All 10 of the family law solicitors interviewed listed various ways in which they believed violence to be relevant in making family law applications; however, in explaining when and how violence would be relevant, their responses varied considerably. In relation to children's matters, 2 solicitors simply said that violence was always relevant (B.2, interview, October 22, 1997, recounting her practice as a solicitor before going to the Bar; J. Peirce, interview, August 21, 1997). Three thought that a history of violence gave an indication of the parties' respective parenting skills and abilities, and of who should be the preferred residence parent (D. Dawson, interview, June 5, 1996; M. Mann, interview, March 8, 1996; J. Trickey, interview, March 20, 1996), while 4 focused on the question of whether the children had actually witnessed or been exposed to physical or verbal violence or intimidation perpetrated by one of their parents against the other, in which case this would have an impact on the residence and contact arrangements proposed (K. Anderson, interview, March 8, 1996; M. Lee, interview, June 3, 1996; S. Macgregor, interview, March 1, 1996; S.2, interview, October 28, 1997). Three thought that a history of violence ought to result in contact (or contact handover) being supervised (B.2, interview, October 22, 1997; M. Mann, interview, March 8, 1996; J. Trickey, interview, March 20, 1996), but only 3 considered that violence should raise the question of whether the father should have any contact at all (B.2, interview, October 22, 1997; M. Lee, interview, June 3, 1996; S.1, interview, January 16, 1997).

Eight of the 10 solicitors also thought violence was relevant in property matters, although only 5 of these explained the relevance of violence under the Family Law Act (1975), either in constituting a "negative contribution" on the part of the perpetrator (B.2, interview, October 22, 1997; D. Dawson, interview, June 5, 1996; S.2, interview,

October 28, 1997), or in increasing the future needs of the victim of violence because of the long-term physical and/or psychological effects of the violence (M. Lee, interview, June 3, 1996; M. Mann, interview, March 8, 1996). Five mentioned the possibility of a cross-vested claim for damages (K. Anderson, interview, March 8, 1996; B.2, interview, October 22, 1997; S. Macgregor, interview, March 1, 1996; S.1, interview, January 16, 1997; S.2, interview, October 28, 1997), although they also noted that there had to be a large enough property pool to make such a claim worthwhile, and 2 further observed that the property pool would have to be large enough to cover the client's legal costs, since legal aid would not fund damages claims (K. Anderson, interview, March 8, 1996; S.1, interview, January 16, 1997). Two noted that although claims for damages were usually made in respect of physical violence and physical injuries, they had also commenced cases based on long-term psychological damage but were unsure how these would turn out (S.1, interview, January 16, 1997; S.2, interview, October 28, 1997). At least one solicitor confessed herself to be rather daunted by the prospect of drawing up pleadings in a damages claim, including particularizing assaults and quantifying damages, since this was not her area of expertise, though she was investigating how to go about it (K. Anderson, interview, March 8, 1996).

Four solicitors expressed the view that the passage of the Family Law Reform Act (1995) would ensure that the issue of domestic violence would receive greater recognition (B.2, interview, October 22, 1997; D. Dawson, interview, June 5, 1996; M. Lee, interview, June 3, 1996; J. Trickey, interview, March 20, 1996). In the words of one, now that violence was listed in section 68F(2) as a specific factor to be taken into account in children's matters, it had been transformed from being simply part of the historical picture of the relationship to being something that could be addressed directly under the rubric of the best interests of the child (J. Trickey, interview, March 20, 1996). Another was convinced that the Reform Act's emphasis on domestic violence in relation to children would flow over into the disposition of property matters as well (M. Lee, interview, June 3, 1996).

Only 2 solicitors mentioned the effects of violence in the solicitor-client relationship. One said that it was very important to know about any history of violence, as she would then have a better understanding of where the client was coming from in making decisions about her children and property (S.1, interview, January 16, 1997). The other said that a history of violence would inform how he dealt with the client and with the other side. If the client was cowed, intimidated, and/or was unable to give clear instructions, he would try to advocate for her, carry and encourage her more than usual, and push for her entitlements (S.2, interview, October 28, 1997).

Asking About Violence

If violence was understood to be relevant for one reason or another, to what extent did solicitors actually ask their clients about a history of violence? Jaffe et al. (2003) have referred to the general "don't ask, don't tell" attitude towards domestic violence in the community and among professionals (p. 38). On the other hand, numerous commentators have argued that lawyers should always ask clients about any history of violence in order to understand fully the client's position and provide proper representation that focuses on ensuring the client's safety (e.g., Bala, 1996, p. 238; Buehl, 1999, p. 725; Dalton, 1997, pp. 367–370; Jaffe et al., 2003, p. 41; Valente, 1995, p. 192; Waits, 1995, pp. 1030–1031, 1042).

The solicitors interviewed placed themselves on a wide spectrum from always waiting for the client to volunteer the information (J. Trickey, interview, March 20, 1996), to always asking about violence directly in the first interview (S.1, interview, January 16, 1997). Those who were hesitant about asking tended to look for cues and use them as a basis for specific questioning (K. Anderson, interview, March 8, 1996; B.2, interview, October 22, 1997; D. Dawson, interview, June 5, 1996; S. Macgregor, interview, March 1, 1996; M. Mann, interview, March 8, 1996), and to express concern for the client's privacy (S. Macgregor, interview, March 1, 1996). One said that if the client did not offer information about violence, whether or not she asked depended on the dynamics established between herself and the client—and she was aware of a few cases where women had not told her about violence, though she had known of their background from other sources (M. Lee, interview, June 3, 1996).

Three solicitors said they would routinely ask if the information was not volunteered and the case concerned children (D. Dawson, interview, June 5, 1996; J. Peirce, interview, August 21, 1997; S.2, interview, October 28, 1997). Only one had a clearly established practice of, and rationale for, always asking about violence (S.1, interview, January 16, 1997). In doing so, she said that she always explained what she meant by "violence"—including physical and nonphysical abuse and intimidation—since different women would have different cultural understandings of violence (see also Jaffe et al., 2003, p. 38). She was also aware that women from different cultural backgrounds might find it easier or more difficult to speak about their experiences of violence, so her practice of always asking and establishing a relationship of trust and respect with the client helped to overcome these barriers. At least one of the women interviewed appears to have had such a relationship with the lawyer who initially represented her in her case, as she described her lawyer as very useful and very good, and as someone she could really talk to (W.L.2, interview, December 18, 1997). By contrast, the majority of women interviewed by Kaye et al. (2003) had found it very difficult to talk to professionals about the violence they had experienced, partly because they were not given the opportunity to do so, and partly because responses tended to be uninterested or disbelieving (p. 41).[7]

Responding to Violence

The evidence from solicitors, and from the files in which a high proportion of cases scheduled for hearing included affidavits containing allegations of violence, suggests that solicitors frequently did hear stories of violence from their clients, and that some would also ask about violence if the information was not volunteered. But how solicitors reacted to that information also appears to have varied widely—particularly in relation to the extent to which they considered it to be relevant to the issues in the case (as mere "background," or actually material), and, as discussed in the previous chapter, how they conducted negotiations and the extent to which they were concerned for the client's safety.

The way in which barristers responded to clients' stories of violence raised the same issues, but also some additional ones by virtue of their advocacy role. This was manifested in the content and nature of their presentation of evidence and argument in court on the client's behalf, and in their "gamesmanship" and interactions with the other side. In one case observed, for example, the wife had been subjected to a long series of incidents of physical and emotional abuse by a dominating, alcoholic husband, each relatively minor in themselves but cumulatively having a significant impact on the wife's physical and mental health. The wife's barrister, however, failed to build up a compelling account of the overall effect of the husband's power and control tactics, and so the wife came across as unreliable and irrational rather than as someone responding to prolonged harassment and undermining of her self-esteem (F.C.2, June 25–26, 1996). In another case, in which the mother was in a very fragile emotional state, her (older, male) barrister got impatient and cross with her—possibly because she was so "wet," or possibly deliberately to make her cry, but either way he intensified her suffering. In a context in which the mother was arguing that she was so fearful of the father that he should have no contact with their child, the barrister also completely failed to understand her fear of being directly cross-examined by the father, who was unrepresented, and would have allowed the case to proceed as normal had not the judge intervened to protect the mother (F.C.3, July 15–18 & 23, 1996).

In the same case, the barrister's single strategy in relation to the self-represented father was to be fairly aggressive towards him. By contrast, in two other cases, the wife's barrister (both female) through her behavior presented a sharp counterpoint to the behavior of the unrepresented husband, which operated very much to the benefit of her client. In one of these cases, the barrister was quiet, calm, and measured, almost understated, while the husband was blustering and belligerent (F.C.5, December 2–6, 1996). In the other, while the husband was utterly fixated on his point of view but clearly struggled with the procedure and presented his case in a chaotic fashion, the wife's barrister was very organized, concise, and helpful to the judge (F.C.11, February 10–14 & March 3–4, 1997). In both cases, the contrast between the styles of the husband and the wife's barrister made the allegations about the husband's violence more believable.

A barrister could also engage in symbolic action outside the courtroom. For example, one of the barristers interviewed said that, if possible (and depending on how terrified her client was), she would confront the husband and his advisers in the public waiting area, raise her voice, and engage in a bit of grandstanding. Her clients found this very affirming, as they saw that a woman could stand up to the man who had been bullying them. She conceded, however, that it could be exhausting at times "being the carer as well as the advocate"—raising clients' consciousness about violence, bolstering and encouraging them, and referring them to other sources of support and assistance (B. Phelan, interview, October 29, 1997).

Thus, unsurprisingly, lawyers' own views and practices in relation to clients who had been subjected to violence mirrored the spectrum of doctrinal approaches to violence available, although, in some cases, they were considerably in advance of the doctrinal high point. Unless women were referred to a lawyer by a refuge, domestic violence outreach service, or other feminist organisation, it was a matter of luck whether the lawyer they chose held to feminist or nonfeminist understandings of domestic violence, and likewise in relation to the barrister chosen by their lawyer. But clearly, other players apart from legal representatives inhabited the family law system, and their understandings of violence also had an important impact on proceedings.

CHILDREN'S REPRESENTATIVES, CHILD EXPERTS, AND FAMILY REPORTS

In cases in which a child's representative was appointed, the views of the child's representative and of the expert who wrote the Family Report were very influential in determining the outcome of the case

(B.2, interview, October 22, 1997; J. Trickey, interview, March 20, 1996; see also "Developments in the Law," 1993, p. 1599; Lapidus, 1998; Shalleck, 1995; Mahoney, 1991, p. 47). This is not to say that the proposals put forward by the child's representative were invariably adopted, but rather that the expert and the child's representative were considered by virtue of their structural position to be more focused on the best interests of the child than were either of the parties (see also Berns, 2000, p. 6; Fineman, 1988). Thus, in effect, if the wife/mother wanted to make an argument about the impact of violence on the welfare of the children, she had to get the Family Report writer and the children's representative on her side, and it would be very difficult for her to succeed if they did not support her.

In only one of the cases observed did the wife succeed against the recommendations of the children's representative (F.C.1, June 20–21 & 24, 1996). In this case, the wife wished to relocate from a country town to Melbourne, with the children, in order to increase her employment prospects. In the country town, the children resided with the mother, but the father enjoyed extensive contact with them. The child psychologist who had written the Family Report favored shared parenting, which he believed, contrary to conventional wisdom, could be sustained even in cases involving a high degree of hostility between the parents (cf. Johnston, 1995, p. 21; Rhoades, 2000, p. 145; Rhoades et al., 2000, p. 44; Zorza, 1996, pp. 1123–1124). However, he conceded that a shared arrangement in either the country town or in Melbourne would be equally appropriate. The children's representative submitted that the mother should be restrained from relocating in order to maintain the current arrangements. However the judge was persuaded that there was a compelling economic argument for the wife to relocate, and made orders accordingly.[8]

Conversely, in only one case did the children's representative support the wife's position, but the judge decided against her (F.C.2, June 25–26, 1996). In the other 5 children's matters that went to hearing, the children's representative and/or the child expert supported the wife/mother, and the judge decided in her favor (F.C.3, July 15–18 & 23,

1996; F.C.5, December 2–6, 1996; F.C.7, January 8–10, 1997; F.C.9, January 20–24, February 10–11 & February 14, 1997; F.C.11, February 10–14 & March 3–4, 1997). This included the case in which both parties were self-represented, the mother wished to relocate interstate, and there was no child's representative (F.C.7, January 8–10, 1997). The judge expressed frustration at the fact that there was no avenue available for him to gain access to the child's wishes, and requested that one of the court counsellors interview the child and come into court to provide an oral report. The counsellor's report made it clear that the child wanted to live with his mother and was happy to move interstate with her. The counsellor also rejected the father's suggestion that the mother had turned the child against him. In his judgment, the judge described the counsellor's evidence as having been of *great* assistance in determining where the child's best interests lay, and it appears to have been the most influential factor in his decision to allow the mother to relocate.

The influential nature of the Family Report in children's matters meant, in turn, that in cases involving allegations of domestic violence, the Family Report writer's understanding of and attitudes towards domestic violence assumed considerable importance. Family Reports were written by social workers, psychologists, or psychiatrists, whose disciplinary backgrounds involved particular—and not necessarily feminist—views on violence against women.[9] Their analyses could minimize or disregard the mother's concerns about violence (e.g., Kaye et al., 2003, pp. 44–45; Rendell et al., 2000, p. 98; see also Buehl, 1999, p. 737; McKeon, 1998, p. 476); construct the interests of the children and their mother as entirely separate (e.g., Kaspiew, 2005, p. 128); have a bias towards at least preserving, and in some instances maximizing, contact between children and both their parents (Kaspiew, 2005, p. 125); and interpret children's fear of their father as the product of parental alienation by the mother (e.g., Rendell et al., 2000, p. 101; see also Berns, 2001; Buehl, 1999, p. 737; Lemon, 2001a, p. 346) (the alienating mother being another version of the feminine "fright" narrative). Some of the Family Reports in the files read during the fieldwork were astonishing in their disregard and dismissal of mothers' concerns about their children's and their own safety. The example previously noted of a child psychologist who favored shared parenting arrangements and believed they could be sustained in high conflict relationships (for which read those involving serious physical violence and threats) (in F.C.1, June 20–21 & 24, 1996) was a relatively mild illustration of this point.

It is notable that the same child psychologist, in another of the cases observed, also recommended an interim shared residence arrangement, in circumstances in which the relationship between the parties had completely broken down. Although it was clear that the wife had been the children's primary carer, the psychologist diagnosed her on the basis of very limited evidence as having a personality disorder, which then appeared to account for all the problems in the relationship (F.C.9, January 20–24, February 10–11 & February 14, 1997).[10] In her decision, the judge noted that the view of the husband taken by the psychologist was very different from the view she had formed of him after seeing him in the witness box. Women interviewed by Kaye et al. (2003) also reported concerns that court counsellors writing Family Reports had obtained only limited evidence, accepted the father's accounts and explanations without question, and failed to observe the children's fear of their father (p. 83).

Moreover, the pool of Family Report writers used by the court tended to be small, comprising the court's own counsellors and a handful of outside experts who were highly respected and received multiple referrals. Thus, these experts' views on violence were expounded repeatedly in numerous cases and had a cumulative impact on the court, as well as an impact on individual cases. At the individual level, an adverse or even unsupportive Family Report could be a reason for a victim of violence to decide to settle for consent orders rather than pursue her case in court. And an adverse Family Report was certainly relied upon by Legal Aid as a reason not to extend a party's grant of aid for trial, providing no opportunity for the validity of its conclusions to be tested (see also Rendell et al., 2000, p. 100).

In one of the cases observed, the mother's legal representatives, to their great credit, took on an unsupportive Family Report and succeeded (F.C.5, December 2–6, 1996); however, such cases appear to have been rare. This was the case involving the vexatious, self-representing husband who wanted equal time with his children. The Family Report indicated some support for his proposal, including the children's wishes that they spend more time with their father and the wife's apparent openness to a shared arrangement. Overall, it appeared that the written report placed too much emphasis on the ideal of shared residence and on the children's wishes taken out of context and did not sufficiently emphasize the evident problems in the parties' relationship, which ought to have qualified its conclusions. Yet this report was written by a social worker who was one of the small group of experienced experts frequently called upon to assist the court in determining the child's best interests.

In her cross-examination of the wife, the barrister for the children's representative asked why the wife now strongly opposed a shared arrangement but had not said this to the social worker. The wife responded that she had felt unable to express her own position and have it accepted in the interview. Rather, she had felt backed into a corner and had not disagreed with the idea in order to appease everyone. In the witness box, the social worker described the wife as initially very hesitant and passive in the interview, and agreed that she could feel overborne by the husband, but hoped (apparently vainly) that he had not himself put her under pressure. He agreed that the husband lacked insight into his impact on others and that he always had to have the upper hand. He also conceded that the wife might have felt pushed by the husband into agreeing to a new arrangement, and then reconsidered and backed off. In response to a question from the judge about how to weigh up competing considerations, he stated that despite the children's good individual relationships with both parents, the impossibility of reasonable communication between the parties was a fundamental problem. And in response to a question from the husband, he stated that joint residence arrangements required flexibility, and he had never seen any such arrangements work successfully if they had been ordered. In her final address, the barrister for the children's representative argued that the social worker's report had been considerably watered down by his oral evidence, and she accordingly supported the wife's position that there should be no change in residence and contact arrangements. Few women, however, would either be in position or would have the support of their lawyers to challenge the Family Report in this way.

Judicial Responses to Allegations of Violence

Judicial Sympathy

Unlike magistrates, Family Court judges presiding over final hearings were not attempting to rush through large numbers of cases. The pace of proceedings was much more measured, and judges did not approach them in a bureaucratic manner. At the same time, there was little direct interaction between judges and litigants, except occasionally when the party was in the witness box.

Interviewees made few comments about the way judicial officers responded to women who had been victims of violence, although the three women judges then sitting in Melbourne received particular praise in this respect (M. Mann, interview, March 8, 1996; S.1, interview, January 16, 1997; W.L.2, interview, December 18, 1997), with one lawyer noting that these judges would raise issues of violence that might have remained unaddressed by male practitioners (M. Mann, interview, March 8, 1996). A barrister and one of the litigants interviewed identified a spectrum of judicial responses, ranging from total lack of sympathy and disbelief, to almost exaggerated concern (B.2, interview, October 22, 1997; W.L.2, interview, December 18, 1997), although most judges were thought to be appropriately sympathetic (B. Phelan, interview, October 29, 1997). Only one interviewee thought that the woman's ethnicity, age, or class made a difference to how judges responded to stories of violence. In her observation, women tended to elicit more sympathy if they were gently spoken, small, and/or middle class, and if their demeanor was devastated rather than strident, so they responded to needling cross-examination by crying rather than by snapping back (B. Phelan, interview, October 29, 1997). Another also noted that women who appeared to be overwhelmed by their experience of violence could create a feeling of irritation rather than empathy in the judge (B.1, interview, October 17, 1997).

All of these points were borne out to some extent in the cases observed. The two women judges observed in defended hearings were attentive to issues of violence and were particularly good at providing appropriate support to distressed women and filling gaps left by those women's male lawyers (F.C.3, July 15–18 & 23, 1996; F.C.8, January 17, 1997; F.C.9, January 20–24, February 10–11 & February 14, 1997). Most of the male judges were also reasonably sympathetic, although one of the mothers had previously encountered a judge mentioned as unsympathetic, and he had held against her and delivered a judgment that, among other things, made adverse findings in scathing terms with regard to her claims about the father's violence (F.C.7, January 8–10, 1997). The women who appeared devastated and cried a lot, and/or were softly spoken, clearly elicited a great deal of sympathy (F.C.3, July 15–18 & 23, 1996; F.C.5, December 2–6, 1996; F.C.9, January 20–24, February 10–11 & February 14, 1997), while the one woman who appeared overwhelmed to the point of dynsfunctionality did indeed generate some degree of irritation and lack of sympathy, and was ultimately unsuccessful (F.C.2, June 25–26, 1996). Two of the women were middle class but more feisty—one with a tendency to snap back (F.C.1, June 20–21 & 24, 1996), the other quietly persistent (F.C.7, January 8–10, 1997). Both of these women were seeking to relocate with the children, however, so it was to the benefit of their cases that they projected an image of autonomy and recovery, whereas a very watery performance might have gained them sympathy but not success. Finally, it was certainly true that in the absence of a devastated demeanor, it was difficult to gain access and respond to the effects of violence on women from non-English speaking backgrounds, something that even the most skilled interpreter could not convey (F.C.8, January 17, 1997; F.C.11, February 10–14 & March 3–4, 1997).

Judicial Understandings of Violence

The Privileging of Physical Violence

Even though the Family Law Reform Act (1995) had introduced a broad definition of "family violence," most of the lawyers interviewed noted that the court was more interested in evidence of physical violence than of other forms of violence (B.1, interview, October 17, 1997; B.2, interview, October 22, 1997; B. Phelan, interview, October 29, 1997; S.1, interview, January 16, 1997; S.2, interview, October 28, 1997; J. Trickey, interview, March 20, 1996). This was both because physical assaults were considered to be more serious or "real" violence, and also because they were easier to corroborate with other evidence, and thus were more believable (B.1, interview, October 17, 1997; D. Dawson, interview, June 5, 1996; B. Phelan, interview, October 29, 1997; S.2, interview, October 28, 1997; J. Trickey, interview, March 20, 1996; see also "Developments in the law," 1993, p. 1619). By contrast, economic abuse might "add flavor" to a case, but would not make much difference in the end (S.2, interview, October 28, 1997). And the court was hard pressed to see the effects or the significance of emotional abuse (D. Dawson, interview, June 5, 1996; S.1, interview, January 16, 1997; J. Trickey, interview, March 20, 1996) or of rape within marriage (S.1, interview, January 16, 1997), although the women judges were said to understand emotional manipulation and other more subtle issues rather than just looking for bruises (M. Mann, interview, March 8, 1996). One lawyer thought that threats and intimidation were simply impossible to prove (D. Dawson, interview, June 5, 1996), while another said that domination, control, and belittling were not considered as reprehensible, and were likely to have little impact on the outcome of a case, unless they could be shown to be pathological (B.2, interview, October 22, 1997). Likewise, if the mother was deeply scarred by an act of violence that had occurred a long time ago, this was difficult to get across in the witness box (S.2, interview, October 28, 1997; see also Jaffe et al., 2003, p. 43).

Similarly, a barrister noted that where women were subjected to ongoing emotional violence, it seemed to take a precipitating event for them to leave the perpetrator, and then they would often go back several times before making the final break. As in the Magistrates' Court, these returns tended to be interpreted as "reconciliations," and as indications that the abuse had not been particularly serious, rather than being seen as evidence of the difficulty of separating from an abusive and controlling partner (B. Phelan, interview, October 29, 1997).

TABLE 16. Forms of nonphysical violence alleged in Family Court cases observed.

Type of Violence	Cases
Harassment	F.C.4, F.C.5, F.C.6, F.C.7, F.C.9, F.C.10, F.C.12, F.C.18, F.C.20
Domination/control	F.C.2, F.C.5, F.C.8, F.C.11, F.C.12, F.C.18
Verbal abuse	F.C.3, F.C.5, F.C.6, F.C.17, F.C.18, F.C.19
Emotional abuse	F.C.2, F.C.3, F.C.8, F.C.11, F.C.16
Coercion	F.C.12, F.C.14, F.C.16, F.C.18
Stalking	F.C.12, F.C.15, F.C.20
Intimidation	F.C.7, F.C.9, F.C.17
Economic abuse	F.C.12, F.C.20
Property damage	F.C.13, F.C.15
Sexual abuse	F.C.15, F.C.16
Imprisonment	F.C.16
Isolation	F.C.18

In all but 2 of the cases observed (F.C.5, December 2–6, 1996; F.C.12, April 7, 1997), physical violence was at the center of the wife/mother's allegations. However, it was also notable that only one of the cases involved only allegations of actual or threatened physical violence (F.C.1, June 20–21 & 24, 1996). In all of the other cases, the wife/mother's affidavits included allegations of other forms of violence, as shown in table 16.

Whether these various allegations of nonphysical violence were included to "add flavor" or to advance a power and control analysis is not clear, particularly since many of the cases did not proceed to hearing.

The Need for Independent Evidence of (Psychological) Harm

One of the barristers suggested that if emotional or economic abuse formed an important part of the mother's case, it would be helpful to have an expert to explain to the court how real and terrifying these forms of abuse were to the mother (B.1, interview, October 17, 1997). Indeed, a notable feature of the court's approach to domestic violence was that abused women needed experts to speak for (or about) them. They could make allegations of violence but could not themselves establish that the violence affected the child's best interests. As one barrister put it, if a mother wanted to deny contact to the father, she needed a high standard of proof—not just her word, but also some sort of expert evidence. In property proceedings, she would need medical and police records (B.2, interview, October 22, 1997). Another barrister noted that if a wife was running an argument about the overall effect of the violence on her parenting or on her contribution to the property, she would need psychological or psychiatric evidence (B. Phelan, interview, October 29, 1997; also J. Trickey, interview, March 20, 1996). In other words, women could not speak authoritatively about the effects of the violence on themselves and their children.

The tendency for the legal system to discount women's own stories and to prefer the evidence of professional "experts" has been critiqued in the context of criminal law (e.g., in relation to "battered woman syndrome" and "rape trauma syndrome": see, e.g., Hunter, 1996a), but it appears to operate in family law as well. In the family law context, the difficulties sometimes encountered in criminal law of persuading the court to admit expert evidence did not arise, but the effect of disqualifying women's voices was the same.

Only one of the cases in my observation sample that proceeded to hearing, however, actually involved the introduction of expert psychological evidence on behalf of the mother (F.C.16, January 6, 1997). In one other case, after her relationship with the father broke up, the mother had had the good fortune to marry a psychology professional, although his evidence on her behalf was purely personal, and the judge did not permit the child's representative to ask him questions about his professional opinion on the effects of violence. Nevertheless, he was a highly credible witness, and his evidence probably carried greater weight than that of an ordinary relative (F.C.3, July 15–18 & 23, 1996).

These 2 cases were also the only two in which the mother was seeking to deny contact altogether, and hence her psychological state was directly relevant. In all the other cases that went to hearing, the Family Report was relied upon as the source of expert evidence (if any) about the ongoing effects of violence on the family dynamic, as previously discussed. In one case, the wife's position would have been considerably helped by the provision of expert evidence on her behalf, but none was tendered (F.C.2, June 25–26, 1996). In this case, the husband had residence of the children and the wife was seeking property orders and an alteration to the contact arrangements. The wife's barrister stated at the outset that the wife's allegations of domestic violence against the husband were relevant to both the contact and property issues. However, after the property issues settled on the second day of the hearing, the wife's representatives made no real attempt to connect the remaining contact issues to the violence she had experienced. The allegations of violence consisted of an accumulation of individually relatively minor incidents of physical pushing, shoving, hitting, verbal abuse, constant put-downs, and incitement of the children to abuse and denigrate her. After years of this treatment, however, combined with the husband's domination and alcohol abuse, the wife argued that her health had been affected and she was an emotional wreck—and indeed in court, she did appear to be emotionally or psychologically disturbed. The husband, on the other hand, denied all but three incidents, and instead sought to construct the wife as chronically untrustworthy, unpunctual, and incapable of organizing herself into a routine to see the children. The wife's representatives could have called expert psychological evidence to demonstrate that her emotional state and apparent disorganization in relation to contact were a consequence of the violence she had experienced. But in the absence of any such evidence, the husband's argument prevailed.

Conceptual Separation Between the Interests of Mothers and Children

The various ways in which children may be harmed by exposure to domestic violence in their household have been noted in chapter 2. In children's matters in the Family Court, however, most judges continued to accept the view that wife abuse did not necessarily harm the children, that a violent father could still be a good parent, and that the needs of women and children subjected to domestic violence were different (see

Bancroft & Silverman, 2002, pp. 115–128; Davidson, 1995; Eriksson & Hester, 2001; Hewitt et al., 1996, p. 23; Kaspiew, 2005, pp. 121–122, 131, 137–138; Kaye et al., 2003, pp. 101–102; Laing, 2000b, p. 21; Levin, 2000, pp. 817–818; Meier, 2003, pp. 675–681; Rendell, 1999; Rhoades, 2002, p. 82; Rosnes, 1997, pp. 33, 50). The woman's account of violence thus merely became part of the historical picture of the relationship, which might have little or no bearing on future parenting arrangements (J. Trickey, interview, March 20, 1996). One lawyer noted that a lot of women found it hard to take when she explained the court's position that even though the woman's ex-partner had been violent towards her in the presence of the children, he was still likely to get access (M. Mann, interview, March 8, 1996). Another reported the court's general approach that if the parties themselves were kept apart, there was no reason for the father not to see the children (S. Macgregor, interview, March 1, 1996). Thus, at best, women might be able to achieve supervised access or supervised handover arrangements for a period of time (S. Macgregor, interview, March 1, 1996; M. Mann, interview, March 8, 1996; J. Trickey, interview, March 20, 1996). Anything more limited than this would only be ordered if it could be shown that the violence had a direct impact on the children—that is, evidence that the father had been violent towards the children as well, evidence of psychological damage to the children from witnessing the father's violence to the mother, or evidence that ongoing contact with the father would seriously impair the mother's parenting abilities to the children's detriment (D. Dawson, interview, June 5, 1996; S. Macgregor, interview, March 1, 1996).

These points were recognized by 2 of the women litigants interviewed. One said that the best interests of the child principle meant that if there was no violence directly towards the child, the court did not want to hear about violence towards the mother (W.L.2, interview, December 18, 1997), while the other observed that while her ex-husband's violence towards her son was mentioned in the Family Court, there was never any mention of the violence against her (W.L.5, interview, December 19, 1997). Both thought that the court failed to understand the wider effects of violence, both in terms of how it affected the mother's parenting ability and what it said about the father's parenting ability, and were concerned that this failure placed women's and children's safety at risk.

The (Ir)relevance of Violence Against Women

The tendency to consider the interests of mothers separately from those of their children had a structural basis in the kinds of legal arguments available to women in the Family Court. In children's matters, if the mother was the applicant, she could argue that the children should reside with her and have no contact, supervised contact, or unsupervised contact with the father, or she could argue that the children should reside with the father and have contact with her. If the mother was the respondent, she could oppose the father's application for residence or contact, according to the same range of options. In all cases in which the mother argued that the father should have at least some form of unsupervised contact with the children, she effectively conceded that he was an adequate parent. In these cases, then, concerns about the father's violence were almost inevitably subordinated to other considerations. It was only when women argued that the father was an unsafe parent, and therefore should have no or only supervised contact, that his violence became a central issue.

In a more recent study of children's cases decided by the Family Court, Kaspiew (2005) distinguished between the role of violence as a "disqualifying" factor, where the mother argued that the father should have no contact with the children because of his violence, and as a "contextual" factor, where the father's violence was one of several arguments raised by the mother to resist the father's claims for residence or increased contact (pp. 114, 122). In "contextual violence" cases, the father's entitlement to ongoing contact with his children was not fundamentally challenged, and hence the family violence provisions in section 68F(2) of the Family Law Act (1975) tended to have only minimal effect in the decision about what arrangement would be in the children's best interests (pp. 123, 132). The majority of cases in Kaspiew's study involving allegations of violence fell into this category. "Disqualifying violence" cases, on the other hand, were rare and required a high standard of proof in terms of the severity of the violence involved and the extent of corroborating evidence (pp. 114, 122–123). Kaspiew contended that the fact that violence was mostly argued as a contextual rather than as a disqualifying factor was "produced by tactical considerations" (p. 122). That is, in the procontact culture after the Family Law Reform Act (1995), an implicit "friendly parent" criterion operated in children's cases, making it "tactically dangerous for women to problematize contact except in the most extreme circumstances" (p. 136).[11]

As in Kaspiew's study, the majority of children's cases that proceeded to hearing in my observation sample involved arguments about "contextual violence" rather than "disqualifying violence." In none of these cases did the mother argue that the father should be restricted to supervised contact, and in only 2 did the mother argue that the father should have no contact with the child because of his violence towards her (F.C.3, July 15–18 & 23, 1996; F.C.16, January 6, 1997). The available evidence suggests that decisions by women and their lawyers about how to argue these cases may have been driven by lawyers' failure to consider the possibility of no contact, lawyers' knowledge of the likely outcome if the case went to court, the reasonableness of allowing contact in the particular circumstances, and/or the woman's support for ongoing contact between the children and their father, provided such contact could be exercised in a way that was safe for the children and for themselves (see discussion above and Kaye et al., 2003, p. 72; Rhoades et al., 2000, pp. 82–83). Whatever the reasons, however, and despite the court's ability to show kindness and sympathy towards traumatized women, their experiences of violence tended to be regarded as being of limited legal relevance in "contextual violence" cases.

One consequence of the fact that evidence of domestic violence was often merely "contextual" rather than central to the exercise of judicial discretion was that the court rarely made affirmative findings about the violence alleged. The court was also reluctant to make findings about violence due to the "no-fault" ethos, and its concern that doing so would have an adverse impact on the parties' future parenting relationship. This was illustrated, for example, in F.C.1 (June 20–21 & 24, 1996), when the judge said that he did not want to have to analyze the personalities of the parties as that would have a polarizing effect, whereas the parties needed to cooperate on future parenting. Thus, while wives/mothers were successful in most of the cases observed, their allegations of violence were not necessarily believed or upheld by the court. Rather, in dealing with allegations of violence, the court tended simply to rehearse the arguments made by each party and then move on (see also Altobelli, 1998, p. 10; Easteal, Behrens & Young, 2000, p. 246; Rhoades et al., 2000, p. 81). As a result, as was the case with intervention orders, women did not gain the acknowledgement of their experience or symbolic statements of disapproval about their ex-partner's violence that they may have been looking for (see also Berns, 2000, pp. 2–3). There was also little institutional affirmation of the existence of violence against women in general, or acknowledgment of its widespread nature.

The court made no findings at all in relation to the allegations of violence in 3 of the cases observed that went to a final hearing. In F.C.2 (June 25–26, 1996), the husband's barrister initially objected to the admission of sections of the wife's affidavit, including the allegations of domestic violence. The wife's barrister responded that they were arguing that domestic violence was relevant to the contact and property issues in the case, and in particular that the wife's earning capacity had been reduced. The judge then queried whether the *cause* of her reduced earning capacity was relevant, or just the fact of it, since the wife was not making a claim for damages in conjunction with her property application. The wife's barrister finally convinced the judge that the issue of domestic violence did need to be raised in the context of their second argument that the husband had made a negative contribution to the property. However, as noted above, once the property matter settled and the issue to be decided became simply whether the current contact arrangements should be maintained or altered, there was no further mention of domestic violence, including in the judge's reasons for deciding to make no change to the current arrangements.

In F.C.9 (January 20–24, February 10–11 & February 14, 1997), both parties were seeking interim residence of the children in the matrimonial home, with contact for the other party. The wife's argument was based on her status as the primary caregiver. Although she alleged that the husband had physically assaulted and intimidated her on several occasions, and engaged in racist abuse of herself and the children, she did not argue that this affected his parenting abilities. The husband's argument was that the wife had been physically abusive towards the children and had behaved inappropriately in their presence, and thus she could not be trusted to care for them alone. As a result, it was necessary for the judge to make findings about the wife's alleged behavior towards the children, but not about the husband's alleged behavior towards the wife. Accordingly, she did not make any findings on domestic violence by the husband, but decided in favor of the wife on the basis that her behavior was not such as to displace the presumption that stability should be maintained for the children on an interim basis by leaving them with their primary carer.

In F.C.1 (June 20–21 & 24, 1996), the wife wished to relocate with the children, which would change the nature and extent of the contact currently enjoyed by the husband. It was alleged that the husband had physically assaulted the wife at the time of separation and subsequently during handovers, had on one occasion tried to choke her, and on another threatened her with a gun. It was also alleged that the wife had stabbed the husband with a knife (she claimed in self-defense). The judge repeatedly steered the husband's barrister away from arguments that would have compelled him to adjudicate on the violence. So long as neither parent cast aspersions on the other's parenting ability, there was no need to go into it. In this case, too, since the wife had been charged in relation to the stabbing incident and was awaiting trial, it would have been difficult for the Family Court to deal with the allegations without running into problems with double jeopardy and the privilege against self-incrimination. Ultimately, the case was decided in the wife's favor on the basis of economic issues alone: she would have a better chance of finding appropriately skilled and remunerated work in Melbourne than in the country town in which they currently lived.

In 3 further cases, only limited findings about violence were made to the extent necessary to dispose of particular arguments. In F.C.11

(February 10–14 & March 3–4, 1997) there were four children: two older girls, who resided with the husband, and two younger boys, who resided with the wife. The husband was seeking residence of the two boys as well as the girls. The wife alleged that the husband had subjected her to verbal and emotional abuse, insisted that he obey her orders, threatened to kill her, and on one occasion had kicked her so hard that she sustained broken ribs. However, the dispute in the case in terms of the children's best interests revolved entirely around whether the wife had sexually abused the children and whether, conversely, the husband's reaction to and obsession with these allegations was equally or more emotionally abusive of the children. The husband's violence towards the wife was mentioned only in the process of working through the various factors listed in section 68F(2), and only in relation to the one serious physical incident. During the wife's barrister's final submissions, the judge queried whether the husband's serious assault on the wife had occurred in the presence of the children. The barrister replied that the wife said they were present, and the judge indicated that that was of interest to him. Ultimately, then, that assault became a further instance of the husband's emotional abuse of the children, which persuaded the judge to maintain the status quo and not to grant residence of all four children to the husband. The remaining allegations of violence, which were contested by the husband, were largely ignored.

In F.C.5 (December 2–6, 1996), the husband sought an order for shared residence, while the mother argued for the maintenance of the existing arrangements in which the children resided with her and had contact with the husband. The husband's overbearing and controlling behavior towards the wife was simply taken by the judge as part of the background to demonstrate that the relationship between the parties was not such as to enable a shared residence arrangement to work effectively, and hence would not be in the children's best interests.

In F.C.8 (January 17, 1997), the wife's allegations about the husband's violence towards her were central to her application to institute property and spousal maintenance proceedings out of time. The husband denied the allegations and argued that they were a recent invention by the wife in order to support her property application. In granting the wife's application, the judge did not make any detailed findings about the alleged violence. She simply stated that she had found the wife to be an honest, forthright, and candid witness, while the husband had been less so. Accordingly, she accepted the wife's evidence as to why she had not initiated property proceedings earlier, including her fear of the husband, which was corroborated by the fact that she had obtained an intervention order against him.

The 2 cases in which detailed findings were made about the father's violence towards the mother were the two in which the mother was arguing that the father should have no contact with the child due to the effects of his violence and of her ongoing fear of him on her parenting capacity, and hence on the child's overall welfare. In F.C.3 (July 15–18 & 23, 1996), the father was applying to regain contact with his young son after a period in jail, and subsequent denial of contact by the mother. The judge found that the evidence overwhelmingly supported a finding that the father had subjected the mother to severe violence during their relationship. She found the mother's evidence to be credible and convincing, and to be corroborated by other witnesses, documentary evidence, and the Family Report. On the other hand, she considered that the father's almost total denial of his violence went against his credit, and she also doubted that he understood that violence to the parent of a child is a form of abuse of the child. She concluded that any attempt to reintroduce contact with the father would put the child and the mother at risk, and accordingly ordered that contact be confined to cards and letters from the father on specified occasions.

In F.C.16 (January 6, 1997), the judge found that the father had subjected the mother to very severe and sustained violence (including the assault during the court counseling session), and noted that while the father had never directly harmed the child, his conduct towards the mother had been such that continued contact would seriously impair the mother's parenting ability. After considering the principles in section 60B(2) and the factors set out in section 68F(2), including those relating to family violence, the judge concluded that direct contact between the child and the father would not be in the child's best interests, subject to further evidence to be obtained from a potential contact supervisor. When that evidence was subsequently heard, the judge ordered that the child have supervised contact with the father three times per year, for 1–2 hr, and without any meeting between the father and the mother. Thus, he made every effort to uphold the principle of ongoing contact with both parents. These orders were overturned on appeal, however, on the basis that there was insufficient evidence on which the trial judge could find that any contact could be exercised safely and securely for the mother and child. This case appears to have foreshadowed the respective influence of sections 60B(2) and 68F(2) at trial level in "disqualifying violence" cases. In her study of cases decided in 1999–2000, Kaspiew (2005) found that "even in the most severe cases, the maintenance of father-child contact [was] very seriously considered" (p. 143), and she cited at least one instance in which an application for no contact supported by ample evidence was refused (pp. 130–132).[12]

CONCLUSION

Apart from the rare case involving an argument for no contact, a series of factors operated to exclude domestic violence from the cognizance of the Family Court. Firstly, lawyers might not ask about or might ignore their clients' experiences of violence. Secondly, issues of violence were often ignored or sidelined in the process of negotiating and approving consent orders, and, consequently, were not evident in the terms of the consent orders made. Thirdly, in children's matters, Family Report writers might dismiss or minimize mothers' concerns about the father's violence, or might analyse the mother's and children's behavior or the family dynamic within nonfeminist frameworks that attributed problems to factors other than the father's violence. Fourthly, the presentation of evidence about violence in court might be more limited than the allegations made in affidavits—for example, because only some incidents of physical violence could be corroborated, because the issues in dispute had narrowed, or in response to the judge's indications as to what they considered relevant. Finally, the judge would make findings in relation to allegations of violence only when and to the extent that it was legally necessary to do so, and, in making those findings, might confine consideration to incidents of physical violence, minimize the violence, or reject the allegations altogether. Thus, despite the reputation of the Family Court as being relatively sympathetic to victims of domestic violence—and despite the fact that the Family Law Reform Act (1995) and decisions of the Full Court spelled out the relevance of violence in children's and property proceedings—on a day-to-day basis, there was little affirmation of individual experiences of abuse or recognition of the social prevalence of domestic violence, and no consistent assertion that violence by one parent towards the other necessarily affected the safety, welfare, and best interests of the child. Against this backdrop, the fact that the "right to contact" came to dominate internal legal culture after the Family Law Reform Act (1995) is hardly surprising.

A recent international review of family law legislation placed the Australian Family Law Act (1975) somewhere towards the bottom of the scale in terms of "international best practice" in safeguarding women and children from domestic violence, due to its failure to "prioritize the safety of adult and child victims of domestic violence as more important than the child's right to stay in contact with both parents, when there is a conflict between these two policies" (Jaffe et al., 2003, p. 87). As discussed in this chapter, violence is also marginalized as an issue where (as in most cases) it is not argued that the violent partner is a totally unfit parent. In order to bring domestic violence from the margins to the center in settlement negotiations, court proceedings, and judicial decision making, the legislation would need to specify women's and children's safety as the primary objective in cases where domestic violence is alleged (Bowermaster, 1998, p. 462; Eriksson & Hester, 2001, p. 793; Laing, 2000b; Rendell et al., 2000, pp. 121–122). Other jurisdictions, for example, incorporate a rebuttable presumption against residence or unsupervised contact being awarded to a violent spouse (Jaffe & Crooks, 2004, p. 921; Lemon, 2001b; see also Behrens, 2002, p. 413). Alternatively, where violence is alleged, the focus of a children's matter should not be on whether and how the violent partner should have contact with the children, but on whether and how contact can be exercised safely for the children and the other partner (see, e.g., Sheeran & Hampton, 1999). It would be more difficult to elevate the issue of violence from being merely one of a number of factors to being a central concern in property proceedings, but the Family Law Council's proposal that it be specified among the factors to be taken into account in both sections 79(4) and 75(2) of the Family Law Act would still be an improvement on the current position.

As explained earlier, however, the recent policy climate surrounding family law in Australia has not favored such proposals relating to property division. To the contrary, up to November 2007, the federal government's major policy preoccupation in the family law area was with the perceived social "problem" of fatherlessness (see, e.g., House of Representatives Standing Committee on Family and Community Affairs, 2004; Smyth, 2004).[13] Further reforms to the Family Law Act (1975) introduced by the Family Law Amendment (Shared Parental Responsibility) Act (2006) increased the Act's emphasis on children maintaining contact with both parents after separation, by creating a presumption of equal shared parental responsibility (s. 61DA) and by strong encouragement for agreements and orders to provide for children to spend equal or substantial time with both parents (s. 65DAA). While the presumption of joint parental responsibility does not apply if there are reasonable grounds to believe that one of the parents has engaged in family violence (s. 61DA(2)), and other elements of the amending legislation also attempted to strengthen the provisions relating to family violence (ss. 60B(1)(b), 60CC(2)(b), 60K), there is still no prioritization of safety in such cases, and the child's right to maintain contact with both parents is still the primary emphasis (ss. 60B(1)(a), 60B(2), 60CC(2)(a)). Moreover, other aspects of the Act, including provisions mandating nonlitigious dispute resolution (s. 60I) and the addition of an explicit "friendly parent" criterion to the section 68F(2) factors (now s. 60CC(3)(c)), all tend to reinforce the view that family violence is exceptional and needs to be taken seriously only in relatively rare cases (see, e.g., House of Representatives Standing Committee on Legal and Constitutional Affairs, 2005; Rathus, 2007; De Simone, 2008). While women's legal services and feminist academics made submissions to the parliamentary inquiries that preceded the 2006 amendments, advocating the kinds of proposals made here, they were consistently rejected (House of Representatives Standing Committee on Family and Community Affairs, 2004; House of Representatives Sanding Committee on Legal and Constitutional Affairs, 2005).

ENDNOTES

1. The same result has been observed following the introduction of the Children Act (1989) in the U.K. (see Lees, 1997, p. 128; Radford, Hester, Humphries, & Woodfield, 1997; Rendell et al., 2000, pp. 32–33).
2. As has been noted in the U.S. context, the inclusion of violence among a list of statutory factors still leaves discretion in the decision maker as to how much weight to give it (Developments in the law, 1993).
3. By contrast, in their U.K. study of 161 separated women, Humphreys and Thiara (2003) found that child contact arrangements "provided the most consistent vulnerability to post-separation violence," and that "[c]hild contact proceedings were used as a legal means to track the woman and sanction unsafe contact arrangements, leaving both women and children unprotected" (pp. 207–208). Jaffe et al. (2003) explain the different impacts of domestic violence on children according to their age and stage of development, from prenatal onwards (pp. 25–27).
4. In her study of unreported judgments, Middleton (2001) found a few cases in which the consequences of violence had been raised in relation to section 75(2), arguing that the adverse effects of the violence on the wife's psychological health and wellbeing had diminished her future earning capacity (p. 245).
5. For U.S. evaluations of the usefulness of tort remedies against abusers, see, for example, Kohler (1992); Scherer (1992).
6. This occurred, for example, in *In the Marriage of Morgan* (1997), when the trial judge, of his own motion, transferred the wife's claims for damages for assault and battery, intentional infliction of nervous shock, and defamation to the Supreme Court of New South Wales, on the basis that the claims were more appropriately dealt with in a State court. Grounds for transferring cases were set out in the Jurisdiction of Courts (Cross-vesting) Act (1987), section 5.
7. The Australian *Best Practice Guidelines for Lawyers Doing Family Law Work* (Family Law Council & Law Council of Australia, Family Law Section, 2004), specify that the lawyer should "provide the client with an opportunity to talk about violence issues if they wish," not be judgemental if violence is disclosed, and be aware that clients may be reluctant to disclose a history of abuse. Thus, "they should develop skills that will help them to facilitate a full and frank disclosure," and equip themselves

to help clients overcome inhibitions in this regard (p. 49). Appendix 3 of the *Guidelines* provides a list of indirect and more direct questions that may be used by lawyers to determine if violence is an issue for their client. Having elicited this information, however, the *Guidelines* focus on the lawyer's role in ensuring the client's physical safety in negotiations, while attending court, and apart from their family law proceedings. However, they are vague as to the substantive relevance of violence in the proceedings, stating only that violence may "impact on children and property matters" (p. 49).

8. It is notable that in the study of relocation cases post–*B and B* conducted by Easteal et al. (2000), women wishing to relocate for reasons of employment had the greatest chances of success (75%) (p. 244).
9. Many other studies both in Australia and overseas have observed that child "experts" used by family courts often fail to understand the dynamics and impact of domestic violence (see, e.g., Buehl, 1999, p. 737; "Developments in the law," 1993, p. 1599; Dick, 1998, p. 64; Jaffe et al., 2003, p. 28; Kaye et al., 2003, pp. 44–45, 83; McKeon, 1998, p. 476; Rendell et al., 2000, pp. 98–101; Scutt, 1990, pp. 252–253). Rhoades et al. (2000) also note that the Family Court counsellors they interviewed were not familiar with the actual provisions of the Family Law Act (1975), the Family Law Reform Act (1995), or the court's case law, and tended to apply a generalized understanding of the law, which was sometimes incorrect (pp. 43, 45). These problems appear to have been recognized by the Family Court in its *Family Violence Strategy* (2004), which states,

> The Family Court aims to ensure that the evidence of independent experts designed to assist in the decision making process is of the highest quality and, in the context of family violence issues, that expert evidence be underpinned by an awareness of the dynamics of violence and its impact upon parents and children. (p. 12)

Actions to be taken in pursuit of this aim included the establishment of a Working Group to review and report on the role of the Family Report writer, the provision of ongoing training in family violence and child protection for mediators, and revision of the court's Guidelines for the preparation of Family Reports as they related to issues of family violence, the criteria for the appointment of expert witnesses, the function and structure of Family Reports and expert reports, and the accreditation and competencies of experts appointed to report to the court.

10. Other studies have also observed psychological assessments of battered women as "hysterical," "histrionic," paranoid, and personality disordered (see, e.g., Jaffe et al., 2003, pp. 45–46; Rendell et al., 2000, p. 38). For an extreme example, see *T v. S* (2001). The trial judge in this case dismissed the mother's evidence of domestic violence largely on the basis of an adverse psychological report. However, as the Full Court accepted, the mother's mental state was also consistent with a history of severe violence and abuse, but since she was unrepresented at trial, it had been impossible for her to challenge through cross-examination the evidence of a professional who had diagnosed her as mentally unfit.
11. Compare the *Best Practice Guidelines for Lawyers Doing Family Law Work* (Family Law Council & Law Council of Australia, Family Law Section, 2004, p. 31), which state that lawyers' advice to clients about how to proceed in children's matters "should be realistic but sufficiently robust to support clients should their individual circumstances raise questions about the appropriateness of residence or contact."
12. Kaspiew's (2005) file sample of 40 cases included 5 in which the mother argued for no contact based on the father's violence. Four of these applications were successful, and one was unsuccessful; however, decisions in favor of the mother in 2 of the cases were made after the father withdrew or failed to appear.
13. The November 2007 federal election brought a change of government, but the Labour government's policy direction in family law had not yet become clear at the time of the writing.

Chapter 7

The Jurisdictional Intersection: Intervention Orders in the Family Court and Children's Issues in the Magistrates' Court

This chapter deals with the interaction between Magistrates' Court intervention order proceedings and Family Court proceedings in relation to domestic violence. As Kaye et al. (2003) have observed, women seeking protection from violence for themselves and their children are compelled to navigate both State and federal jurisdictions, in a context in which there is little coordination between the two. Indeed, they argue that the existence of a family law dispute can reduce the protection available from a State domestic violence order, while the existence of such an order carries little or no weight in family law proceedings (p. 91).

The same conclusion arose from my interviews and observations. While the Family Law Act (1975) sought to achieve coordination between the two systems, the relevant provisions have been widely ignored in favor of more entrenched understandings about the appropriate relationship between the Magistrates' Courts and the Family Court, and the appropriate relationship between children and violent fathers, held by magistrates, judges, and legal practitioners.

THE LEGISLATION: PART VII, DIVISION 11 OF THE FAMILY LAW ACT

In Theory

As part of its report on *Equality Before the Law* (1994), the ALRC referred to the issue of conflict between intervention orders and Family Court orders, and noted that pursuant to section 109 of the Australian Constitution (1901), the latter prevailed over the former to the extent of any inconsistency (p. 183). This situation was seen to be less than satisfactory, and the Commission recommended that a procedure be established for bringing intervention orders to the Family Court's attention and for the court to ensure that its orders did not detract from the protection given to women by intervention orders (p. 184). Following this recommendation, the Family Law Reform Act (1995) inserted a new Division 11 into Part VII of the Family Law Act (1975), which attempted to eliminate inconsistencies between State domestic violence protection orders and Family Court orders, although in an excessively complex and convoluted way, and not exactly as the ALRC had suggested (Crawford, 2003, p. 9; Family Law Council, 2004, p. 5; Kearney McKenzie & Associates, 1998, ¶ 21.4).[1]

The purposes of Division 11 were set out in section 68Q of the Family Law Act (1975).

> The purposes of this Division are:
>
> (a) to resolve inconsistencies between [Family Court contact orders] and [State] family violence orders; and

(b) to ensure that [Family Court contact orders] do not expose people to family violence; and
(c) to respect the right of a child to have contact, on a regular basis, with both the child's parents where:
   (i) contact is diminished by the making or variation of a [State] family violence order, and
   (ii) it is in the best interests of the child to have contact with both parents on a regular basis.

As the first report on the operation of Division 11 noted, purpose (c) (like other sections of the Family Law Reform Act (1995) discussed in the previous chapter) suggested that it was sometimes in the child's best interests to have regular contact with a violent parent, and undermined the importance of ensuring the safety of that child and their residence parent (Kearney McKenzie & Associates, 1998, ¶ 2.4; see also Alexander, 1996, p. 279). In other words, Division 11 was consistent with the procontact ethos of the rest of the new Part VII and did not absolutely prioritize the safety of those who had been subjected or exposed to domestic violence.

The procedure established by Division 11 was one of priority in time. Under section 68R, if the Family Court encountered an existing State family violence order, it was empowered to override it with a contact order. The court was not required to decide *whether* to make an inconsistent contact order. Rather, the Act simply assumed that inconsistent orders would be made, subject only to certain procedural conditions concerning explanations to the parties as to what the contact order required and why it had been made (ss. 68R, 68S).[2] On the other hand, under section 68T, if a State court encountered an existing contact order (or the absence of any Family Court orders) it was empowered to make a contact order or to "revive, vary, discharge or suspend" the Family Court order as appropriate (s. 68T(1)). In doing so, the State court was required to "have regard" to the best interests of the child or children involved, but the best interests of the child were not made the paramount consideration (s. 68T(2)(b), (3)). The power to make or vary a contact order could be exercised upon application or upon the court's own initiative (s. 68T(4)).[3]

In Practice

In practice, however, neither section 68R nor section 68T were given any effect. During my fieldwork shortly after the introduction of the Family Law Reform Act (1995), support workers and lawyers commented that section 68T was being routinely ignored in Magistrates' Courts in intervention order applications (Field notes, Broadmeadows Magistrates' Court, February 21, 1997; Sunshine Magistrates' Court, July 2, 1996; H. Assafiri, interview, June 24, 1997; F. Culpen, interview, March 17, 1997; J. Peirce, interview, August 21, 1997; S.1, interview, January 16, 1997; S.W.1, interview, December 23, 1997; also Geelong Focus Group, interview, December 19, 1997). Partly this was because women usually sought an intervention order before commencing Family Court proceedings, so there were few contact orders in place that might require variation, suspension, or discharge (F. Culpen, interview, March 17, 1997; J. Peirce, interview, August 21, 1997). But section 68T also gave magistrates power to *make* contact orders in appropriate circumstances, which was also never invoked.

In the course of my observations in Magistrates' Courts, there was not a single case in which section 68T was raised, either by lawyers or by the magistrate, although there were several cases in which it could usefully have been employed. For example, in M.C.23 (July 2, 1996), the magistrate was making a final intervention order by consent that, among other things, restricted the defendant's ability to telephone the applicant. The applicant's solicitor pointed out that there was in place a Family Court order for contact with the children that apparently provided for telephone calls to make arrangements in relation to contact visits. The magistrate clearly did not consider the fact that he was making an intervention order to protect the applicant from future violence and harassment to have any bearing on the defendant's contact with the children, as he directed the defendant's interpreter to tell the defendant that he could still collect the children as before, but must not breach the intervention order in the process. Neither did he take any responsibility for varying the contact order so as to dovetail better with the intervention order. Instead, he suggested that perhaps the applicant could arrange for a mutual friend to do the telephoning, and directed the parties to work it out between themselves outside the courtroom.

In M.C.45 (October 31, 1996)—one of the contested cases—the parties clearly had ongoing problems with contact orders, with the ex-wife alleging ongoing abuse and harassment in connection with contact, and the ex-husband claiming that she was physically and verbally abusive during handovers. This would appear to have been a classic case in which clearly unworkable Family Court orders needed to be varied to establish a safer contact regime for the child as well as for the parents, which avoided any need for them to come into contact with each other. But rather than doing anything of the sort, the magistrate queried why the parties could not themselves organize some other handover arrangement, and lectured them on the need for commonsense to prevail. He also made an order limited to restraining the respondent from assaulting, harassing, molesting, and so forth, the applicant, rather than the more extensive order the applicant sought, in order to enable the current contact regime to continue to (dys)function.

The fact that section 68T did not accord with magistrates' notions of how to resolve conflicts between intervention orders and Family Court orders was made explicit in the magistrate's comments in another case. Here, a woman had an intervention order against her ex-husband, and he was now seeking an order against her, to which she consented without admitting the allegations. The magistrate was at pains to point out that nothing in the intervention order would interfere with the exercise of contact in accordance with the parties' Family Court orders, since the Family Court orders were decisive in relation to contact, and the parties must comply with them. If they wanted any change in contact arrangements, they could go to the Family Court, and if there was any change in the Family Court orders, they could return to the Magistrates' Court to have their intervention orders correspondingly varied (M.C.92, June 27, 1997).

Likewise, section 68R was not raised in any of the cases observed in the Family Court.[4] Where intervention orders were in place, they were never made an issue in the process of approving consent orders (e.g., F.C.12, April 7, 1997; F.C.14, August 9, 1996; F.C.15, December 5, 1996; F.C.17, January 20, 1997), and were often not mentioned at all in the course of contested hearings (e.g., F.C.1, June 20–21 & 24, 1996; F.C.2, June 25–26, 1996; F.C.5, December 2–6, 1996; F.C.9, January 20–24, February 10–11 & February 14, 1997), let alone any consideration being given to whether the contact orders being made were inconsistent with the intervention orders.

Subsequent research on the operation of Division 11 confirmed the continuing accuracy of these findings (e.g., Dewar & Parker, 1999, p. 105; Kaye, 2003; VLRC, 2004a, p. 170). The nonuse of section 68R has been ascribed to the fact that the Family Court may not have been notified of the existence of a domestic violence order, or may not have been aware of any inconsistency in the case of consent orders (Kearney McKenzie & Associates, 1998, ¶ 3.5–3.6). Lawyers appear not to have taken responsibility for bringing these matters to the court's attention, and self-represented litigants may have been unaware of any requirement to do so. Neither did the court itself take any responsibility for raising the issue. In my reading of Family Court files, the existence of intervention orders was usually manifest (of the 80 files read involving allegations of domestic violence, 56% included details of one or more intervention orders), and in such cases, the court could have sought submissions from the parties' representatives on the application of section 68R, as it routinely did on the application of the section 68F(2) factors. Other reasons put forward as to why section 68R was rarely used were that intervention orders provided little detail about the nature or history of violence involved, they may not have been accepted as proof that the alleged violence occurred, or the existence of an intervention order may have been viewed as a strategic ploy in Family Court proceedings (Kearney McKenzie & Associates, 1998, ¶ 3.7). These reasons are discussed further later in the chapter.

The nonuse of section 68T has been variously ascribed to lack of awareness among magistrates, legal practitioners, and police prosecutors;

the complexity and opacity of the legislative provisions; and the fact that magistrates, already pressed for time in hearing intervention order applications, did not wish to entertain section 68T applications that would have the effect of prolonging proceedings (Crawford, 2003, pp. 8–9; Family Law Council, 2004, p. 5; Kearney McKenzie & Associates, 1998, ¶ 2.14, 3.14–3.15, 3.18).[5] So too, domestic violence court support workers interviewing women before court on the return date may not have had time to obtain instructions from clients on contact issues (Crawford, 2003, p. 9), and applicants appearing in person were highly unlikely to be aware that they could request the magistrate to make or vary a contact order (Kearney McKenzie & Associates, 1998, ¶ 3.21). Again, however, these procedural obstacles need to be supplemented by a recognition of cultural factors—in particular, that magistrates were generally reluctant to delve into family law issues, and might also be suspicious of applicants' motives in seeking an intervention order (Kearney McKenzie & Associates, 1998, ¶ 3.18–3.19).

Magistrates' Views of Family Law

Exceptions Allowing for Child Contact

Magistrates' preferred means of avoiding inconsistency between intervention orders and any present or future Family Court orders was to insert—usually of their own initiative and without consulting the applicant—into every intervention order where children were involved an exception to allow for the exercise of child contact, either by agreement between the parties or pursuant to Family Court orders. Such an exception, of course, reduced the protection provided to the aggrieved family member and potentially compromised her safety and that of her children during contact and contact handovers (Nunn & D'Arcy, 2001, pp. 23–24; VLRC, 2004a, p. 170; Wearing, 1992, p. 29; Wearing, 1996, pp. 121–122). It also made the intervention order more difficult to enforce, as defendants could argue that they were simply trying to arrange or exercise contact and therefore had not breached the order (Kaye et al., 2003, p. 97; Nunn & D'Arcy, 2001, p. 23; VLRC,

2004a, p. 171). But the use of such exceptions was a long-standing and consistent practice among magistrates (see, e.g., Alexander, 1996, p. 279; Kearney McKenzie & Associates, 1998, ¶ 3.9).[6]

Two of the women interviewed referred to their experience in this regard. One noted that the Magistrates' Court had insisted on inserting an exception in her intervention order giving her ex-husband the right to contact her in relation to seeing the children (W.L.2, interview, December 18, 1997). The other had an intervention order containing the standard exception and, as noted earlier, was clearly confused by it. The order stated that her ex-husband was not to contact or approach her except to have access with their child as agreed with her or pursuant to court order. Since she did not have a Family Court order relating to access, she was not sure whether the exception meant that she had to agree to access if her ex-husband demanded it (W.L.8, interview, November 7, 1997).

Exceptions for child contact were included in a number of the intervention orders made during the course of my court observations. For example, in M.C.18 (June 18, 1996), the applicant explained that she was seeking an order so that her son would not be exposed to her husband's violence. Her son was fearful of his father but had also started behaving aggressively in imitation of him. Despite these concerns, the magistrate automatically made the order with an exception to enable the father to exercise agreed or court-ordered contact. In M.C.46 (November 6, 1996), the magistrate asked whether there was any residence or contact order in place. The applicant replied "not yet," but indicated that she planned to apply for such orders. The magistrate then asked whether the applicant had any objection to the defendant seeing the children. When she said "no," the magistrate made an order that (among other things) restrained the defendant from coming within 100 meters of the applicant's premises, except for the purposes of child contact. He did not canvass the possibility of structuring contact so as to maintain the applicant's protection from further violence. The same problematic outcome occurred in another case on the same day (M.C.50, November 4, 1996). In M.C.93 (June 27, 1997), the allegations specifically concerned the defendant's harassment of the applicant over the telephone, but the magistrate refused to make an order restraining the defendant from telephoning the applicant in order to enable "necessary" contact between the parties in relation to their children, and in M.C.110 (June 27, 1997), the same magistrate unilaterally amended the terms of the orders to which the defendant had consented to provide the standard exception for child contact by agreement or pursuant to Family Court orders.

Similarly, in one of the Family Court cases observed (F.C.15, December 5, 1996), there was evidence that the husband suffered from a paranoid delusional disorder and had subjected the wife to life-threatening violence, to the extent that she was being treated for posttraumatic stress disorder. Nevertheless, the intervention order she had obtained against him in the Magistrates' Court included an exception allowing the husband to approach, telephone, or contact her in order to participate in counseling or to exercise child contact by agreement with her or by direction or order of the Family Court. And in another Family Court file, the wife had obtained two contested intervention orders against the husband, the first of which he had breached, resulting in a conviction and fine. The wife had suffered serious and frequent violent assaults that were witnessed by the children, along with physical injuries, verbal abuse, property damage, and threats to kill. She was very fearful that the husband would assault her again or abduct the children. Nevertheless, her second intervention order contained the standard exception for child contact.

The Father's Right of Contact

In making these exceptions, some magistrates clearly believed that fathers had a right of contact with their children (the right being seen to reside in the father rather than in the child), and either had no conception that ongoing contact might compromise the child's or the mother's safety, or considered that the right of ongoing contact overrode safety considerations (e.g., F. Culpen, interview, March 17, 1997; see also Kaye et al., 2003, p. 53; Kearney McKenzie & Associates, 1998, ¶ 2.15; Kinports & Fischer, 1992, pp. 195, 197). A court support worker noted that women who had been lectured by the magistrate about allowing contact often came out of court asking, "Do I have to let him see the kids?" (F. Culpen, interview, March 17, 1997).

One of the women interviewed had applied for two intervention orders and had encountered different attitudes from the magistrate on each occasion. The first (woman) magistrate had said that her daughter did not have to go on contact visits with her father if she did not wish to (she was 12 years old, had been physically assaulted by him, and was scared of seeing him). The second (male) magistrate, however, said, "Rubbish; a father has the right to see his children." As a consequence, her daughter had been further traumatized, and the woman herself had suffered additional stress in trying to offer some kind of protection to her daughter while being undermined in this way (W.L.7, interview, October 28, 1997).

Family Law Belongs in the Family Court

More broadly, magistrates evinced a general distaste for family law matters and a belief that such matters were not appropriate for their courts and should all be referred to the Family Court. This was despite the fact that all Magistrates' Courts had jurisdiction, not only under section 68T but also more generally, to make interim and consent orders under the Family Law Act (1975) (see also Kinports & Fischer, 1992; Rhode, 2002, p. 85). Thus, as noted earlier, magistrates would deal only with the narrow intervention order application before them and instruct parties to take any child residence and contact issues to the Family Court (e.g., Field notes, Sunshine Magistrates' Court, July 7, 1996; see also Dewar & Parker, 1999, p. 105; Wearing, 1996, p. 153). According to one lawyer interviewed, most magistrates were frightened of family law and did not want to touch the issues (S.1, interview, January 16, 1997; also S.W.1, interview, December 23, 1997). A support worker considered that magistrates saw their role as being crisis intervention, while the Family Court offered processes for longer-term dispute resolution, including counseling and mediation services (H. Assafiri, interview, June 24, 1997). A magistrate explained to me that the advantage of being able to send people back to the Family Court was that the dispute could be relocated where it belonged—as a family dispute that happened to give rise to an intervention order application (Field notes, Moonee Ponds Magistrates' Court, November 1, 1996).

In my court observations, magistrates frequently advised applicants to go to the Family Court to get their residence issues resolved. For example, in M.C.50 (November 4, 1996), after making the intervention order including the standard exception for child contact, the magistrate asked what arrangements had been made for the children. The applicant responded that although she had made various offers, there was no agreement as yet. The magistrate then unhelpfully advised that once there was an agreement, she should get it formalized in the Family Court. In M.C.35 (July 4, 1996), the magistrate asked whether the applicant and defendant had been married and had any children. On receiving an affirmative answer, the magistrate told the applicant that she needed to see a lawyer and get the family law aspects of their separation sorted out. The applicant, who was unrepresented, then queried whether the intervention order applied to the custody of the children. The magistrate replied that it did not and should not because custody was a separate issue.

Some magistrates appeared to have quite an unrealistic view of the Family Court process. For example, in M.C.55 (November 4, 1996), the applicant explained that after she and the defendant first separated, the defendant had kidnapped the children in order to coerce her into taking him back. The magistrate asked whether she understood that she could get a residence order from the Family Court. The applicant replied that she had been attempting to do so for the last 2 years. The magistrate dismissed the notion that it could take that long, and advised the applicant that she had to make a decision as to whether she wanted the defendant back or not, and if not, she should get a residence order.

Magistrates might also decide that the matter before them was "really" a residence and/or contact dispute, and be very reluctant to make an intervention order (Geelong Focus Group, interview, December 19, 1997). In one of the contested matters (M.C.108, July 11, 1997), in which the applicant sought an order to restrain the defendant from bombarding her and her family with crazy, threatening letters several times a week, his conduct also happened to be in breach of Family Court orders that prohibited him from communicating in any way with his wife and children. The magistrate told me that his initial view had been that this was just a Family Court matter and he had had to be convinced by the clerk that he should hear the application. He thought that the applicant should have brought contempt proceedings in the Family Court rather than effectively attempting to enforce the orders in the Magistrates' Court.

The Strategic Use of Intervention Orders

Finally, many magistrates subscribed to the "fright" narrative that women make false allegations of violence and apply for intervention orders only in order to gain a tactical advantage in family law proceedings—either by depriving men of residence of and contact with their children or gaining exclusive possession of the property, and thereby establishing a "status quo" that is difficult to dislodge in the Family Court (e.g., S.W.1, interview, December 23, 1997; see also Hickey & Cumines, 1999, pp. 35, 37; Kaye & Tolmie, 1998a, pp. 53–59; Kaye & Tolmie, 1998b, p. 54; Kearney McKenzie & Associates, 1998, ¶ 3.19). The notion that women's primary goal in applying for intervention orders was to punish or persecute their ex-partners rather than to secure their own safety has been identified overseas as well as in Australia (e.g., Römkens, 2001, p. 282). Women always had to contend with this suspicion, despite empirical evidence to the contrary, and it operated as a disincentive for lawyers to make applications for intervention orders in cases that may have warranted an order (J. Peirce, interview, August 21, 1997).[7]

The issue of ulterior motives for intervention order applications arose in several ways in my Magistrates' Court observations. In the case mentioned earlier in which the unrepresented applicant queried whether the intervention order applied to the custody of the children, the magistrate replied that it did not, but added that he thought that was "why a lot of women come in and get an order" (M.C.35, July 4, 1996). In one of the contested cases (M.C.21, June 27, 1996), the defendant's barrister managed to extract an admission from the applicant that her motivation for seeking an order was to get the defendant out of the house for the purposes of their family law property dispute, that she had received legal advice to that effect, and that she had embarked on a strategy of provoking the defendant in order to create grounds for an order. The magistrate picked up on this admission and queried the applicant further on her motivations, noting that the recent amendments to the Family Law Act (1975) (i.e., the Family Law Reform Act, 1995) demonstrated the potential for intervention order proceedings to affect outcomes in the Family Court—although this was in fact true only in relation to children's matters, not property matters. During the lunch break in this case, the defendant's solicitor and barrister took the opportunity to tell me about how intervention order proceedings were being abused "all the time" in order to gain advantage in family law property cases, although the solicitor conceded that he did not have much personal experience of this occurring as he did not usually practise in the family law field.

In M.C.104 (July 11, 1997), the application for an intervention order was refused because the magistrate believed the applicant was merely seeking a strategic advantage in the Family Court. The applicant sought an order against her son-in-law, who had recently separated from her daughter. She claimed that since the separation, he had constantly rung her house and harassed her with threats and abuse, including a threat to remove the children so that their mother and grandmother would never see them again. Under questioning by the magistrate, it emerged that the daughter also had an intervention order against her ex-partner, which contained the usual exception for child contact and allowed him to contact the mother through the grandmother in case of emergency. However, the contact was by agreement with the mother (there were no Family Court orders in place), and she had recently stopped contact on the advice of a counsellor. The magistrate then pointed out that if the grandmother obtained an intervention order, the father would not be able to contact her or the mother to make arrangements to see the children. This, he considered, "would be unfortunate," since "children do have a right to have contact with both parents," and it would be "counterproductive to cut [the father] adrift from the children." Consequently, the magistrate decided that it would be inappropriate to grant the order sought.

Outside the hearing room, the magistrate explained to me that there had been another agenda at work in the case. In his view, the application was a power play against the father. They were trying to cut off all his contact with his children so as to get sole custody. However they had forgotten that the Family Law Reform Act (1995) said that children have rights to see both parents (Field notes, Broadmeadows Magistrates' Court, July 11, 1997). This reasoning misrepresented both the Family Law Reform Act (1995) and the Family Court process. The domestic violence court support program coordinator gave me a different explanation. She noted that the applicant had felt bullied by the magistrate during the hearing and had broken down in tears outside. The refusal of an order was remarkable given that this was the return date and there was no appearance by the defendant. If he was concerned about seeing his children, he could have appeared to defend the order, or could commence proceedings in the Family Court (Field notes, Broadmeadows Magistrates' Court, July 11, 1997). Here, then, the magistrate had shown more concern for the absent defendant's contact with his children than for the present applicant's concerns about harassment. And rather than staying out of family law, the magistrate had interpolated his views on fathers' rights to contact and applicants' ulterior motives.

INTERVENTION ORDERS IN THE FAMILY COURT

The fact that intervention orders count for very little in Family Court proceedings has been observed by numerous commentators. The existence of a family violence order is not generally treated as evidence that violence has occurred (Family Law Council & Law Council of Australia, Family Law Section, 2004, p. 51), especially where the order is made by consent without admitting the allegations (Altobelli, 1998, p. 12; Family Law Council, 2004, p. 4), or where mutual orders have been made (F. Culpen, interview, March 17, 1997). Only if a party has been charged and convicted for breach of an order will it carry much weight—which, as noted earlier, is a relatively rare occurrence (Katzen & Kelly, 2000, p. 194; Kaye et al., 2003, p. 105). According to the practitioners interviewed by Dewar and Parker (1999),

> The existence of a state domestic violence order was not considered good evidence, because the orders (a) frequently [were perceived to have] little evidential basis; and (b) were seen by Family Court judges as being too easily made and not necessarily indicative of violence. (p. 105; see also Kaspiew, 2005, p. 119)

This raises a further social narrative in relation to intervention orders—that they are handed out in the Magistrates' Court like "lollies at a children's party" (Kaye & Tolmie, 1998b).

This attitude was evident in the Family Court case observed (F.C.7, January 8–10, 1997) that had involved a previous contested hearing, as a result of which the mother had been restrained from relocating interstate with the child. The reasons for judgment in this previous case referred to the fact that the mother had obtained an interim intervention order in the Magistrates' Court. The judge concluded that in applying for the intervention order, she had misused the legal system in order to promote her position in the Family Court, and went on to question the practice of magistrates issuing intervention orders on an ex parte basis (although this is clearly provided for in the Crimes (Family Violence) Act, 1987). He stated, "Frequently, in this court, I find these orders have been issued by a magistrate with little supporting evidence and without any satisfactory reason apparently being given to the magistrate as to why a party is not served."

One of the lawyers interviewed considered that an intervention order would be of assistance if the mother's case was that the father should have no contact with the child/ren. However, this was not borne out in the no-contact cases observed. In F.C.3 (July 15–18 & 23, 1996), there was no intervention order in place against the father. In F.C.16 (January 6, 1997), there had been an intervention order in place, and the father had been convicted of breaching it, but it was not clear if it was still current. Either way, there was no mention of either the order or the breach in the judgment of either the trial judge or the Full Court.

Similarly, and consistent with the notion that the issue of domestic violence was merely "contextual" rather than directly relevant in most cases, the existence of an intervention order was either not mentioned at all, or mentioned only very briefly, in most of the contested cases in which orders were in place (F.C.1, June 20–21 & 24, 1996; F.C.2, June 25–26, 1996; F.C.5, December 2–6, 1996; F.C.9, January 20–24, February 10–11 & February 14, 1997). In only 2 of the cases observed was anything made of the intervention order by either counsel or the judge, and in one of these, the order appeared to be material only in relation to the sequence of events. In F.C.11 (February 10–14 & March 3–4, 1997), the wife had obtained an intervention order against the husband in response to previous assaults and his recent attempt to force her to relinquish their two sons to him. The day after she obtained the interim order, however, the husband made a notification to the State child welfare department alleging that the wife had sexually abused and neglected the children, and subsequently appeared to have put pressure on the children to "disclose" abuse by the wife. The question was whether these notifications had a genuine basis or were simply in retaliation to her attempt to invoke the legal system against him. The intervention order itself had expired almost 12 months before the Family Court hearing commenced. As discussed in chapter 6, it was ultimately found that the husband had subjected the children to serious emotional abuse in maintaining and pursuing the allegations against the wife, and his abuse of her faded into the background.

In F.C.8 (January 17, 1997), in which the wife was seeking leave to institute property proceedings out of time, she had obtained two final intervention orders against the husband: one for 12 months, which had expired, and a further order for 2 years, which was still in place. The husband's barrister sought to attack the process by which the first intervention order had been made, questioning whether the husband had been represented and whether there had been an interpreter present through whom he could speak. The barrister also tried to suggest that once the wife had obtained the intervention order, she should no longer have been afraid of the husband, and when she mentioned that she had called the police on one occasion, the barrister quickly established that the husband had not been charged with a breach of the order. In deciding in favor of the wife, however, the judge considered that the intervention orders corroborated her claim to be in fear of the husband. This was the only case observed in which the existence of an intervention order was accepted as evidence in the wife's favor.

Conclusion

As the foregoing discussion demonstrates, consideration of the interaction between the two civil jurisdictions in relation to domestic violence raises a further set of implementation problems for the legislation. Firstly, there is the structural problem that women are compelled to bring proceedings in two separate courts, with attendant disadvantages of time and cost (Kaye, 2003, p. 4). Secondly, as well as some of the previously identified social and legal narratives coming into play (such as women's tendency to exaggerate, lie, and abuse the system, and the importance of ongoing contact between children and their fathers), new narratives emerged relating specifically to the relationship between the two jurisdictions—that family law belongs in the Family Court and that Magistrates' Courts hand out intervention orders too freely. These narratives, in turn, frequently operated to undermine even the minimal legislative attempts that had been made to produce better coordination between Magistrates' Court and Family Court proceedings in relation to domestic violence.

ENDNOTES

1. Division 11 has subsequently been wholly repealed and replaced by the Family Law Amendment (Shared Parental Responsibility) Act (2006), Schedule 6.
2. The court was also required to provide a copy of the contact order to the Commissioner of Police in the State in which the family violence order was made (s. 68R(4)).
3. A copy of the contact order made or varied by the State court was also required to be registered with the Family Court (s. 68T(6)).
4. One of the cases in the file sample, which proceeded to hearing but was not observed, included mention in the written judgment of the intervention order in place and the role of section 68R. However, in that case, any Family Court orders would not conflict with the intervention order since the latter contained an exception to cater for the former, as discussed further later in this chapter.
5. A 2004 amendment to the Crimes (Family Violence) Act (1987) positively requires magistrates to determine whether any Family Court orders are in force and draws their attention to section 68T—but only in relation to the possible variation, discharge, or suspension of Family Court orders (not in relation to the potential to make a contact order), and only if the proposed intervention order specifically extends protection to a child or children (Crimes (Family Violence) Act (1987), s. 4A(4)). The VLRC subsequently recommended that magistrates receive training in relation to section 68T, and that the legislation be further amended to provide that magistrates must suspend contact if they made an intervention order including a child, and must consider altering any contact orders and ensure safe handover arrangements if they made an intervention order in favor of an applicant residing with children (2006, p. xlii). These recommendations are taken up in the Family Violence Protection Bill (2008).
6. The VLRC recommended that magistrates should be barred from including an "except for child contact" exception in intervention orders unless they also included a condition in the order specifying how and when contact was to occur (2006, p. xliii), but the Family Violence Protection Bill (2008) proposes a less directive provision that would still permit the use of such exceptions.
7. For Australian and U.S. research indicating that the majority of women applying for intervention orders had experienced repeated violence before

first approaching the court, see Fischer and Rose (1995, p. 416), Stubbs and Powell (1989, p. 43), Trimboli and Bonney (1997, p. 30), Wearing (1992, p. 363, 1996, p. 133). While this evidence does not establish that women never apply for orders for strategic reasons, it does suggest that applicants are far more likely than not to have genuine need of an order, and supports Jaffe & Crooks' (2004) contention that underreporting of partner violence and false denials by perpetrators are far more likely to occur than false allegations by women (p. 920).

Chapter 8

Conclusion

This study began with a question about whether the feminist claim that the criminal law silences women is also true of new civil claims specifically designed to respond to women's experiences. The research into intervention order proceedings and family law proceedings relating to domestic violence has shown, on the one hand, that the great majority of women applying for intervention orders in the cases observed were successful, as were the majority of the women in the Family Court cases that went to trial. Women got their intervention orders, were permitted to relocate with their children or to institute property proceedings out of time, and were successful in preventing violent ex-partners from having contact with or gaining joint or sole residence of the children. These outcomes are a clear improvement over the results of reform efforts in criminal law, where, for example, rape law reform has failed to produce any statistical improvement in conviction rates (see, e.g., Heath & Naffine, 1994; Stubbs, 2003), and battered women's self-defense claims are still frequently rejected (see chapter 1, note 6). From this perspective, civil jurisdictions have indeed given survivors of violence a better hearing.

On the other hand, the study has also shown that while many survivors of violence may have achieved successful legal results, they did not experience a supportive and affirming legal process, and they were compelled to return to court repeatedly in order to deal with all of the issues arising from the separation from their violent partner. Moreover, it is questionable whether the intervention orders obtained actually secured the safety of applicants and their children in many cases, and doubtful whether the Family Court orders obtained did so if they were made by "consent." In addition, the discursive effects of the proceedings were often disappointing. The provision of venues to hear women's stories about domestic violence did not result in any general revision of traditional conceptions and myths about what constitutes violence, what causes violence, and how it affects women and children. Rather, women's stories tended to be heard, filtered, and interpreted through nonfeminist social and legal narratives about domestic violence. Those narratives were often reinforced rather than replaced.

As predicted on the basis of socio-legal experience, the evidence from this study demonstrates that feminist law reforms relating to domestic violence have not been implemented as intended, due to a combination of legal forms, structures, and culture, particularly the "internal" legal culture of lawyers, magistrates, and judges. Also as predicted at the outset of this study, the precise implementation problems have varied between jurisdictions.

STRUCTURAL FACTORS

Potential structural factors identified in chapter 2 were the limitations of existing legal forms, categories, doctrines, procedures, and evidentiary rules, as well as lawyers' domination of their clients, women's intimidation by courtroom practices, and communication difficulties resulting from ethnicity, class, and disability. Of these, the issue of legal forms and categories really only arose in intervention order proceedings, with the assimilation of intervention orders to equitable injunctions and the associated addition of magisterial discretion to the statutory criteria for an order, and the concern to distinguish "real," "deserving" victims of violence from those who did not fall into that category and hence did not merit an order. In addition, magistrates were concerned to distinguish "intervention order" matters from "family law" matters, and to deal only with the former, meaning that women attempting to seek safety for themselves and their children were compelled to engage in multiple proceedings and sometimes found themselves falling between jurisdictional boundaries. Family law, by contrast, was not particularly plagued by restrictive forms or categories, being much more open textured and based on standards and principles rather than bright-line rules.

The particular doctrinal frame did have an impact in both jurisdictions. Under the Crimes (Family Violence) Act (1987), the specified grounds for an order emphasized individual incidents rather than patterns of behavior, and particular types of actions by the perpetrator (especially recent physical violence) rather than the cumulative effect of the perpetrator's actions on the aggrieved family member. They also required a likelihood of repetition, which was arguably unnecessary, and operated to the disadvantage of women who had managed to secure some level of safety for themselves but required further protection. The specified terms of orders also limited the protection available to abused women, particularly in relation to duration, sole occupancy, and exceptions for child contact. In children's cases in family law, the principles of no-fault and the child's right of ongoing contact with both parents, together with the listing of domestic violence as merely one of a number of factors to be taken into account in making a parenting order, served to de-emphasize the issue of domestic violence and to subordinate it to other considerations in the great majority of cases in which the mother did not argue that the father should be denied contact with the children altogether. In property cases, the Family Law Act (1975) did not specify domestic violence as a factor to be taken into account at all.

On the other hand, the rules of evidence did not operate as barriers in either jurisdiction. They were not strictly observed in the Magistrates' Court, particularly given the brevity of proceedings and the high proportion of self-representing litigants. They were observed in contested hearings in the Family Court, but they did not in themselves prevent accounts of violence from being heard. Their impact was rather on the weight that would be given to testimony that could not be corroborated with other evidence. The rules of procedure in the Family Court did create some difficulties. The practice of giving evidence in chief in affidavit form, with oral proceedings dominated by cross-examination, left women feeling that their experiences had not been properly presented or heard. And the ability of abusive men to bring numerous applications and to use the Family Court process as a further tactic of power, control, and harassment of their former partners—including the opportunity for direct cross-examination if they were self-represented—also left survivors of violence particularly vulnerable.

Lawyers did not do all the speaking on behalf of their clients in intervention order proceedings. Most applicants did not, in fact, have legal representation, and those who did were often grateful to be relieved of the need to say very much or to run their own case. Solicitors and barristers played a much greater role in the Family Court. Lawyers also demonstrated the potential to dominate, misunderstand, and misrepresent their clients in both courts, although the research indicated a wide spectrum of approaches by lawyers, so that at best, lawyers could offer understanding and empowerment, and achieve results that protected their client's safety and autonomy. A further structural feature operating in both courts was the tendency for lawyers to have more of an ongoing relationship with the court than with the client, so that if there was a conflict between the court's expectations and the client's needs or instructions, the former might prevail.

Unfamiliarity and intimidation in court certainly affected women applying for intervention orders and appearing in the Family Court, while communication problems for women whose first language was not English also occurred in both courts. In the Magistrates' Court, the rushed nature of intervention order proceedings made it particularly difficult for women to understand the proceedings or to convey their story through an interpreter, even if a competent interpreter was made available. In the Family Court, although proceedings took place at a more measured pace, women speaking through interpreters struggled to understand and answer convoluted questions, and hence to convey their case effectively, and also struggled to convey their experience of violence and its impact.

In addition to the structural factors identified in the existing literature, the study also revealed four additional structural factors operating in intervention order and family law proceedings that had the effect of suppressing women's stories of violence, perpetuating the abuse against them, or negating their chances of future safety. The primary example producing all three effects was the prevalence of consent orders, which were actively promoted in both jurisdictions. While consent orders are an essential mechanism to enable courts to manage their caseloads, they also operate within a substantive context that appears to have been largely ignored in both courts. The encouragement of consent without admissions in the Magistrates' Court, and the failure of most lawyers and judges to pay attention to power relations and safety considerations in negotiating and approving consent orders in the Family Court, meant that consent orders often produced adverse material and symbolic consequences for survivors of violence.

In both jurisdictions, too, women's intimidation in court was compounded by the intimidation and lack of safety they experienced in court waiting areas. In the Magistrates' Court, women's stories and the protection they sought were initially filtered and rewritten by the clerk/registrar, and the overload of cases and consequent routinization of intervention order proceedings, and the bureaucratic style adopted by magistrates, contributed significantly to the silencing of women's voices and the lack of support and affirmation given to applicants.

Internal Legal Culture

Clearly, nonfeminist narratives about domestic violence predominated in many lawyers', magistrates', and judges' minds, and were highly influential in the way they went about their representative and adjudicative roles. These narratives flourished in both doctrinal and discretionary spaces in the two jurisdictions. The nonfeminist narratives about domestic violence identified in chapter 2 were that violence is manifested in isolated incidents of physical assault and occurs exceptionally; that women tend to lie or exaggerate about abuse; that violence is caused by provocation, relationship conflict, alcohol, and cultural norms among "ethnic" communities; that there is no relationship between a man's violence towards his partner and his parenting capacity; and that victims of violence suffer from a psychological disorder. Broader social narratives that might also have a bearing on proceedings relating to domestic violence included "fright" narratives about bad, neglectful mothers and vindictive, bitter ex-wives; and beliefs in the sanctity of the nuclear family, with associated encouragement for couples in conflict to take steps to resolve their differences and reestablish a happy family.

A focus on individual incidents and physical violence, the consequent inability to comprehend fear resulting from accumulated experience of abuse, and the belief that "real" violence is exceptional, emerged as part of the dominant discourse about violence in both jurisdictions. The tendency of violent men to deny or minimize their violence was shared by some magistrates, Family Report writers, and judges. Similarly, many lawyers and magistrates, as well as some Family Court judges, appeared to hold the view that women tend to exaggerate or lie about violence, and this view was particularly apparent in the belief that women applied for intervention orders only in order to gain a tactical advantage in Family Court proceedings. Attribution of violence to relationship conflict or to the woman's provocation was a common theme among magistrates and Family Report writers. Alcohol and ethnic communities' cultural norms also figured in accounts of violence accepted in the Magistrates' Court, together with class-based explanations and excuses for violence.

The perceived disjunction between domestic violence and parenting played a prominent role in the Family Court. Although the jurisprudence of the Full Court suggested that there was a relationship between the two (albeit limited in scope), the influence of the old no-fault principle and the new right-to-contact principle, together with the structural issue of the kinds of legal arguments available in children's cases, tended to squeeze out that recognition in practice. The same perceived disjunction also played a prominent role in the Magistrates' Court, in magistrates' failure to implement section 68T of the Family Law Act (1975) in intervention order proceedings, preferring instead to insert exceptions into intervention orders to allow for defendants to have contact with their children.

The propensity to view victims of violence as psychologically disordered also appeared in both jurisdictions. This was a double-edged sword for women. On the one hand, if they could establish that their parenting capacity was diminished by overwhelming fear of their abuser, this would be grounds for a no-contact order in the Family Court. On the other hand, they could be perceived as dysfunctional, irrational, and untrustworthy, or could find their accounts of violence disbelieved if they did not produce the expert evidence of a counsellor or psychologist to testify to their genuine victim status.

"Fright" narratives were a notable feature of both jurisdictions, with bad mothers and vindictive wives making appearances in magistrates' decisions in contested intervention order cases and in Family Reports in particular. In the Family Court, these two roles combined in the dangerous figure of the alienating parent—the mother who sought to gain revenge against her ex-partner by turning the children against him.[1] Some magistrates also demonstrated a preference for maintaining the nuclear family by encouraging parties to reconcile and failing to recognize that, in some cases, "reconciliations" may have resulted from separation assaults.

As was the case with structural factors, social and legal narratives other than the ones previously identified also turned out to play a role—in some cases quite a significant one—in civil proceedings relating to domestic violence. In the Magistrates' Court, a paternalistic concern to minimize applicants' speaking roles for their own benefit, regardless of their actual wishes, contributed to applicants' difficulties in having their voices heard, and the strongly held view that family law belongs in the Family Court created additional costs for applicants and had the potential to compromise their safety. In the Family Court, survivors of violence encountered the view that intervention orders are made too easily.

And in both courts, they faced the beginnings of a procontact culture that held, variously, that fathers had a right of ongoing contact with their children, or that regular contact with both parents was presumptively in the best interests of the child.

MOVING FORWARD

Detailed analysis of the two jurisdictions revealed that the combination of structural and cultural factors operating in each one was both complex and extensive. The study demonstrates—if further demonstration were needed—that feminist law reformers cannot take implementation for granted or ignore the importance of both legal structures and cultures. It suggests a need for careful and comprehensive analysis of the operation of existing systems before reform proposals are made.

The study also provides support for the argument of critical feminist theorists that feminist reformers should not invest too much faith in legal solutions, but rather should be concerned to challenge nonfeminist narratives, both within law and wherever else in society they appear. We cannot expect counter-narratives to be created simply through legislative change—at least not without change that incorporates measures to address the structural factors that prevent counter-narratives being heard at all, and the internal legal cultures that continue to support nonfeminist accounts of the world and of the women seeking to invoke the legislation.

Combating the cultural and structural barriers to justice for survivors of violence identified in this study would involve a combination of legal, judicial, and community education; legislative reforms; procedural reforms; changes to court design; and more comprehensive provision of support services for survivors of violence accessing the court system. Legal education (both in law schools and for practising lawyers) should include the need to screen for domestic violence in all family law cases and to be nonjudgemental and supportive of clients who have experienced violence; understanding domestic violence and the dynamics of violent relationships in terms of power and control tactics and separation assault; the interrelationship of domestic violence and child abuse; the need to represent victims of violence in negotiations in a way that is empowering rather than dominating, and that promotes their safety and autonomy; and issues in the representation of victims of violence from culturally and linguistically diverse backgrounds. Such education would reach children's representatives in family law cases, but not the social workers, child psychologists, and counsellors who write Family Reports. Under its current *Family Violence Strategy*, however, the Family Court is reviewing all aspects of the ordering and preparation of Family Reports, with a view to ensuring "in the context of family violence issues, that expert evidence [is] underpinned by an awareness of the dynamics of violence and its impact upon parents and children" (Family Court of Australia, 2004, p. 12).

Amendments to the Crimes (Family Violence) Act (1987) suggested by this study include the addition of a statement of objectives in the legislation; revised grounds for an intervention order to incorporate a definition of domestic violence in terms of a pattern of controlling behavior producing fear for the victim's safety, and removal of the requirement for likely repetition; separate mention of sole occupancy orders among the kinds of orders available, with greater encouragement for the making of such orders; a requirement that the defendant notify his intention to consent to or contest an order ahead of the return date, with the order automatically becoming final if he fails to respond within a specified period; and abolition of the option of consent without admissions. The creation of a judicial discretion whether or not to grant an order after the statutory grounds for an order have been made out has also been problematic, but it could be equally problematic to abolish the discretion. There is a possibility, for example, that an excessively rigid application of the grounds for an order may result in more mutual orders being made (although the chances of this occurring should be reduced by the suggested amendments to the grounds for an order). If the discretion is retained, however, its exercise should be guided by the statement of objectives. Alternatively, there could be an explicit provision stating that in exercising their discretion, magistrates' paramount consideration should be the safety of the aggrieved family member.

Amendments to the Family Law Act (1975) suggested by the study would involve specifying domestic violence as a factor to be taken into account under both sections 79(4) and 75(2) in property proceedings, and making domestic violence a central concern rather than a mere factor in proceedings relating to child residence and contact. The latter could be achieved by means of a rebuttable presumption that a parent found to have perpetrated domestic violence should not be awarded residence or unsupervised contact, or by means of a provision stating that where domestic violence is found to have occurred, the best interests of the child require the court to give absolute priority to ensuring the safety of the child and the other parent, and ensuring their protection from future violence. In addition, the court should have an unqualified duty to ensure that its orders do not expose a person to an unacceptable risk of violence, which should extend to its approval of consent orders. As well as making domestic violence far more relevant in family law cases, these amendments would require the court to make positive findings about the existence of violence in a wider range of cases, and would educate lawyers about how they should approach the issue of violence in settlement negotiations. Finally, in order to limit the opportunity for violent men to use repeated Family Court proceedings as a further means of harassing and controlling their former partners, the Family Law Act (1975) could be amended to enable the court to order that a person not institute any new proceedings for a specified period of years.

Judicial and community education, procedural reforms, changes to court design, and the provision of greater support services for victims of violence may all be achieved through the creation of specialized domestic violence courts. A specialized court would ideally include dedicated and trained judicial officers, registrars, and court staff; safe, secure waiting areas for victims of violence; hearing venues that provide privacy and otherwise minimize the intimidation often experienced by women in court; the provision of expert advocacy services for all victims of violence, whether in the form of lawyers, domestic violence court support workers, or police acting as complainants; and the provision of reliable, sensitive interpreting services for women from non-English speaking backgrounds. Proceedings should be efficient without being bureaucratic. Victims of violence should be given the opportunity to explain their experiences and express their views in all cases, including in the making of consent orders, and the terms and duration of orders should be tailored to suit the specific circumstances of each case. All personnel in the court, including defense lawyers, should work as a team towards the substantive goals of hearing victims of violence, ensuring women's and children's safety, encouraging violent men to take responsibility for their actions and to relinquish controlling behavior, and sending appropriate messages to the community about the unacceptability of domestic violence. In addition, a specialized court should provide staff and support services to facilitate and encourage use of the court by Indigenous women, lesbians, and women with disabilities experiencing domestic violence.

In Australia, specialized domestic violence courts would have to be instituted at the State level, since only State courts would be able to exercise State criminal and civil jurisdictions, while also having power to make interim orders, consent orders, and contact orders under the Family Law Act (1975). This would be the closest option to a "one stop shop" for victims of violence, which would involve considerable time and cost savings, as well as greater satisfaction with court processes, increased safety for women and children, and consistent decision making within a feminist framework.

The introduction of broadly accessible, specialized courts is all the more important given that at the federal level, family law policy has become increasingly dominated by the narratives of fathers' rights and shared parenting after separation. These social narratives have grown in strength over the years since this study was undertaken, and are now firmly lodged within the culture of family law. There is some scope for change in family law processes via the Family Court's family violence strategy, which proposes a range of procedural reforms for the benefit of victims of violence (Family Court of Australia, 2004)—although, as argued in chapter 5, these are not comprehensive (particularly in relation to the making of consent orders). Another recent procedural initiative,

Less Adversarial Trials, aims to provide a more child-focused method of dealing with children's cases, and includes, among other things, greater scope for parties to speak directly to the judge about their experiences and concerns (Family Law Amendment (Shared Parental Responsibility) Act, 2006, sched. 3; Practice Direction No. 2 of 2006). It thus has the potential to solve some of the problems identified in relation to women's intimidation in court, their dissatisfaction with being unable to give oral evidence in chief, and the capacity for cross-examination to be at best traumatic for a victim of violence, and at worst destructive of her credibility. But it will still be necessary to ensure that the issue of violence, and its effects on women's ability to speak, are not marginalized in the process (see Hunter, 2006, pp. 231–233). And changes in some judges' understandings of domestic violence and doctrinal amendments are also required. Since these would involve cutting against the current cultural grain in family law, however, the chances of achieving them in practice appear, at this juncture, to be limited.

ENDNOTE

1. Kaspiew (2005) notes the gendered nature of this figure and the apparent double standard whereby fathers' criticisms, or even vilification, of mothers was tolerated to a much greater degree than mothers' criticisms of fathers (p. 136).

Appendix A

Court Observation Form

IO / FC / DATE:

Location: Presiding:

Observation point:

Applicant/Complainant's representation:

solicitor - M/F barrister - M/F support worker - M/F
self other ___________________________________

Perpetrator present: Y / N ; notified: Y / N

Perpetrator's representation:

solicitor - M/F barrister - M/F self other _________

Perpetrator's relationship to applicant ___________________________

Allegations of violence (including mutual):

Proof tendered/required:

Witnesses for A (number, relationships):

Witnesses for P (number, relationships):

Legal issues:

Previous/associated proceedings:

Outcome:

Time:

- waiting
- in court

Demeanour

- Applicant
- A's representatives
- Interpreter
- Perpetrator
- P's representatives
- Judge/Magistrate (incl. elicit information from A; empathy w. A in court; individualized consideration; w. interpreter)

Nonverbal communication

Swearing procedure: ____________________________________

Language of court:

formal   conversational   technical   other ________

Language of applicant: ____________________________________

Physical facilities (incl. waiting areas: formality, privacy, accessibility)

Speaking Roles

Who	Time	Nature

Applicant data:

- approximate age: 18–20 21–30 31–40 41–50 51–60 61+
- occupation
- source of financial support

  full-time work part-time work

  partner other family member

  social security–UB/Jobsearch

  –pension ______________________________
- ethnicity

  Anglo-Australian ______________________________

  NESB ______________________________

  Aboriginal/Torres Strait Islander/other Indigenous ________
- English language ability ______________________________

  interpreter used Y / N

  attitude of interpreter ______________________________
- number of children and ages
- residence

  inner city suburban regional rural
- physical disabilities
- deserving/undeserving factors in the eyes of the court

APPENDIX B

INTERVIEW SCHEDULE FOR LAWYERS AND SUPPORT WORKERS

1. Consent form

A. FAMILY COURT

2. Extent of experience - a few/a number/a lot/main area?

   Any particular groups of clients?

3. When is violence relevant in family law proceedings? Do you ask if your client has been the target of violence, or wait for the client to volunteer the information?

4. What is the significance of your client having obtained an intervention order against her partner? Would you advise a client who reported violence to obtain an intervention order?

5. In what circumstances would you make an application for damages under cross-vesting legislation? Have you ever done so?

6. Many family law matters result in interim or final consent orders. What are the advantages and disadvantages of consent orders? How do you protect the interests of a client who has been the target of violence in arriving at consent orders?

7. What advice/information do you give to clients regarding a hearing in the Family Court?

8. How does the court respond to women's experiences of violence?
   What prevents women from being heard?
   What helps them to be heard?

What requirements of proof of violence?
What effect of pleadings/the rules of evidence?
What differences within the jurisdiction?

9. What is the influence of the following factors:
   - nature of violence?
   - existence of an intervention order?
   - race, ethnicity, age, class, sexual preference of the woman?
   - any other variables I should take into account?

10. Experience with non-English speaking clients?
    - how do you find working with an interpreter in court?

11. Are there any safety issues for women in attending court?

B. INTERVENTION ORDERS

2. Extent of experience - a few/a number/a lot/main area?

   Any particular groups of clients?

3. What advice/information do you give to clients about the process of obtaining an intervention order?

4. Do you focus on a particular incident to get the order, or do you take instructions and lead evidence on any history of violence?

5. On the return date of an interim order, defendants are given the choice either to contest the application, or to consent to the order being made (without admitting the allegations).
   What is your view of allowing defendants to consent without admitting the allegations of violence?
   What are the advantages and disadvantages of making orders by consent (if allegations denied or not)?
   Do you think applicants should have a say in whether the defendant is allowed to consent without admitting the allegations?

6. How does the court respond to women's experiences of violence?
   What prevents women from being heard?
   What helps them to be heard?
   What requirements of proof of violence?
   What effect of application process/form, rules of evidence?
   What differences within the jurisdiction?

7. What is the influence of the following factors:
   - relationship between perpetrator and target of violence?
   - nature of violence?
   - race, ethnicity, age, class, sexual preference of the woman?
   - existence of Family Court orders? (have you applied for or seen a Magistrate modify any Family Court orders?)
   - any other variables I should take into account?

8. Experience with non-English speaking clients?
   - how do you find working with an interpreter in court?

9. Are there any safety issues for women in attending court?

---

12. Do you have any specialist expertise or training in the area of domestic or sexual violence?

13. Are you aware of any other research being done in the area of this study?
    Is there anyone else you'd recommend I speak to?

14. Thank-you's

Appendix C

Interview Schedule for Women Litigants

1. Consent forms
2. What kind of legal proceedings have you been involved in:
   - Family Court?
   - intervention order?
3. Did your case settle or did it go to a hearing? If it settled:
   - were you happy with the outcome?
   - did you feel pressured to agree?
   - did the perpetrator of the violence against you simply get his own way again?
   - (for intervention orders) what do you think about perpetrators being able to consent to an order without admitting the allegations?
4. Was the perpetrator of violence against you present in the court when you attended?
5. Did you have any fears for your safety in attending (any) court?
6. Did you understand everything that was happening in (each) court? Were you confused about anything?
7. What did you expect to happen in (each) court?
8. Was it any different from your expectations? How?
9. How did you feel speaking about violence in (each) court? - nervous, scared, embarrassed, confident...?

   Did you feel in control, or was it all out of your hands?

Was there anything that prevented you from telling your story the way you wanted?

10. Did you have a lawyer? How important/helpful were they?
11. How did the judge/Magistrate in (each) court respond to your story?
    – understanding, sympathy, disbelief, hostility, lack of interest, blaming you for violence, stereotyping...?
12. How did the judge/Magistrate respond to the person who was violent towards you? How do you feel about their treatment compared to yours?
13. Did you have a support person present? How important/helpful were they?
14. What was the best aspect of (each) court proceedings?
15. What was the worst aspect of (each) court proceedings?
16. Were you satisfied with the outcome of your case(s)?
17. Have there ever been any criminal charges against the perpetrator of violence against you? What was the outcome?
18. Can you make any comparisons between the court proceedings you experienced?
19. (If relevant) In your experience, how much coordination is there between Family Court orders and intervention orders? (complement each other? contradictory? ignored?)
20. Would you go through the process(es) again?
21. What advice would you give to another woman in your situation?
22. Any other comments?

Appendix D

Demographic Data Questionnaire for Women Litigants

Confidential Questionnaire

Thank you for participating in today's session. Your contribution to this study is very valuable.

So that I can prepare the report of this study, I would appreciate getting some information about you. This information is completely confidential. I do not need your name or other identifying details on this form. If you have any queries about the questions, please ask me.

1. What is your age group? (please circle)

   18–20   21–30   32–40   41–50   51–60   61+

2. What is your occupation? ____________________

3. What is your source of financial support? (please circle)

   full-time work   part-time work   your partner

   another family member   social security

   other ____________________

4. What kind of area do you live in? (please circle)

   inner city Melbourne   a suburb of Melbourne

   a Victorian regional centre   a Victorian rural area

   outside Victoria

5. How many children do you have? ____________________

   What are their ages? ____________________

6. Are you (please circle YES or NO):

   an Aborigine or Torres Strait Islander? YES NO

   from a non-English speaking background? YES NO

   from an Anglo-Australian background? YES NO

   none of the above? ______________________________

7. Do you speak English as your first language? YES NO

8. What is or was your relationship with the person who was violent towards you?

   ____

9. Was that person: MALE FEMALE (please circle)

10. Did you experience any of the following kinds of treatment? (please circle)

    coercion and threats intimidation

    emotional abuse isolation

    economic abuse physical abuse

    sexual abuse sexual harassment

    using the children to exercise control over you

11. How long did the violence last before you first took legal action?

    ____

12. How many times have you:

    – applied for an interim intervention order? ______________

    – applied for a full intervention order? ______________

    – been in the Family Court? ______________

APPENDIX E

POWER AND CONTROL WHEEL

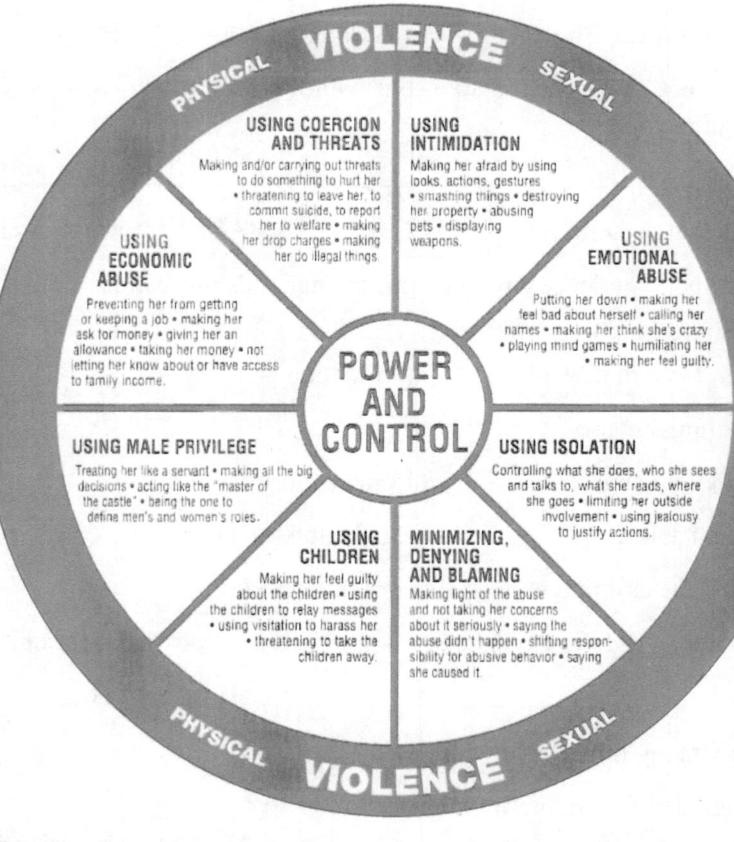

List of Cases

A *v.* A: Relocation Approach, 26 Fam. L.R. 382 (Full Ct. Fam. Ct. Austl. 2000)

AMS *v.* AIF, 199 C.L.R. 160 (Austl. 1999)

B and B: Family Law Reform Act 1995, 21 Fam. L.R. 676 (Full Ct. Fam. Ct. Austl. 1997)

Fisher *v.* Fisher, 1988 V.R. 1028 (S. Ct. Vict.)

In the Marriage of Blanch, 24 Fam. L.R. 325 (Full Ct. Fam. Ct. Austl. 1998)

In the Marriage of Chandler, 6 Fam. L.R. 736 (Full Ct. Fam. Ct. Austl. 1981)

In the Marriage of Doherty, 1996 F.L.C. 92–652 (Full Ct. Fam. Ct. Austl.)

In the Marriage of Ferguson, 4 Fam. L.R. 312 (Full Ct. Fam. Ct. Austl. 1978)

In the Marriage of Fisher, 13 Fam. L.R. 806 (Full Ct. Fam. Ct. Austl. 1990)

In the Marriage of Grant, 1994 F.L.C. 92–505 (Fam. Ct. Austl.)

In the Marriage of Hack, 6 Fam. L.R. 425 (Fam. Ct. Austl. 1980)

In the Marriage of Heidt, 11 A.L.R. 594 (Fam. Ct. Austl. 1976)

In the Marriage of Jaeger, 18 Fam. L.R. 126 (Full Ct. Fam. Ct. Austl. 1994)

In the Marriage of Kennon, 22 Fam. L.R. 1 (Full Ct. Fam. Ct. Austl. 1997)

In the Marriage of Lythow, 1976 F.L.C. 90–007 (Fam. Ct. Austl.)

In the Marriage of Mead, 9 Fam. L.R. 193 (Fam. Ct. Austl. 1983)

In the Marriage of Morgan, 22 Fam. L.R. 79 (Fam. Ct. Austl. 1997)

In the Marriage of Patsalou, 18 Fam. L.R. 426 (Full Ct. Fam. Ct. Austl. 1995)

In the Marriage of Schenck, 7 Fam. L.R. 170 (Full Ct. Fam. Ct. Austl. 1981)

In the Marriage of Sheedy, 1979 F.L.C. 90–719 (Fam. Ct. Austl.)

In the Marriage of Smythe, 8 Fam. L.R. 1029 (Full Ct. Fam. Ct. Austl. 1983)

In the Marriage of Soblusky, 12 A.L.R. 699 (Full Ct. Fam. Ct. Austl. 1976)

JG and BG, 18 Fam. L.R. 255 (Fam. Ct. Austl. 1994)

Kay *v*. McIntosh, 2003 V.S.C. 373 (S. Ct. Vict.)

Kingsland *v*. McIndoe, 1989 V.R. 273 (S. Ct. Vict.)

Kirby *v*. Phelan, 2003 V.S.C. 43 (S. Ct. Vict.)

Marsh *v*. Marsh, 17 Fam. L.R. 289 (Fam. Ct. Austl. 1993)

Osland *v*. R., 197 C.L.R. 316 (Austl. 1998)

R. *v*. Watson; ex parte Armstrong, 136 C.L.R. 248 (Austl. 1976)

R. *v*. Whalen, unreported (S. Ct. N.S.W. April 5, 1991)

Re JJT; ex parte Victoria Legal Aid, 195 C.L.R. 184 (Austl. 1998)

Re K, 17 Fam. L.R. 537 (Full Ct. Fam. Ct. Austl. 1994)

Re Wakim; ex parte McNally, 198 C.L.R. 511 (Austl. 1999)

Stephens *v.* Melis, 2002 V.S.C. 263 (S. Ct. Vict.)

T *v*. N, 31 Fam. L.R. 257 (Fam. Ct. Austl. 2003)

T *v*. S, 28 Fam. L.R. 342 (Full Ct. Fam. Ct. Austl. 2001)

Tsutsulis *v.* Tsutsulis, unreported (Broadmeadows Mag. Ct. January 30, 1997)

U *v*. U, 211 C.L.R. 238 (Austl. 2002)

List of Statutes

Australian Constitution 1901

Children Act 1989 (U.K.)

Crimes Act 1900 (N.S.W.)

Crimes Act 1958 (Vict.)

Crimes (Amendment) Act 1994 (Vict.)

Crimes (Family Violence) Act 1987 (Vict.)

Domestic Violence Act 1986 (A.C.T.)

Domestic Violence Act 1992 (N.T.)

Domestic Violence Act 1995 (N.Z.)

Domestic Violence Act 1994 (S. Austl.)

Domestic Violence (Family Protection) Act 1989 (Queensl.)

Family Law Act 1975 (Austl.)

Family Law Amendment Act 1983 (Austl.)

Family Law Amendment Act 1991 (Austl.)

Family Law Amendment (Shared Parental Responsibility) Act 2006 (Austl.)

Family Law Reform Act 1995 (Austl.)

Family Violence Act 2004 (Tas.)

Family Violence Protection Bill 2008 (Vict.)

Jurisdiction of Courts (Cross-vesting) Act 1987 (Austl.)

Justices Act 1959 (Tas.)

Law and Justice Legislation Amendment Act 1997 (Vict.)

Legal Profession Act 2004 (Vict.)

Magistrates' Court (Family Violence) Act 2004 (Vict.)

Matrimonial Causes Act 1959 (Austl.)

Practice Direction No. 2 of 2006—Child-related proceedings (Division 12A) (Fam. Ct. Austl. July 7, 2006)

Restraining Orders Act 1997 (W. Austl.)

United Nations Convention on the Rights of the Child 1989

Violence Against Women Act 1994, 42 U.S.C.A. Ch. 136

References

Abela, L., Opat, A., Wilkes, G., & van Moorst, E. (1994). *Crimes (Family Violence) Act 1987 intervention order support project: Background and information paper*. Melbourne: Women's Legal Resources Group, Inc.

Aboriginal and Torres Strait Islander Social Justice Commissioner. (1997). *Indigenous deaths in custody (1989–96)*. Canberra: Aboriginal and Torres Strait Islander Commission.

Aboriginal and Torres Strait Islander Women's Task Force on Violence. (2000). *The Aboriginal and Torres Strait Islander Women's Task Force on Violence report* (Rev. ed.). Brisbane: Aboriginal and Torres Strait Islander Women's Task Force on Violence.

Access Economics. (2004). *The cost of domestic violence to the Australian economy: Pt. 1*. Canberra: Office for the Status of Women.

Alexander, R. (1992). Mediation, violence and the family. *Alternative Law Journal, 17*, 271–273.

Alexander, R. (1996). New mantras in family law. *Alternative Law Journal, 21*, 276–279.

Alexander, R. (2002). *Domestic violence in Australia: The legal response* (3rd ed.). Sydney: Federation Press.

Altobelli, T. (1998). Family violence in children's cases—implications in practice: Pt. I. *Australian Family Lawyer, 13*(1), 6–12.

Ammons, L. L. (1995). Mules, madonnas, babies, bath water, racial imagery and stereotypes: The African-American woman and the battered woman syndrome. *Wisconsin Law Review*, 1003–1080.

Antonios, Z. (1996). Opening speech: Violence against NESB women. In *Not the same: Conference proceedings and a strategy on domestic violence and sexual assault for non-English speaking background women* (pp. 5–7). Melbourne: Domestic Violence & Incest Resource Centre.

Armstrong, S. M. (2001). "We told you so…": Women's legal groups and the Family Law Reform Act 1995. *Australian Journal of Family Law, 15*, 129–154.

Assafiri, H., & Dimopoulos, M. (1995). The legal system's treatment of NESB women victims of male violence. *Criminology Australia, 6*(4), 20–22.

Astor, H. (1994a). Swimming against the tide: Keeping violent men out of mediation. In J. Stubbs (Ed.), *Women, male violence and the law* (pp. 147–173). Sydney: Institute of Criminology.

Astor, H. (1994b). Violence and family mediation: Policy. *Australian Journal of Family Law, 8*, 3–21.

Atkinson, J. (1990). Violence against Aboriginal women: Reconstitution of community law—the way forward. *Aboriginal Law Bulletin, 46*, 6–9.

Atkinson, J. (1997, Summer). Telling stories and healing trauma, *DVIRC Newsletter*, 3–9.

Attorney General for Victoria. (2004, June 13). *Media release: Domestic violence courts for Heidelberg, Ballarat*. Melbourne: Attorney General for Victoria.

Australian Bureau of Statistics. (1996). *Women's safety Australia* (Cat. 4128.0). Canberra: Australian Bureau of Statistics.

Australian Law Reform Commission. (1994). *Report No. 69, Pt. I—Equality before the law: Justice for women*. Sydney: Australian Law Reform Commission.

Babbel, J. (2002, Winter). Balancing the Act: Survivors of family violence, intervention orders and Victorian Magistrates' Courts. *DVIRC Newsletter*, 12–19.

Backer, L. C. (1998). Tweaking facts, speaking judgment: Judicial transmogrification of case narrative as jurisprudence in the United States and Britain. *Southern California Interdisciplinary Law Journal, 6*, 611–662.

Bailey, A. (1995, November). Women's understandings of violence in their everyday relationships. *DVIRC Newsletter*, 5–11.

Bala, N. (1996). Spousal abuse and children of divorce: A differentiated approach. *Canadian Journal of Family Law, 13*, 215–285.

Bancroft, L., & Silverman, J. G. (2002). *The batterer as parent: Addressing the impact of domestic violence on family dynamics*. Thousand Oaks, CA: Sage.

Beaman-Hall, L. (1996). Abused women and legal discourse: The exclusionary power of legal method. *Canadian Journal of Law and Society, 11*(1), 125–139.

Behrendt, L. (1993). Aboriginal women and the white lies of the feminist movement: Implications for Aboriginal women in rights discourse. *Australian Feminist Law Journal, 1*, 27–44.

Behrens, J. (1993). Domestic violence and property adjustment: A critique of "no fault" discourse. *Australian Journal of Family Law, 7*, 9–28.

Behrens, J. (1995). Violence in the home and family law: An update. *Australian Journal of Family Law, 9*, 70–75.

Behrens, J. (1996). Ending the silence, but…: Family violence under the Family Law Reform Act 1995. *Australian Journal of Family Law, 10*, 35–47.

Behrens, J. (2002). The form and substance of Australian legislation on parenting orders: A case for the principles of care and diversity and presumptions based on them. *Journal of Social Welfare and Family Law, 24*, 401–421.

Behrens, J., & Bolas, K. (1997). Violence and the Family Court: Cross-vested claims for compensation. *Australian Journal of Family Law, 11*, 164–195.

Bennet, W. (1997). Barriers to support for lesbians in abusive relationships. In *Out of Limbo: First National Conference on Violence in Lesbian Relationships* (pp. 17–24). Adelaide.

Berns, S. (1999). *To speak as a judge: Difference, voice and power.* Aldershot, U.K.: Ashgate.

Berns, S. (2000). Folktales of legality: Family law in the procedural republic. *Law & Critique, 11*, 1–24.

Berns, S. (2001). Parents behaving badly: Parental alienation syndrome in the Family Court—magic bullet or poisoned chalice? *Australian Journal of Family Law, 15*, 191–214.

Bezdek, B. (1992). Silence in the court: Participation and subordination of poor tenants' voices in legal process. *Hofstra Law Review, 20*, 533–608.

Blashki, S. M. (1997, February). Family law: Some issues following recent legislative amendments. *DVIRC Newsletter*, 4–10.

Blazejowska, L. (1996). *Domestic violence court assistance: An information and training kit.* Sydney: Redfern Legal Centre Publishing.

Bolger, A. (1991). *Aboriginal women and violence.* Darwin: North Australia Research Unit, Australian National University.

Bordow, S. (1994). Defended custody cases in the Family Court of Australia: Factors influencing the outcome. *Australian Journal of Family Law, 8*, 252–263.

Bowermaster, J. M. (1998). Relocation custody disputes involving domestic violence. *University of Kansas Law Review, 46*, 433–463.

Bowker, L. H., Arbitell, M., & McFerron, J. R. (1988). On the relationship between wife beating and child abuse. In K. Yllo & M. Bograd (Eds.), *Feminist perspectives on wife abuse* (pp. 158–174). Thousand Oaks, CA: Sage.

Braithwaite, J., & Daly, K. (1995). Masculinities, violence and communitarian control. In D. Chappell & S. Egger (Eds.), *Australian violence: Contemporary perspectives II* (pp. 221–251). Canberra: Australian Institute of Criminology.

Bricker, D. (1993). Fatal defense: An analysis of battered woman's syndrome expert testimony for gay men and lesbians who kill abusive partners. *Brooklyn Law Review, 58*, 1379–1437.

Brooks, P., & Gewirtz, P. (Eds.). (1996). *Law's stories: Narrative and rhetoric in the law*. New Haven, CT: Yale University Press.

Brown, W. (1995). *States of injury: Power and freedom in late modernity*. Princeton, NJ: Princeton University Press.

Brown, T., Frederico, M., Hewitt, L., & Sheehan, R. (1998). *Child abuse and the Family Court* (Trends & Issues in Crime and Criminal Justice No. 91). Canberra: Australian Institute of Criminology.

Buehl, S. M. (1999). Domestic violence and the law. *Family Law Quarterly, 33*, 719–744.

Bumiller, K. (1988). *The civil rights society: The social construction of victims*. Baltimore: Johns Hopkins University Press.

Burke, A. S. (2002). Rational actors, self-defense, and duress: Making sense, not syndromes, out of the battered woman. *North Carolina Law Review, 81*, 211–316.

Busch, R. (1994). "Don't throw flowers at me…(judges) will say we're in love": An analysis of New Zealand judges' attitudes towards domestic violence. In J. Stubbs (Ed.), *Women, male violence and the law* (pp. 104–146). Sydney: Institute for Criminology.

Busch, R., & Robertson, N. (1994). "Ain't no mountain high enough (to keep me from getting to you)": An analysis of the Hamilton Abuse Intervention Pilot Project. In J. Stubbs (Ed.), *Women, male violence and the law* (pp. 34–63). Sydney: Institute for Criminology.

Busch, R., Robertson, N., & Lapsley, H. (1995). The gap: Battered women's experience of the justice system in New Zealand. *Canadian Journal of Women and the Law, 8*, 190–222.

Cahn, N. R. (1993). Inconsistent stories. *Georgetown Law Journal, 81*, 2475–2531.

Cahn, N. R. (2000). Policing women: Moral arguments and the dilemmas of criminalization. *DePaul Law Review, 49*, 817–829.

Cain, M. (1994). The symbol traders. In M. Cain & C. B. Harrington (Eds.), *Lawyers in a postmodern world: Translation and transgression* (pp. 15–48). New York: New York University Press.

Cain, M., & Harrington, C. B. (Eds.). (1994). *Lawyers in a postmodern world: Translation and transgression*. New York: New York University Press.

Carpenter, B., Currie, S., & Field, R. (2001, February). *Domestic violence: Views of Queensland magistrates*. Paper presented at Australian and New Zealand Society of Criminology Annual Conference, Melbourne.

Cavanagh, K., Dobash, R. E., Dobash, R. P., & Lewis, R. (2001). "Remedial work": Men's strategic responses to their violence against intimate female partners. *Sociology, 35*, 695–714.

Cecere, D.J. (1986). The second closet: Battered lesbians. In K. Lobel (Ed.), *Naming the violence: Speaking out about lesbian battering* (pp. 21–31). Emeryville, CA: The Seal Press.

Chaudhuri, M., & Daly, K. (1992). Do restraining orders help? Battered women's experience with male violence and the legal process. In E. S. Buzawa & C. G. Buzawa (Eds.), *Domestic violence: The changing criminal justice response* (pp. 227–252). Westport, CT: Auburn House.

Chief Justice's Taskforce on Gender Bias. (1994). *Report of the Chief Justice's taskforce on gender bias*. Perth: Supreme Court of Western Australia.

Cobb, S. (1997). The domestication of violence in mediation. *Law & Society Review, 31*, 397–440.

Coker, D. K. (1999). Enhancing autonomy for battered women: Lessons from Navajo peacemaking. *UCLA Law Review, 47*, 1–111.

Coker, D. K. (2000). Shifting power for battered women: Law, material resources, and poor women of color. *UC Davis Law Review, 33*, 1009–1055.

Collins, P.H. (1991). *Black feminist thought: Knowledge, consciousness and the politics of empowerment*. New York: Routledge.

Conley, J. M., & O'Barr, W. M. (1990). *Rules versus relationships: The ethnography of legal discourse*. Chicago: University of Chicago Press.

Conley, J. M., & O'Barr, W. M. (1998). *Just words: Law, language, and power*. Chicago: University of Chicago Press.

Cooke, M. (1995). Aboriginal evidence in the cross-cultural courtroom. In D. Eades (Ed.), *Language in evidence: Issues confronting Aboriginal and multicultural Australia* (pp. 55–96). Sydney: University of New South Wales Press.

Coombs, M. I. (1993). Telling the victim's story. *Texas Journal of Women and the Law, 2*, 277–315.

Coughlin, A. M. (1994). Excusing women. *California Law Review, 82*, 1–93.

Crawford, V. (2003, September). *Section 68T Family Law Act 1975 and family violence proceedings*. Paper presented at the National Community Legal Centres Conference: Peace Justice Community, Hobart.

Creed, B. (1993). *The monstrous-feminine: Film, feminism, psychoanalysis*. London: Routledge.

Crenshaw, K. W. (1991). A Black feminist critique of antidiscrimination law and politics. In D. Kairys (Ed.), *The politics of law: A progressive critique* (pp. 195–218). New York: Pantheon Books.

Crenshaw, K. W. (1994). Mapping the margins: Intersectionality, identity politics, and violence against women of color. In M. A. Fineman & R. Mykitiuk (Eds.), *The public nature of private violence: The discovery of domestic abuse* (pp. 94–118). New York: Routledge.

Cunneen, C., & Stubbs, J. (1997). *Gender, "race" and international relations: Violence against Filipino women in Australia*. Sydney: Institute of Criminology.

Dalton, C. (1997). Domestic violence, domestic torts and divorce: Constraints and possibilities. *New England Law Review, 31*, 319–395.

Davidson, H.A. (1995). Child abuse and domestic violence: Legal connections and controversies. *Family Law Quarterly, 29*, 357–373.

Davies, M., & Seuffert, N. (2000). Knowledge, identity, and the politics of law. *Hastings Women's Law Journal, 11*, 259–290.

Delgado, R. (1989). Storytelling for oppositionists and others: A plea for narrative. *Michigan Law Review, 87*, 2411–2441.

De Simone, T. (2008). The friendly parent provisions in Australian family law—How friendly will you need to be? *Australian Journal of Family Law, 22*, 56–71.

Dessau, L. (2000, July). *Family violence and other conduct in property cases: Life after Kennon*. Paper presented at the Family Law Section Ninth National Conference, Sydney.

Developments in the law: Legal responses to domestic violence. (1993). *Harvard Law Review, 106*, 1498–1620.

Dewar, J., & Parker, S. (1999). The impact of the new Part VII Family Law Act 1975. *Australian Journal of Family Law, 13*, 96–116.

Dick, T. (1998). She gave as good as she got? Family violence, interim custody/residence and the Family Court. *QUT Law Journal, 14*, 40–72.

Dobash, R. E., & Dobash, R. P. (1977–78). Wives: The "appropriate" victims of marital violence. *Victimology, 2*, 426–442.

Domestic Violence Advocacy Service (N.S.W.). (1998). *Annual report 1997–98*. Sydney: Domestic Violence Advocacy Service.

Domestic Violence Legislation Working Group. (1997). *Model domestic violence laws: Discussion paper*. Canberra: Attorney-General's Department.

Douglas, H., & Godden, L. (2003). The decriminalisation of domestic violence: Examining the interaction between the criminal law and domestic violence. *Criminal Law Journal, 27*, 32–43.

Douzinas, C., & Warrington, R. (1995). A well-founded fear of justice: Law and ethics in postmodernity. In J. Leonard (Ed.), *Legal studies as cultural studies: A reader in (post) modern critical theory* (pp. 197–229). Albany, NY: SUNY Press.

Doyne, S. E., Bowermaster, J. M., Meloy, J. R., Dutton, D., Jaffe, P., Temko, S., et al. (1999). Custody disputes involving domestic violence: Making children's needs a priority. *Juvenile and Family Court Journal, 50*(2), 1–12.

Dutton, M. A. (1992). *Empowering and healing the battered woman.* New York: Springer.

Dziggel, C. (1986). The perfect couple. In K. Lobel (Ed.), *Naming the violence: Speaking out about lesbian battering* (pp. 62–69). Emeryville, CA: The Seal Press.

Eades, D. (Ed.). (1995). *Language in evidence: Issues confronting Aboriginal and multicultural Australia.* Sydney: University of New South Wales Press.

Easteal, P. (1996). *Shattered dreams: Marital violence against overseas-born women in Australia.* Canberra: Australian Government Publishing Service.

Easteal, P. (Ed.). (1998). *Balancing the scales: Rape, law reform and Australian culture*. Sydney: Federation Press.

Easteal, P., Behrens, J., & Young, L. (2000). Relocation decisions in Canberra and Perth: A blurry snapshot. *Australian Journal of Family Law, 14*, 234–257.

Eastwood, S., & Phillips, K. (1996, March). But was he a good father? Parenting and male violence. *DVIRC Newsletter*, 12–16.

Eaton, M. (1994). Abuse by any other name: Feminism, difference, and intralesbian violence. In M. A. Fineman & R. Mykitiuk (Eds.), *The public nature of private violence: The discovery of domestic abuse* (pp. 195–223). New York: Routledge.

Edwards, R., for N.S.W. Strategy to Reduce Violence Against Women. (2004). *Violence excluded: A study into exclusion orders, south east Sydney, final report*. Sydney: Attorney General's Department of New South Wales.

Egger, S., & Stubbs, J., for the National Committee on Violence Against Women. (1993). *The effectiveness of protection orders in Australian jurisdictions*. Canberra: Australian Government Publishing Service.

Epstein, D. (1999). Effective intervention in domestic violence cases: Rethinking the roles of prosecutors, judges, and the court system. *Yale Journal of Law and Feminism, 11*, 3–50.

Eriksson, M., & Hester, M. (2001). Violent men as good enough fathers? A look at England and Sweden. *Violence Against Women, 7*, 779–798.

Erlanger, H. S., Chambliss, E., & Melli, M. S. (1987). Participation and flexibility in informal processes: Cautions from the divorce context. *Law and Society Review, 21*, 585–604.

Espinoza, L. G. (1997). Legal narratives, therapeutic narratives: The invisibility and omnipresence of race and gender. *Michigan Law Review, 95*, 901–937.

Ewick, P., & Silbey, S. S. (1995). Subversive stories and hegemonic tales: Toward a sociology of narrative. *Law & Society Review, 29*, 197–226.

Family Court of Australia. (1993, January). *Chief Justice's direction as to the management of cases involving family violence*. Melbourne: Family Court of Australia.

Family Court of Australia. (2004). *Family violence strategy 2004–2005*. Canberra: Family Court of Australia.

Family Court of Australia, Research and Evaluation Unit. (1992). *Review of Family Court research: Submission to the Joint Select Committee on Certain Aspects of the Operation and Interpretation of the Family Law Act*. Canberra: Family Court of Australia.

Family Law Council. (1998). *Violence and the Family Law Act: Financial remedies: Discussion paper*. Canberra: Family Law Council.

Family Law Council. (2001, August). *Letter of advice: Violence and property proceedings*. Canberra: Family Law Council.

Family Law Council. (2004, November). *Letter of advice to the Attorney-General on the operation of Division 11 in Part VII of the Family Law Act 1975*. Canberra: Family Law Council.

Family Law Council & Law Council of Australia, Family Law Section. (2004). *Best practice guidelines for lawyers doing family law work*. Canberra: Commonwealth of Australia.

The Family Court Lobby Group. (1990). *"In whose best interest?" A report of the South Australian phone in on women, domestic violence and the Family Court*. Adelaide: Family Court Lobby Group of South Australia.

Fedders, B. (1997). Lobbying for mandatory-arrest policies: Race, class, and the politics of the battered women's movement. *New York University Review of Law and Social Change, 23*, 281–300.

Fenton, Z. E. (1998). Domestic violence in black and white: Racialized gender stereotypes in gender violence. *Columbia Journal of Gender and Law, 8*, 1–65.

Fenton, Z. E. (1999). Mirrored silence: Reflections on judicial complicity in private violence. *Oregon Law Review, 78*, 995–1060.

Fenton, Z. E. (2003). Silence compounded: The conjunction of race and gender violence. *American University Journal of Gender, Social Policy and Law, 11*, 271–285.

Ferrante, A., Morgan, F., Indemaur, D., & Harding, R. (1996). *Measuring the extent of domestic violence*. Perth: Hawkins Press.

Ferraro, K. J. (1996). The dance of dependency: A genealogy of domestic violence discourse. *Hypatia, 11*(4), 77–91.

Field, R., Carpenter, B., & Currie, S. (2001). *Issues for magistrates in the making of ouster orders under the Domestic Violence (Family Protection) Act, 1989 (Qld)*. Unpublished manuscript.

Fineman, M. A. (1988). Dominant discourse, professional language, and legal change in child custody decisionmaking. *Harvard Law Review, 101*, 727–774.

Fineman, M. A., & Mykitiuk, R. (Eds.). (1994). *The public nature of private violence: The discovery of domestic abuse*. New York: Routledge.

Finley, L. (1989). Breaking women's silence in law: The dilemma of the gendered nature of legal reasoning. *Notre Dame Law Review, 64*, 886–910.

Fischer, K., & Rose, M. (1995). When "enough is enough": Battered women's decision making around court orders of protection. *Crime & Delinquency, 41*, 414–429.

Fischer, K., Vidmar, N., & Ellis, R. (1993). The culture of battering and the role of mediation in domestic violence cases. *Southern Methodist University Law Review, 46*, 2117–2174.

Fleming, D. (2000). Australian legal aid under the first Howard government. *UBC Law Review, 33*, 343–382.

Flick, B. (1990). Colonisation and decolonisation: An Aboriginal experience. In S. Watson (Ed.), *Playing the state: Australian feminist interventions* (pp. 61–66). Sydney: Allen & Unwin.

Friedman, L. M. (1984). Rights of passage: Divorce law in historical perspective. *Oregon Law Review, 63*, 649–669.

Friedman, L. M. (1985). Legal culture and the welfare state. In G. Teubner (Ed.), *Dilemmas of law in the welfare state* (pp. 13–27). Berlin: Walter de Gruyter.

Friedman, L. M. (1990). The concept of the self in legal culture. *Cleveland State Law Review, 38*, 517–534.

Friedman, L. M. (1994). Is there a modern legal culture? *Ratio Juris, 7*, 117–131.

Friedman, L. M. (2002). *American law in the 20th century*. New Haven, CT: Yale University Press.

Friedman, L. M. (2004). *Private lives: Families, individuals, and the law*. Cambridge, MA: Harvard University Press.

Friedman, L. M., & Scheiber, H. N. (Eds.). (1996). *Legal culture and the legal profession*. Boulder, CO: Westview Press.

Frohmander, C. (2001). Violence against women with disabilities. In *Out of the fire: Domestic violence and homelessness* (p. 28). Sydney: New South Wales Women's Refuges Resource Centre, Domestic Violence & Incest Resource Centre, & Council to Homeless Persons.

Frohmann, L. (1998). Constituting power in sexual assault cases: Prosecutorial strategies for victim management. *Social Problems, 45*, 393–407.

Frug, M. J. (1992). *Postmodern legal feminism*. New York: Routledge.

Funder, K., Harrison, M., & Weston, R. (Eds.). (1993). *Settling down: Pathways of parents after divorce* (AIFS Monograph No. 13). Melbourne: Australian Institute of Family Studies.

Galanter, M. (1974). Why the "haves" come out ahead: Speculations on the limits of legal change. *Law and Society Review, 9*, 95–160.

Genovese, A. (1997, April). The battered body. *Australian Feminist Studies, 25*, 91–102.

Genovese, A. (2000). The politics of naming: '70s feminisms, genealogy and "domestic violence." In R. Walker, K. Brass, & J. Byron (Eds.), *Anatomies of violence: An interdisciplinary investigation* (pp. 115–129). Sydney: Research Institute of Humanities and Social Sciences, University of Sydney.

Geraci, L. (1986). Making shelters safe for lesbians. In K. Lobel (Ed.), *Naming the violence: Speaking out about lesbian battering* (pp. 77–79). Emeryville, CA: The Seal Press.

Giddings, J. (Ed.). (1998). *Legal aid in Victoria: At the crossroads again*. Melbourne: Fitzroy Legal Service Publishing.

Gilchrist, E., & Blissett, J. (2002). Magistrates' attitudes to domestic violence and sentencing options. *Howard Journal, 41*, 348–363.

Gilkerson, C. P. (1992). Poverty law narratives: The critical practice and theory of receiving and translating client stories. *Hastings Law Journal, 43*, 861–945.

Goldfarb, S. F. (1996). The civil rights remedy of the Violence against Women Act: Legislative history, policy implications, and litigation strategy. *Journal of Law and Policy, 4*, 391–399.

Goldfarb, S. F. (2000). Violence against women and the persistence of privacy. *Ohio State Law Journal, 61*, 1–87.

Goldflam, R. (1995). Silence in court! Problems and prospects in Aboriginal legal interpreting. In D. Eades (Ed.), *Language in evidence: Issues confronting Aboriginal and multicultural Australia* (pp. 28–54). Sydney: University of New South Wales Press.

Gondolf, E. W., & Fisher, E. (1988). *Battered women as survivors: An alternative to treating learned helplessness*. Lanham, MD: Lexington Books.

Gondolf, E. W., McWilliams, J., Hart, B., & Stuehling, J. (1994). Court response to petitions for civil protection orders. *Journal of Interpersonal Violence, 9*, 503–517.

Goodall, H., & Huggins, J. (1992). Aboriginal women are everywhere: Contemporary struggles. In K. Saunders & R. Evans (Eds.), *Gender relations in Australia: domination and negotiation* (pp. 388–424). Sydney: Harcourt Brace Jovanovich.

Gordon, L. (1988). *Heroes of their own lives: The politics and history of family violence*. New York: Penguin Books.

Gordon Clark, H. (1997). Damages for domestic violence. *Victorian Family Law, 37*, 17–18.

Graycar, R. (1995). The relevance of violence in family law decision making. *Australian Journal of Family Law, 9*, 58–69.

Graycar, R. (1996a). Telling tales: Legal stories about violence against women. *Australian Feminist Law Journal, 7*, 79–93.

Graycar, R. (1996b). Telling tales: Legal stories about violence against women. *Cardozo Studies in Law and Literature, 8*, 297–315.

Graycar, R., & Morgan, J. (1990). *The hidden gender of law*. Sydney: Federation Press.

Graycar, R., & Morgan, J. (2002). *The hidden gender of law* (2nd ed.). Sydney: Federation Press.

Greenwood, K. (1996). Painday. *Meanjin, 55*, 573–576.

Greer, P. (1994). Aboriginal women and domestic violence in New South Wales. In J. Stubbs (Ed.), *Women, male violence and the law* (pp. 64–78). Sydney: Institute of Criminology.

Greer, P. (1997, May). Creating better services for Aboriginal people. *DVIRC Newsletter*, 13–18.

Gunn, R., & Linden, R. (1997). The impact of law reform on the processing of sexual assault cases. *Canadian Review of Sociology and Anthropology, 34*(2), 155–177.

Hall, J. (1999, Winter). "The court is not a sausage machine": Learning about intervention orders in a mock court. *DVIRC Newsletter*, 10–11.

Hampton, R., Oliver, W., & Magarian, L. (2003). Domestic violence in the African American community: An analysis of social and structural factors. *Violence Against Women, 9*, 533–556.

Harrison, M. (1986). Attitudes to lawyers and the legal process. In P. McDonald (Ed.), *Settling up: Property and income distribution on divorce in Australia* (pp. 241–258). Sydney: Prentice Hall.

Hart, B. J. (1990). Gentle jeopardy: The further endangerment of battered women and children in custody mediation. *Mediation Quarterly, 7*, 317–330.

Heath, M., & Naffine, N. (1994). Men's needs and women's desires: Feminist dilemmas about rape law "reform." *Australian Feminist Law Journal, 3*, 30–52.

Heberle, R. (2001). Law's violence and the challenge of "the feminine." *Studies in Law, Politics, and Society, 22*, 49–73.

Heenan, M., & McKelvie, H. (1997). *Rape law reform evaluation project, report No. 2—The Crimes (Rape) Act 1991: An evaluation report.* Melbourne: Attorney General's Legislation and Policy Branch, Department of Justice.

Heerey, P. (1996). Truth, lies and stereotype: Stories of Mary and Louis. *Newcastle Law Review, 1*(3), 1–31.

Heerey, P. (2000). Storytelling, postmodernism and the law. *Australian Law Journal, 74*, 681–691.

Hekman, S. J. (1999). *The future of differences: Truth and method in feminist theory.* Cambridge, U.K.: Polity Press.

Hekman, S. J. (2000). Beyond identity: Feminism, identity and identity politics. *Feminist Theory, 1*, 289–308.

Henderson, L. (1987). Legality and empathy. *Michigan Law Review, 85*, 1574–1653.

Hensler, D. R. (1988). Researching civil justice: Problems and pitfalls. *Law and Contemporary Problems, 51*(3), 55–65.

Hensler, D. R. (1993). Studying gender bias in the courts: Stories and statistics. *Stanford Law Review, 45*, 2187–2193.

Hensler, D. R. (2003–2004). Reflections on the use of empirical research in legal policy reform. *Newcastle Law Review, 7*(2), 1–12.

Hewitt, L., Brown, T., Frederico, M., & Martyn, R. (1996, August). Family violence in the Family Court. *DVIRC Newsletter*, 19–25.

Hickey, J., & Cumines, S. (1999). *Apprehended violence orders: A survey of magistrates* (Monograph Series No. 20). Sydney: Judicial Commission of New South Wales.

Hitter, M. (1996). Enhancing access for immigrant and refugee women. In *Not the same: Conference proceedings and a strategy on domestic violence and sexual assault for non-English speaking background women* (pp. 46–48). Melbourne: Domestic Violence and Incest Resource Centre.

Holder, R. (2001). *Domestic and family violence: Criminal justice interventions* (Issues Paper 3). Sydney: Australian Domestic and Family Violence Clearinghouse.

Hore, E., Gibson, J., & Bordow, S. (1996). *Domestic homicide* (Research Report No. 13). Melbourne: Family Court of Australia.

Horney, J., & Spohn, C. (1991). Rape law reform and instrumental change in six urban jurisdictions. *Law and Society Review, 25*, 117–153.

House of Representatives Standing Committee on Family and Community Affairs. (2004). *Every picture tells a story: Report on the inquiry into child custody arrangements in the event of family separation.* Canberra: House of Representatives Standing Committee on Family and Community Affairs.

House of Representatives Standing Committee on Legal and Constitutional Affairs. (2005). *Exposure draft of the Family Law Amendment (Shared Parental Responsibility) Bill 2005.* Canberra: House of Representatives Standing Committee on Legal and Constitutional Affairs.

Howe, A. (1998). Notes from a "war" zone: Reporting domestic/family/home/epidemic (men's) violence. In A. Howe (Ed.), *Sexed crime in the news* (pp. 29–55). Sydney: Federation Press.

Huggins, J. (1991). Black women and women's liberation. In S. Gunew (Ed.), *A reader in feminist knowledge* (pp. 6–12). London: Routledge.

Huggins, J. (1994). A contemporary view of Aboriginal women's relationship to the white women's movement. In N. Grieve & A. Burns (Eds.), *Australian women: Contemporary feminist thought* (pp. 70–79). Melbourne: Oxford University Press.

Human Rights and Equal Opportunity Commission. (1991). *Racist violence: Report of the national inquiry into racist violence in Australia.* Sydney: Author.

Human Rights and Equal Opportunity Commission. (1997). *Bringing them home: Report of the national inquiry into the separation of Aboriginal and Torres Strait Islander children from their families*. Sydney: Author.

Humphreys, C., & Thiara, R. K. (2003). Neither justice nor protection: Women's experiences of post-separation violence. *Journal of Social Welfare and Family Law, 25*, 195–214.

Hunter, R. (1996a). Gender in evidence: Masculine norms vs. feminist reforms. *Harvard Women's Law Journal, 19*, 127–167.

Hunter, R. (1996b). Deconstructing the subjects of feminism: The essentialism debate in feminist theory and practice. *Australian Feminist Law Journal, 6*, 135–162.

Hunter, R. (1998). Litigants in person in contested cases in the Family Court. *Australian Journal of Family Law, 12*, 171–178.

Hunter, R. (1999a). *Family law case profiles*. Sydney: Justice Research Centre.

Hunter, R. (1999b). Having her day in court? Violence, legal remedies and consent. In J. Breckenridge & L. Laing (Eds.), *Challenging silence: Innovative responses to sexual and domestic violence* (pp. 59–68). Sydney: Allen & Unwin.

Hunter, R. (2003). Adversarial mythologies: Policy assumptions and research evidence in family law. *Journal of Law and Society, 30*, 156–176.

Hunter, R. (2006). Child-related proceedings under Pt VII Div 12A of the Family Law Act: What the children's cases pilot program can and can't tell us. *Australian Journal of Family Law, 20*, 227–248.

Hunter, R., Genovese, A., Chrzanowski, A., & Morris, C. (2002). *The changing face of litigation: Unrepresented litigants in the Family Court of Australia*. Sydney: Law and Justice Foundation of New South Wales.

Hunter, R., with Genovese, A., Melville, A., & Chrzanowski, A. (2000). *Legal services in family law*. Sydney: Justice Research Centre.

Hunter, R., Giddings, J., & Chrzanowski, A. (2003). *Legal aid and self-representation in the Family Court of Australia*. Brisbane: Socio-Legal Research Centre, Griffith University.

Hunter, R., & Mack, K. (1997). *Exclusion and silence: Procedure and evidence*. In N. Naffine & R. J. Owens (Eds.), *Sexing the subject of law* (pp. 171–192). Sydney: LBC Information Services.

Hunter, R., & Stubbs, J. (1999). Model laws or missed opportunity? *Alternative Law Journal, 24*, 12–16.

Ireland, M. (2002, Summer). "An almost endless list of injustices": Violence against women with disabilities. *DVIRC Newsletter*, 9–14.

Jaffe, P. G., & Crooks, C. V. (2004). Partner violence and child custody cases: A cross-national comparison of legal reforms and issues. *Violence Against Women, 10*, 917–934.

Jaffe, P. G., Lemon, N. K. D., & Poisson, S. E. (2003). *Child custody and domestic violence: A call for safety and accountability*. Thousand Oaks, CA: Sage.

Jhappan, R. (1998). The equality pit or the rehabilitation of justice. *Canadian Journal of Women and the Law, 10*, 60–107.

Johnson, H. (1998). Rethinking survey research on violence against women. In R. E. Dobash & R. P. Dobash (Eds.), *Rethinking violence against women* (pp. 23–51). Thousand Oaks, CA: Sage.

Johnston, J. R. (1995). Domestic violence and parent-child relationships in families disputing custody. *Australian Journal of Family Law, 9*, 12–25.

Kahan, D. M. (2000). Gentle nudges vs. hard shoves: Solving the sticky norms problem. *University of Chicago Law Review, 67*, 607–645.

Kaspiew, R. (2005). Violence in contested children's cases: An empirical exploration. *Australian Journal of Family Law, 19*, 112–143.

Katsabanis, M. (1993). *Access and equity report.* Melbourne: Women's Refuge Referral Service.

Katzen, H., & Kelly, L. (2000). *"How do I prove I saw his shadow?" Responses to breaches of apprehended violence orders: A consultation with women and police in the Richmond Local Area Command of NSW.* Lismore, Australia: Northern Rivers Community Legal Centre.

Kaye, M. (2003). Section 68T Family Law Act 1975: Magistrates' powers to alter Family Court contact orders when making or varying ADVOs. *Judicial Officers' Bulletin, 15*(1), 3–4.

Kaye, M., Stubbs, J., & Tolmie, J. (2003). *Negotiating child residence and contact arrangements against a background of domestic violence* (Research Report 1). Brisbane: Families, Law and Social Policy Research Unit, Griffith University.

Kaye, M., & Tolmie, J. (1998a). Fathers' rights groups in Australia and their engagement with issues in family law. *Australian Journal of Family Law, 12*, 19–68.

Kaye, M., & Tolmie, J. (1998b). "Lollies at a children's party" and other myths: Violence, protection orders and fathers' rights groups. *Current Issues in Criminal Justice, 10*(1), 52–72.

Kearney McKenzie & Associates. (1998). *Report: Review of the operation of Division 11 of the Family Law Reform Act.* Canberra: Office of the Status of Women.

Kelly, L. (1988). How women define their experiences of violence. In K. Yllo & M. Bograd (Eds.), *Feminist perspectives on wife abuse* (pp. 114–132). Thousand Oaks, CA: Sage.

Kelly, L. (1998). Stories from the front: Seeking refuge for battered immigrants in the Violence Against Women Act. *Northwestern University Law Review, 92*, 665–705.

Kewley, A. (1996). Pragmatism before principle: The limitations of civil law remedies for the victims of domestic violence. *Journal of Social Welfare and Family Law, 18*, 1–10.

Keys Young. (1994). *Quarter way to equal: A report on barriers to access to legal services for migrant women*. Sydney: Women's Legal Resources Centre.

Keys Young. (1996). *Research/evaluation study of family mediation practice and the issue of violence: Final report*. Canberra: Attorney General's Department.

Kinports, K., & Fischer, K. (1992). Orders of protection in domestic violence cases: An empirical assessment of the impact of the reform statutes. *Texas Journal of Women and the Law, 2*, 163–276.

Klein, C. F., & Orloff, L. E. (1993). Providing legal protection for battered women: An analysis of State statutes and case law. *Hofstra Law Review, 21*, 801–1189.

Kline, M. (1989). Race, racism, and feminist legal theory. *Harvard Women's Law Journal, 12*, 115–150.

Kohler, R. L. (1992). Comment, the battered woman and tort law: A new approach to fighting domestic violence. *Loyola Los Angeles Law Review, 25*, 1025–1072.

Krug, E. G., Dahlberg, L. L., Mercy, J. A., Zwi, A. B., & Lozano, R. (2002). *World report on violence and health.* Geneva: World Health Organization.

Laing, L. (2000a). *Progress, trends and challenges in Australian responses to domestic violence* (Issues Paper 1). Sydney: Australian Domestic and Family Violence Clearinghouse.

Laing, L. (2000b). *Children, young people and domestic violence* (Issues Paper 2). Sydney: Australian Domestic and Family Violence Clearinghouse.

Langer, R. (1995). Male domestic abuse: The continuing contrast between women's experiences and juridical responses. *Canadian Journal of Law and Society, 10*, 65–89.

Lapidus, L. M. (1998). Maintaining the status quo: Institutional obstacles in a child custody dispute. In G. Bellow & M. Minow

(Eds.), *Law stories* (pp. 51–76). Ann Arbor: University of Michigan Press.

Lawless, E. F. (2000). Transformative re-membering: De-scribing the unspeakable in battered women's narratives. *Southern Folklore, 57*, 65–79.

Lazreg, M. (1990). Feminism and difference: The perils of writing as a woman on "women in Algeria". In M. Hirsch & E. Fox Keller (Eds.), *Conflicts in feminism* (pp. 326–348). New York: Routledge.

Lees, S. (1994). Lawyers' work as constitutive of gender relations. In M. Cain & C. B. Harrington (Eds.), *Lawyers in a postmodern world: Translation and transgression* (pp. 124–154). New York: New York University Press.

Lees, S. (1996). *Carnal knowledge*. Harmondsworth: Penguin.

Lees, S. (1997). *Ruling passions: Sexual violence, reputation and the law*. Buckingham, U.K.: Open University Press.

Lemon, N. K. D. (2001a). *Domestic violence law*. St. Paul, MN: West Group.

Lemon, N. K. D. (2001b). Statutes creating rebuttable presumptions against custody to batterers: How effective are they? *William Mitchell Law Review, 28*, 601–676.

Leonard, J. (Ed.). (1995). *Legal studies as cultural studies: A reader in (post) modern critical theory*. Albany, NY: SUNY Press.

Levin, A. B. (2000). Comment, child witnesses of domestic violence: How should judges apply the best interests of the child standard in custody and visitation cases involving domestic violence? *UCLA Law Review, 47*, 813–857.

Levitt, S. (1995). Rethinking harm: A feminist essay. *Washburn Law Review, 34*, 531–538.

Littleton, C. A. (1989). Women's experience and the problem of transition: Perspectives on male battering of women. *University of Chicago Legal Forum, 1989*, 23–57.

Logan, T. K., Walker, R., Horvath, L. S., & Leukefeld, C. (2003). Divorce, custody, and spousal violence: A random sample of circuit court docket records. *Journal of Family Violence, 18*(5), 269–279.

Loke, T. (1997). Note, trapped in domestic violence: The impact of United States immigration laws on battered immigrant women. *Boston University Public Interest Law Journal, 6*, 589–628.

MacCrimmon, M. (1991). The social construction of reality and the rules of evidence. *UBC Law Review, 25*, 36–50.

Mack, K. (1993). Continuing barriers to women's credibility: A feminist perspective on the proof process. *Criminal Law Forum, 4*, 327–353.

MacKinnon, C. A. (2000). Disputing male sovereignty: On United States v. Morrison. *Harvard Law Review, 114*, 135–177.

Magistrates' Court of Victoria. (2003). *Family violence and stalking protocols* (Rev. ed.). Melbourne: Magistrates Court of Victoria.

Mahoney, M. R. (1991). Legal images of battered women: Redefining the issue of separation. *Michigan Law Review, 90*, 1–94.

Mahoney, M. R. (1994). Victimization or oppression? Women's lives, violence and agency. In M. A. Fineman & R. Mykitiuk (Eds.), *The public nature of private violence: The discovery of domestic abuse* (pp. 59–92). New York: Routledge.

Marginson, M. (1996). Increasing access for Filipina survivors of domestic violence. In *Not the same: Conference proceedings and a strategy on domestic violence and sexual assault for non-English speaking background women* (pp. 18–22). Melbourne: Domestic Violence and Incest Resource Centre.

Martin, D. L., & Mosher, J. E. (1995). Unkept promises: Experiences of immigrant women with the neo-criminalization of wife abuse. *Canadian Journal of Women and the Law, 8*, 3–44.

Mason, G. (1995). (Out)laws: Acts of proscription in the sexual order. In M. Thornton (Ed.), *Public and private: Feminist legal debates* (pp. 66–88). Melbourne: Oxford University Press.

Mazza, D., Dennerstein, L., & Ryan, V. (1996). Physical, sexual and emotional violence against women: A general practice-based prevalence study. *Medical Journal of Australia, 164*, 14–17.

McCarthy, T. (1995). "Battered woman syndrome": Some reflections on the invisibility of the battering man in legal discourse, drawing on *R v Raby*. *Australian Feminist Law Journal, 4*, 141–151.

McDonald, E. (1994). Her sexuality as indicative of his innocence: The operation of New Zealand's "rape shield" provision. *Criminal Law Journal, 18*, 321–336.

McDonald, P. (Ed.). (1986). *Settling up: Property and income distribution on divorce in Australia*. Sydney: Prentice-Hall.

McGregor, H., & Hopkins, A. (1991). *Working for change: The movement against domestic violence*. Sydney: Allen & Unwin.

McIntosh, J. (2002). Thought in the face of violence: A child's need. *Child Abuse and Neglect, 26*, 229–241.

McKeon, M. (1998). The impact of domestic violence on child custody determination in California: Who will understand? *Whittier Law Review, 19*, 459–486.

Meier, J. S. (2003). Domestic violence, child custody, and child protection: Understanding judicial resistance and imagining the solutions. *American University Journal of Gender, Social Policy and the Law, 11*, 657–731.

Memmott, P., Stacy, R., Chambers, C., & Keys, C. (1999). *Violence in Indigenous communities*. Canberra: Attorney-General's Department.

Merry, S. E. (1997a). Global human rights and local social movements in a legally plural world. *Canadian Journal of Law and Society, 12*(2), 247–271.

Merry, S. E. (1997b). Wife battering and the ambiguities of rights. In A. Sarat & T. R. Kearns (Eds.), *Identities, politics, and rights* (pp. 271–306). Ann Arbor: University of Michigan Press.

Middleton, S. (2001). Domestic violence, contributions and s.75(2) considerations: An analysis of unreported property judgments. *Australian Journal of Family Law, 15*, 230–260.

Middleton, S. (2002). Family Court property proceedings: Rethinking the approach to the "financial consequences" of domestic violence. *UNSW Law Journal, 25*, 704–720.

Mileski, M. (1971). Courtroom encounters: An observational study of a lower criminal court. *Law and Society Review, 5*, 473–538.

Mills, L. G. (1996). On the other side of silence: Affective lawyering for intimate abuse. *Cornell Law Review, 81*, 1225–1263.

Min-ha, T. T. (1989). *Woman, native, other: Writing postcoloniality and feminism*. Bloomington: Indiana University Press.

Minow, M. (1990). Words and the door to the land of change: Law, language, and family violence. *Vanderbilt Law Review, 43*, 1665–1699.

Mirchandani, R. (2005). What's so special about specialized courts? The state and social change in Salt Lake City's domestic violence court. *Law and Society Review, 39*, 379–418.

Mnookin, R. S., & Kornhauser, L. (1979). Bargaining in the shadow of the law: The case of divorce. *Yale Law Journal, 88*, 950–997.

Moore, E. (2002, February). *Not just court: Indigenous families, violence and apprehended violence orders in rural New South Wales*. Paper presented at Expanding Our Horizons: Understanding the Complexities of Violence Against Women: Meanings, Cultures, Difference Conference, University of Sydney.

Moreton-Robinson, A. (2000). *Talkin' up to the white woman: Indigenous women and feminism*. Brisbane: University of Queensland Press.

Mouzos, J., & Makkai, T. (2004). *Women's experiences of male violence: Findings from the Australian component of the International Violence Against Women Survey (IVAWS)* (Research and Public Policy Series No. 56). Canberra: Australian Institute of Criminology.

Mullane, G. R. (1998). Evidence of social science research: Law, practice, and options in the Family Court of Australia. *Australian Law Journal, 72*, 434–464.

Murphy, J. C. (1998). Legal images of motherhood: Conflicting definitions from welfare "reform", family, and criminal law. *Cornell Law Review, 83*, 688–766.

Murray, K. A. (1995). Domestic violence and the judicial process: A review of the past 18 years—should it change direction? *Australian Journal of Family Law, 9*, 26–40.

Naffine, N. (1985). *Domestic violence and the law: A study of s.99 of the Justices Act (SA)*. Adelaide: South Australian Department of Premier and Cabinet, Women's Adviser's Office.

Narayan, U. (1989). The project of feminist epistemology: Perspectives from a nonwestern feminist. In A. M. Jaggar & S. R. Bordo (Eds.), *Gender/body/knowledge: Feminist reconstructions of being and knowing* (pp. 256–269). New Brunswick, NJ: Rutgers University Press.

National Committee on Violence Against Women. (1993). *Access to services for women with disabilities*. Canberra: Australian Government Publishing Service.

Neave, M. (1994). Resolving the dilemma of difference: A critique of the role of private ordering in family law. *University of Toronto Law Journal, 44*, 97–131.

New South Wales Department for Women. (1996). *Heroines of fortitude: The experiences of women in court as victims of sexual assault—summary report*. Sydney: Department for Women.

Nicholson, A. (1995). Foreword. *Australian Journal of Family Law, 9*, 1–4.

Noone, M. A. (2001). The state of Australian legal aid. *Federal Law Review, 21*, 37–56.

Nosek, M. A., Howland, C. A., & Hughes, R. B. (2001). The investigation of abuse and women with disabilities: Going beyond assumptions. *Violence Against Women, 7*, 477–499.

Not the same: Conference proceedings and a strategy on domestic violence and sexual assault for non-English speaking background women. (1996). Melbourne: Domestic Violence and Incest Resource Centre.

Nourse, V. F. (1996). Where violence, relationship, and equality meet: The Violence Against Women Act's civil rights remedy. *Wisconsin Women's Law Journal, 11*, 1–36.

Nourse, V. (2000) The "normal" successes and failures of feminism and the criminal law. *Chicago-Kent Law Review, 75*, 951–978.

Nunn, J. (2001). "Sole occupancy" orders. In *Out of the fire: Domestic violence and homelessness* (p. 35). Sydney: New South Wales Women's Refuge Resources Centre, Domestic Violence & Incest Resource Centre, Council to Homeless Persons.

Nunn, J., & D'Arcy, M. (2001, Spring). Legal responses to family violence: The need for a critical review. *DVIRC Newsletter*, 15–25.

O'Barr, W. M., & Conley, J. M. (1985). Litigant satisfaction versus legal adequacy in small claims court narratives. *Law and Society Review, 19*, 661–701.

O'Donovan, K. (1993). Law's knowledge: The judge, the expert, the battered woman, and her syndrome. *Journal of Law and Society, 20*, 427–437.

O'Donovan, K. (1997). With sense, consent, or just a con? In N. Naffine & R. J. Owens (Eds.), *Sexing the subject of law* (pp. 47–64). Sydney: LBC Information Services.

Oh, C. J. (1992). Questioning the cultural and gender-based assumptions of the adversary system: The voices of Asian-American law students. *Berkeley Women's Law Journal, 7*, 125–180.

O'Shane, P. (1976). Is there any relevance in the women's movement for Aboriginal women? *Refractory Girl, 12*, 31–34.

Out of Limbo: First National Conference on Violence in Lesbian Relationships. (1997, April). Adelaide.

"Out" of sight. (2000, March). *DVAR: Journal of the DVRC Inc., 7*, 2–18.

Out of the fire: Domestic violence and homelessness. (2001). Sydney: New South Wales Women's Refuge Resources Centre, Domestic Violence and Incest Resource Centre, Council to Homeless Persons.

Pagelow, M. D. (1993). Justice for victims of spouse abuse in divorce and child custody cases. *Violence & Victims, 8*, 69–83.

Parkinson, P. (1995). Custody, access and domestic violence. *Australian Journal of Family Law, 9*, 41–57.

Payne, S. (1990). Aboriginal women and the criminal justice system. *Aboriginal Law Bulletin, 46*, 9–11.

Pe-Pua, R., & Echevarria, A. S. (1998). *Cultural appropriateness, or plain customer service? Legal needs of NESB residents in Fairfield.* Sydney: Ettinger House.

Pence, E., & Paymar, M. (1993). *Education groups for men who batter: The Duluth model*. New York: Springer.

Pettman, J. (1992). *Living in the margins: Racism, sexism and feminism in Australia*. Sydney: Allen & Unwin.

Ptacek, J. (1999). *Battered women in the courtroom: The power of judicial responses*. Boston: Northeastern University Press.

Putt, J., & Higgins, K. (1997). *Violence against women in Australia: Key research and data issues* (Research & Public Policy Series No. 6). Canberra: Australian Institute of Criminology.

Radford, L., Hester, M., Humphries, J., & Woodfield, K. (1997). For the sake of the children: The law, domestic violence and child contact in England. *Women's Studies International Forum, 20*, 471–482.

Randall, M. (1995). Domestic violence. *Alternative Law Journal, 20*, 3–6.

Rathus, Z. (2007). Shifting the gaze: Will past violence be silenced by a further shift of the gaze to the future under the new family law system? *Australian Journal of Family Law, 21*, 87–112.

Razak, S. H. (1998). *Looking white people in the eye: Gender, race, and culture in courtrooms and classrooms*. Toronto: University of Toronto Press.

Rendell, K. (1999, Autumn). Current responses to children and young people affected by domestic violence: Beyond dichotomies. *DVIRC Newsletter*, 3–10.

Rendell, K., Rathus, Z., Lynch, A., for the Abuse Free Contact Group. (2000). *An unacceptable risk: A report on child contact arrangements where there is violence in the family*. Brisbane: Women's Legal Service Inc.

Report of the taskforce on women and the Criminal Code. (2000). Brisbane: Department of Justice and Attorney-General, & Office of Women's Policy.

Resnik, J. (1991). "Naturally" without gender: Women, jurisdiction, and the Federal Courts. *New York University Law Review, 66*, 1682–1772.

Rhoades, H. (2000). Posing as reform: The case of the Family Law Reform Act. *Australian Journal of Family Law, 14*, 142–159.

Rhoades, H. (2002). The "no contact" mother: Reconstructions of motherhood in the era of the "new father". *International Journal of Law, Policy and the Family, 16*, 71–94.

Rhoades, H., Graycar, R., & Harrison, M. (2000). *The Family Law Reform Act 1995: The first three years*. Sydney: University of Sydney, & Family Court of Australia.

Rhode, D. L. (Ed.). (1990). *Theoretical perspectives on sexual difference*. New Haven, CT: Yale University Press.

Rhode, D. L. (1997). *Speaking of sex: The denial of gender inequality*. Cambridge, MA: Harvard University Press.

Rhode, D. L. (2002). Law, lawyers and the pursuit of justice. *Fordham Law Review, 70*, 1543–1562.

Rhode, D. L. (2003a). Equal justice under law: Connecting principle to practice. *Washington University Journal of Law and Policy, 12*, 47–62.

Rhode, D. L. (2003b). Defining the challenges of professionalism: Access to law and accountability of lawyers. *South Carolina Law Review, 54*, 889–895.

Rhode, D. L. (2004). *Access to justice*. New York: Oxford University Press.

Rimonte, N. (1999). A question of culture: Cultural approval of violence against women in the Pacific-Asian community and the cultural defense. *Stanford Law Review, 43*, 1311–1326.

Rivera, J. (1994). Domestic violence against Latinas by Latino males: An analysis of race, national origin, and gender differentials. *Boston College Third World Law Journal, 14*, 231–257.

Roberts, G. (1995). Domestic violence victims in emergency departments. In D. Chappell & S. Egger (Eds.), *Australian violence: Contemporary Perspectives II* (pp. 87–103). Canberra: Australian Institute of Criminology.

Römkens, R. (2001). Law as a Trojan horse: Unintended consequences of rights-based interventions to support battered women. *Yale Journal of Law and Feminism, 13*, 265–290.

Rosnes, M. (1997). The invisibility of male violence in Canadian child custody and access decision-making. *Canadian Journal of Family Law, 14*, 31–60.

Royal Commission into Aboriginal Deaths in Custody. (1991). *Final Report*. Canberra: Australian Government Publishing Service.

Ruttenberg, M. H. (1994). A feminist critique of mandatory arrest: An analysis of race and gender in domestic violence policy. *American University Journal of Gender and Law, 2*, 171–199.

Sarmas, L. (1994). Storytelling and the law: A case study of *Louth v Diprose*. *Melbourne University Law Review, 19*, 701–728.

Sarmas, L. (1998). A response to Justice Peter Heerey. *Newcastle Law Review, 3*(1), 82–93.

Scarry, E. (1985). *The body in pain: The making and unmaking of the world*. New York: Oxford University Press.

Schafran, L. H. (1995). There's no accounting for judges. *Albany Law Review, 58*, 1063–1085.

Scheppele, K. L. (1992). Just the facts ma'am: Sexualized violence, evidentiary habits and the revision of truth. *New York Law School Law Review, 37*, 123–172.

Scheppele, K. L. (1994). Manners of imagining the real. *Law and Social Inquiry, 19*, 995–1022.

Scherer, D. D. (1992). Tort remedies for victims of domestic violence. *South Carolina Law Review, 43*, 543–579.

Schneider, E. M. (1991). The violence of privacy. *Connecticut Law Review, 23*, 973–999.

Schneider, E. M. (2000). *Battered women and feminist lawmaking*. New Haven, CT: Yale University Press.

Scutt, J. A. (1990). *Even in the best of homes: Violence in the family*. Melbourne: McCulloch Publishing.

Scutt, J. A. (1995). Judicial bias or legal bias? Battery, women and the law. In J. Bessant, K. Carrington, & S. Cook (Eds.), *Cultures of crime and violence: The Australian experience* (pp. 130–143). Bundoora, Australia: LaTrobe University Press.

Scutt, J. A. (1997). *The incredible woman*. Melbourne: Artemis Publishing.

Seddon, N. (1993). *Domestic violence in Australia: The legal response* (2nd ed.). Sydney: Federation Press.

Seidman, L. M. (1996). Some stories about confessions and confessions about stories. In P. Brooks & P. Gewirtz (Eds.), *Law's stories: Narrative and rhetoric in the law* (pp. 162–164). New Haven, CT: Yale University Press.

Seuffert, N. (1994). Lawyering and domestic violence: A feminist integration of experiences, theories and practices. In J. Stubbs (Ed.), *Women, male violence and the law* (pp. 79–103). Sydney: Institute of Criminology.

Seuffert, N. (1995). Hanging out at the gap: A dialogue reading of experiences of survivors of domestic violence with legal representation. *Canadian Journal of Women and the Law, 8*, 290–336.

Seuffert, N. (1996). Locating lawyering: Power, dialogue and narrative. *Sydney Law Review, 18*, 523–552.

Seuffert, N. (1997). Battered women and self-defence. *New Zealand Universities Law Review, 17*, 292–328.

Seuffert, N. (1999). Domestic violence, discourses of romantic love, and complex personhood in the law. *Melbourne University Law Review, 23*, 211–240.

Shalleck, A. (1995). Child custody and child neglect: Parenthood in legal practice and culture. In M.A. Fineman & I. Karpin (Eds.), *Mothers in law: Feminist theory and the legal regulation of motherhood* (pp. 308–327). New York: Columbia University Press.

Sheehan, G., Carson, R., Fehlberg, B., Hunter, R., Tomison, A., Ip, R., et al. (2005). *Children's contact services: Expectation and experience*. Brisbane, Melbourne and Canberra: Griffith University, The University of Melbourne, Australian Institute of Family Studies, & Commonwealth Attorney-General's Department.

Sheehy, E. (1994). Battered woman syndrome: Developments in Canadian law after *R v Lavallee*. In J. Stubbs (Ed.), *Women, male violence and the law* (pp. 174–191). Sydney: Institute of Criminology.

Sheehy, E. (1996). Legalising justice for all women: Canadian women's struggles for democratic rape law reforms. *Australian Feminist Law Journal, 6*, 87–113.

Sheehy, E. A., Stubbs, J., & Tolmie, J. (1992). Defending battered women on trial: The battered woman syndrome and its limitations. *Criminal Law Journal, 16*, 369–394.

Sheeran, M., & Hampton, S. (1999). Supervised visitation in cases of domestic violence. *Juvenile and Family Court Journal, 50*(2), 13–25.

Siegel, R. B. (1996). "The rule of love": Wife beating as prerogative and privacy. *Yale Law Journal, 105*, 2117–2207.

Simon, L. M. J. (1995). A therapeutic jurisprudence approach to the legal processing of domestic violence cases. *Psychology, Public Policy, and Law, 1*, 43–79.

Smart, C. (1989). *Feminism and the power of law*. London: Routledge.

Smart, C. (1990). Law's truth/women's experience. In R. Graycar (Ed.), *Dissenting opinions: Feminist explorations in law and society* (pp. 1–20). Sydney: Allen & Unwin.

Smart, C. (1995). *Law, crime and sexuality: Essays in feminism*. London: Sage.

Smyth, B. (Ed.). (2004). *Parent-child contact and post-separation parenting arrangements* (Research Report No. 9). Melbourne: Australian Institute of Family Studies.

Sous, S. (1996). Mimosa House: A refuge for Indo-Chinese women. In *Not the same: Conference proceedings and a strategy on domestic violence and sexual assault for non-English speaking background women* (pp. 14–15). Melbourne: Domestic Violence and Incest Resource Centre.

Southwell, J. (2002, Spring). Family violence and homelessness: Removing the perpetrator from the home. *DVIRC Newsletter*, 3–10.

Spohn, C., & Horney, J. (1992). *Rape law reform: The grassroots revolution and its impact*. New York: Plenum Press.

Spowart, H., & Neil, R. (1997). Stop in the name of love. *Alternative Law Journal, 22*, 81–85.

Stanko, E.A. (1985). *Intimate intrusions: Women's experience of male violence*. London: Unwin Hyman.

Stewart, A. (2000). Who are the respondents of domestic violence protection orders? *Australian and New Zealand Journal of Criminology, 33*, 77–90.

Stewart, J. (2005). *Specialist domestic/family violence courts within the Australian context* (Issues Paper 10). Sydney: Australian Domestic and Family Violence Clearinghouse.

A strategy on domestic violence and sexual assault for non-English speaking background women. (1996). In *Not the same: Conference proceedings and a strategy on domestic violence and sexual assault for non-English speaking background women* (pp. 84–98). Melbourne: Domestic Violence & Incest Resource Centre.

Straus, M. A., & Gelles, R. J. (1990). Societal change and change in the family from 1975 to 1985 as revealed by two national surveys. In M. A. Straus & R. J. Gelles (Eds.), *Physical violence in American families: Risk factors and adaptations to violence in 8,145 families* (pp. 113–131). New Brunswick, NJ: Transaction Publishers.

Stubbs, J. (Ed.). (1994). *Women, male violence and the law*. Sydney: Institute of Criminology.

Stubbs, J. (2003, February). *Sexual assault, criminal justice and law and order*. Paper presented at Practice and Prevention: Contemporary Issues in Adult Sexual Assault in New South Wales Conference, Sydney.

Stubbs, J., & Powell, D. (1989). *Domestic violence: Impact of legal reform in New South Wales*. Sydney: New South Wales Bureau of Crime Statistics and Research.

Stubbs, J., & Tolmie, J. (1994). Battered woman syndrome in Australia: A challenge to gender bias in the law? In J. Stubbs (Ed.), *Women, male violence and the law* (pp. 192–225). Sydney: Institute of Criminology.

Stubbs, J., & Tolmie, J. (1999). Falling short of the challenge? A comparative assessment of the use of expert evidence on the battered woman syndrome. *Melbourne University Law Review, 23*, 709–748.

Tan, K. L. (1998). Rape law reform in Canada: The success and limits of legislation. *International Journal of Offender Therapy and Comparative Criminology, 42*, 258–270.

Taylor, B. (2001, Summer). Clearing pathways, reforming systems: A reflection on the achievements and existing challenges of the Gold Coast domestic violence integrated response. *DVIRC Newsletter*, 21–24.

Temkin, J. (2000). Prosecuting and defending rape: Perspectives from the Bar. *Journal of Law and Society, 27*, 219–248.

Thornton, M. (1991). Feminism and the contradictions of law reform. *International Journal of the Sociology of Law, 19*, 453–474.

Threadgold, T. (1997). Performativity, regulative fictions, huge stabilities: Framing battered woman's syndrome. *Law Text Culture, 3*, 210–231.

Tjaden, P., & Thoennes, N. (2000). *Extent, nature, and consequences of intimate partner violence: Findings from the national violence against women survey* (NCJ 181867). Washington, DC: U.S. Department of Justice, Office of Justice Programs.

Tobin, J. (1992). Family violence: Opening up the silence. *Melbourne University Law Review, 18*, 851–866.

Tolmie, J. (1997). Pacific-Asian immigrant and refugee women who kill their batterers: Telling stories that illustrate the significance of specificity. *Sydney Law Review, 19*, 472–513.

Tomison, A. M. (2000). *Exploring family violence: Links between child maltreatment and domestic violence* (National Child Protection Clearinghouse Issues in Child Abuse Prevention Paper No 13). Melbourne: Australian Institute of Family Studies.

Trimboli, L., & Bonney, R. (1997). *An evaluation of the NSW apprehended violence order scheme*. Sydney: New South Wales Bureau of Crime Statistics and Research.

Troup, M. (1993). Rupturing the veil: Feminism, deconstruction and the law. *Australian Feminist Law Journal, 1*, 63–88.

Troup, M. (1995). The Family Law Reform Bill No. 2 and its ramifications for women and children. *Australian Feminist Law Journal, 5*, 111–122.

Tsai, B. (2000). The trend towards specialized domestic violence courts: Improvements on an effective innovation. *Fordham Law Review, 68*, 1285–1327.

United States Department of Justice, Bureau of Justice Statistics. (2000, July 14). *Intimate partner violence* (NCJ 178247). Retrieved March 2005 from http://www.ojp.usdoj.gov/bjs/pub/ascii/ipv.txt.

Upton, J. C. R. (1992). By violence, by silence, by control: The marginalization of Aboriginal women under white and "black" law. *Melbourne University Law Review, 18*, 867–873.

Valente, R. L. (1995). Addressing domestic violence: The role of the family law practitioner. *Family Law Quarterly, 29*, 187–196.

Vickers, L. (1996). The second closet: Domestic violence in lesbian and gay relationships: A Western Australian perspective. *E Law—Murdoch University Electronic Journal of Law, 3*(4). Retrieved March 2005 from http://www.murdoch.edu.au/elaw/issues/v3n4/vickers.txt.

Victorian Community Council Against Violence. (1991). *The legal system and family violence: Inquiry into services for those affected by family violence* (Report No. 2). Melbourne: Victorian Community Council Against Violence.

Victorian Community Council Against Violence. (2002). *Victorian family violence database: First report*. Melbourne: Victorian Community Council Against Violence.

Victorian government response to the Victorian Indigenous family violence task force final report. (2004). Melbourne: Government of Victoria.

Victorian Law Reform Commission. (2004a). *Review of family violence laws: Consultation paper*. Melbourne: Victorian Law Reform Commission.

Victorian Law Reform Commission. (2004b). *Defences to homicide: Final report*. Melbourne: Victorian Law Reform Commission.

Victorian Law Reform Commission. (2006). *Review of family violence laws: Report*. Melbourne: Victorian Law Reform Commission.

Victorian Women's Policy Coordination Unit. (1985). *Criminal assault in the home: Social and legal responses to domestic violence*. Melbourne: State of Victoria.

Volpp, L. (1994). (Mis)identifying culture: Asian women and the "cultural defense." *Harvard Women's Law Journal, 17*, 57–101.

Vucko, M. (2001, Winter). Women's experiences of the legal system: Domestic violence, relationship expectations and legal intervention. *DVIRC Newsletter*, 9–15.

Waits, K. (1995). Battered women and family lawyers: The need for an identification protocol. *Albany Law Review, 58*, 1027–1062.

Walker, L. E. (1987). *Terrifying love: Why battered women kill and how society responds*. New York: Harper Collins.

Walker, M. (1995). Interpreting the figures: Increases in women's violence or just more masculinist legal tactics? *Australian Feminist Law Journal, 5*, 123–125.

Wan, A. M. (2000). Battered women in the restraining order process: Observations on a court advocacy program. *Violence Against Women, 6*, 606–632.

Wanganeen, R. (1990). The Aboriginal struggle in the face of terrorism. In S. Watson (Ed.), *Playing the state: Australian feminist interventions* (pp. 67–70). Sydney: Allen & Unwin.

Watson, S. (Ed.). (1999). *Playing the state: Australian feminist interventions*. Sydney: Allen & Unwin.

Wearing, R. (1992). *Monitoring the impact of the Crimes (Family Violence) Act 1987*. Bundoora, Australia: LaTrobe University.

Wearing, R. (1996). *Monitoring the Crimes (Family Violence) Act 1987: A study of those who do not proceed*. Bundoora, Australia: LaTrobe University.

Wearing, R. (2001, Spring). A search for legal protection from family violence. *DVIRC Newsletter*, 8–14.

West, R. L. (2000). The difference in women's hedonic lives: A phenomenological critique of feminist legal theory (reprint). *Wisconsin Women's Law Journal, 15*, 149–215.

Westlund, A. C. (1999). Pre-modern and modern power: Foucault and the case of domestic violence. *Signs, 24*, 1045–1066.

White, L. E. (1990). Subordination, rhetorical survival skills, and Sunday shoes: Notes on the hearing of Mrs G. *Buffalo Law Review, 38*, 1–58.

Womendez, C., & Schneiderman, K. (1991). Escaping from abuse: Unique issues for women with disabilities. *Sexuality and Disability, 9*, 273–279.

Women's Coalition Against Family Violence. (1994). *Blood on whose hands? The killing of women and children in domestic homicides*. Melbourne: Women's Coalition Against Family Violence.

Yue, A. (1996). Battered homes: Some NESBian que(e)ries. In *Not the same: Conference proceedings and a strategy on domestic violence and sexual assault for non-English speaking background women* (pp. 24–26). Melbourne: Domestic Violence and Incest Resource Centre.

Zorza, J. (1995). Recognizing and protecting the privacy and confidentiality needs of battered women. *Family Law Quarterly, 29*, 273–311.

Zorza, J. (1996). Protecting the children in custody disputes when one parent abuses the other. *Clearinghouse Review, 29*, 1113–1127.

Index

www.ingramcontent.com/pod-product-compliance
Lightning Source LLC
LaVergne TN
LVHW101457200926
848483LV00001B/152
* 9 7 8 1 6 0 4 9 7 5 7 5 8 *